AFRICA ON FILM

Of Related Interest from Continuum

For more information on these and other titles on the arts, write to:

Continuum
370 Lexington Avenue
New York, NY 10017

Africa on Film

Beyond Black and White

Kenneth M. Cameron

CONTINUUM • NEW YORK

1994
The Continuum Publishing Company
370 Lexington Avenue
New York, NY 10017

Printed in the United States of America

Library of Congress Cataloging-in-Publication Data

Cameron, Kenneth M., 1931–
    Africa on film : beyond black and white / Kenneth M. Cameron.
       p.   cm.
    Includes bibliographical references and index.
    ISBN 0–8264–0658-0 (acid-free paper)
    1. Africa in motion pictures.   I. Title.
PN1995.9.A43C36   1994
791.43'626—dc20   94-10211
                                        CIP

to
Kenhelm W. Stott, Jr.,
who loves Africa and films

CONTENTS

(Photographs may be found between pages 96 and 97 and 160 and 161.)

ACKNOWLEDGMENTS _____

Above all, I am indebted to Ken Stott, to whom this book is dedicated; he has been a support and help throughout its research and writing, and his comments on the manuscript were invaluable.

As well, I am particularly grateful to three other people: to my editor, Cynthia Eller, who is that rara avis, a *real* editor; to Madeline Matz of the Motion Picture Division of the Library of Congress, who is—luckily for the rest of us— always willing to sacrifice her own time to do our work for us; and to David Kerr, for advice on African sources during a year spent in Botswana. In addition, I want to thank Rosemary Hanes of the Motion Picture Division of the Library of Congress; the South African National Film, Video and Sound Archive in Pretoria, and especially Trevor Moses there; the UCLA Film Archive; the International Museum of Photography at Eastman House, Rochester, and Paolo Cherchi Uchai in particular; and the British Film Institute, London. For help and generosity with stills, I must thank Kathy Lendech of Turner Entertainment as well as that corporation; Warner Brothers; the Museum of Modern Art; Janet Lorenz and the Margaret Herrick Library of the American Academy of Motion Picture Arts and Sciences; Lumiere Pictures, Ltd.; J. de Lange of the Toron Screen Corporation; Mimosa Films (South Africa); MCA, Inc.; the Martin and Osa Johnson Safari Museum and Conrad Froehlich, its director; Mr. Sydney Samuelson, for both a photograph and information otherwise unavailable to me about the 1925 *She;* and Pat Gallahan.

As always, the errors in the book are my own. Wherever possible, I have used the films as their own evidence; however, I regret that many films about Africa are now lost. The filmography is as complete as I could make it, but I am sure there are omissions, and I apologize for them.

INTRODUCTION

A frica is a very old site for European projection, a location of myths and fantasies for which the North seemed not to have the uncharted space. "I speak of Africa and golden joys," Shakespeare's Pistol rants. It is little wonder, then, that "Africa" came into filmmaking almost with cinema's beginnings, seizing there much of the same territory that it occupied in poetry, the novel, and travel literature. At that initial filmic moment—c. 1895–1900—some areas of the continent were still unmapped; African languages and their literatures were unknown, or were known only to specialists; and African cultures were ignored, often deliberately. These attitudes and ignorances affected everybody in cinema's universe: those who used the camera and those who edited the film; those who marketed motion pictures and those who showed them; those who reviewed motion pictures and those who consumed them. Yet all shared certain common ideas of "Africa," and around this body a considerable cinema arose.

In the late seventeenth century, visual imagery of Africa was rich and detailed and conveyed quite dense fields of information about geography and history, with Africans often presented as heroic and beautiful. By the late nineteenth century, on the other hand, illustrations in books and magazines had created a conventional "Africa" that was fairly sparse in information and that depended on a few repeated motifs, especially "jungle," "darkness," and "savagery," the latter nowadays seen as particularly suspect because of its dehumanizing content. Between the seventeenth and the twentieth centuries lay slavery and the greedy carving up of Africa by the European powers. The lowering of real information suited such exploitation: the highly reductive iconography of "savagery," which showed Africans as childlike, violent, superstitious, and uncivilized, matched nineteenth-century theories of racial superiority (e.g., Gobineau's *Essay On the Inequality of the Human Races)* that "provided a pseudo-scientific justification of the subsequent expansion of colonialism and imperialism."

The inherited twentieth-century notion of Africa, then (which, of necessity, was the notion underlying commercial films), was the one brought down from the nineteenth century. Indeed, the primary means of transmission of that notion were either still fresh or were being created even as the first cameras turned: the best-selling books by and about H. M. Stanley; the travel accounts of the first African tourists, among whom Theodore Roosevelt was preeminent; and the older works of Europeans from Du Chaillu to Thompson. Underlying these works were European attitudes toward Africa that had changed dramatically over the previous two hundred years, from one of wonder and a philosophical admiration to one of greed and something like contempt.

With the chief colonial powers also among the important creators of early motion pictures, it was not surprising that the content of cinema would reflect the content of a colonial "received wisdom." In the case of Great Britain, imperial content was sharpened by the coincidence of very early films and the Boer War, as well as by the coincidence of early films and Britain's expansion into its last African area, British East Africa. Although Britain triumphed in the Boer War, the resulting South Africa was culturally as much Boer as British; and, perhaps deliberately, a British iconography of diamonds, English language, and classism dominated early film imagery of South Africa. The United States was not an African colonial power, but its received ideas were the same as Britain's and were in fact derived from Britain's. American views, as expressed in such early films as *The Negro Kiss* and *A Nigger in the Woodpile,* as well as the later *Birth of a Nation,* showed no interest in a more detailed or more generous idea of Africa or Africans.

Censorship, too, must always be considered in looking at these motion pictures as an influence on the perpetuation of nineteenth-century iconography, at least until the collapse of colonialism. It was also an influence in hiding such subjects as miscegenation from the camera. Where governments did not censor directly, they often caused industry to censor itself.

Another restrictive factor was the filmmakers' own limited vision. For early filmmakers and many later ones who worked in the studio and never visited the real Africa, "Africa" was this complex of received ideas and censored subjects, the Dark Continent of Stanley's violent mind. For filmmakers working on location in Africa, the window through which they saw the continent was a colonial one; in the English-language industry, this meant West Africa, South Africa, and "British East," later Kenya and Uganda. Those who filmed on location, especially the Americans, were usually newcomers to Africa, and they were necessarily the captives of their colonial hosts: this situation influenced both the linguistic and the iconographic vocabularies in which they presented "Africa." The East African language Swahili became in a bastardized form the "spoken African" of virtually every sound film. The effect of such constraints was an even further reduction in real information about the real Africa, with all Africans called Zulus in early films, and with, in the sound era, one language and one landscape and a few physical types replacing the hundreds of languages and cultures and physical environments of that enormous continent.

Nor should we forget the audience of motion pictures as a factor in their arrested content. Commercial movies are not made in a vacuum, nor are they meant to appeal to idealized humans; they are made for very real audiences about whom, it is thought, something is known. What is known, although it may not be so defined, is the prior knowledge of that audience, what Pierre Sorlin has called its "capital," its stock of fairly general, even incorrect *but broadly believed* "knowledge" of a time or place. The film audience's knowledge of Africa has until recently been an even further reduction of the reductive nineteenth-century ideas, and it is questionable whether it is much better today.

The "Africa" of film, then, was from the beginning an Africa seen through several filters. When the filmic "Africa" and Africa are compared, a disjunction can always be found. Some of this disjunction is the result of ignorance, some of indifference, some of wilfull blindness, some of governmental or industrial interference or even censorship; but some of it is inevitable—the impossibility of ever capturing an almost infinite complexity with the camera.

IT HAS BECOME a truism of recent criticism that commercial motion pictures about Africa are racist. Contemporary scholarship has abandoned the language of what used to be called objectivity and has embraced a rhetoric that includes such terms as "'master race' narcissism" and "the voyeuristic gaze" to describe films about Africa. Thus, the established fact of a repulsive racism rises between viewer and films like a colored glass, through which, we are told, we must look if we are to view them properly.

The studies that have produced the notion of the racist monolith have been primarily studies of images, although their sense of "image" has been a very loose one that often referred least of all to *cinematic image*. Indeed, a failure to take full account of the primary sense of "image" as *picture* and to depend instead on a sometimes slippery notion of image as figure of speech has led to such recourses as using another person's plot summary as a source for a racist "image." Failure to use cinematic images has also led to some misreading of key films, particularly those whose nonracist cinematography was a critique of their racist scripts.

But is racism the only thing to be seen in these films? That is the question with which this book began. It, however, gave rise to a prior question: Why has Africa been such an important location for commercial filmmaking (more than four hundred titles)? Then, are there varieties and degrees of racism in these films? Is there significance, for example, in the emergence and development of black actors and producers? Is it not important to follow the change—surely for the better—in the way in which black Africans have been shown in films, and also to trace how contemporary black film artists themselves define and use "Africa"? As well, do these films change over time or are they merely replications of received attitudes and prejudices, everlastingly "colonialist," forever "entrenched in the dehumanizing spirit of slavery?"

A body of scholarship has shown links outside Africa among issues of race, gender, and class. Are these issues also linked in films about Africa? For example, women are conspicuously absent from some pictures, splendidly present in others; have the repetitive discoveries of racism obscured sexism—both in films and in modern Africa?

How is class represented in films about Africa, and do issues of class support or contradict issues of race and gender? Is class important to distinctions between American and British films at certain periods, or is it important to political questions raised by certain films?

Finally, how do the films reveal things other than racism in the societies that produced them? How do these films illuminate social history, both of Africa and of the producing countries, especially the United States and Great Britain? Are the African films of these last two nations different? If so, why? Are there significant differences in the films of the third major producer, South Africa?

This book, then, is an attempt to answer these questions through a critical evaluation of feature-length, English-language films set in, or about, Africa. My approach is often thematic, but I am also concerned with the quality of the films, with actors, and with particular problems whose solutions produced particular performances, because these matters affected both the cinematic image of major issues and the audience perception of them. I am also concerned with dominant myths and the archetypes who populate them, and with the relationship between the myths and archetypes of individual films and their historical moments. I have used "myth" and "archetype" throughout in a critical rather than an anthropological or psychological sense and have relied particularly on identifying archetypes that are significant embodiments of ideas or attitudes.

Restricting the body of films to those in English and released in the United States or Great Britain isolates a coherent body of work: films made in the United States, Great Britain, and (selectively), South Africa (although South African film is a distinct entity that deserves, and is beginning to receive, separate study). Further restricting these films to those having to do with Sub-Saharan Africa gives even greater coherence and identifies more than four hundred films, although some decisions along this geographic line are almost arbitrary (the inclusion, for example, of *Khartoum* but not of *Sudan*). The majority of the resulting films are American, because the American industry has long dominated the English-language market, sometimes outproducing the British nine to one. Rivalry between the two national industries has produced a xenophobia on both sides that sometimes tilted critical appraisal and that has caused such trade restrictions as the British Quota Act of 1927 and its successors; nonetheless, neither trade rivalry nor critical xenophobia has made it illogical to group the films for study, and so I have considered them pretty much together, pretty much chronologically, pointing out such distinctions as I have found significant.

The result, I hope, goes beyond discoveries of racism.

PART 1
The Beginnings

1 THE WHITE QUEEN AND THE HUNTER

The lights go down, the shrill voices of children still, and to the throbbing of drums, a woman takes shape on the screen of the neighborhood movie house. Her nature—magic, erotic, powerful—defies all sense, but the movies make her real.

The White Goddess is a key filmic archetype of the white idea of Africa. However much we patronize her, however much we see her as a cliché and not a myth figure, she is in the consciousness and the unconsciousness; in the very worst sense, she is in the blood. Beautiful (by white standards), magical, powerful, she is a goddess to be sought through the horrors of movie jungle and desert: ruler of hordes of black people by virtue of her whiteness—itself her magic and her power—she is the embodiment of a gut-level racialism. Whether she is the wild woman of *Trader Horn* or the white-robed Vestal of *Jungle Queen*, she is a proof of white might in Africa, and she descends from a single female ancestor: Ayesha, She-Who-Must-Be-Obeyed, the immortal white beauty of *She*.

She was an Edison title of 1908, directed by E. S. Porter. It was filmed again by other makers in 1911, 1916, 1917, and 1925. It signalled the fascination of a single source for early movie-makers, one that quickly dominated cinematic ideas of Africa: the writings of Rider Haggard.

Henry Rider Haggard was born in 1856. Unlike many who would write or make films about Africa, he knew parts of the continent well. He had "with [my own hands] hoisted the British flag over the Transvaal" at the annexation of 1877. The locations he was to write about, the male characters—white hunters and black warriors—came out of personal observation. The filter through which this observation reached page and screen, however—Haggard's imagination—was at the outer edge of the exotic. The resulting novels, above all *She*, *Allan Quatermain*, and *King Solomon's Mines*, all published in the 1880s, were a dizzying mixture of realism and racial and erotic wish-fulfillment.

Whether Haggard created the Victorian idea of Africa, or whether the Victorian subconscious created Haggard, these three novels became the best-selling wellsprings of African fiction, then of film. Originally taken as serious adult works, they were by the early twentieth century "boys' books," but their influence was nonetheless profound. For better or worse, they gave movie-makers an Africa so imaginatively rich that it can be argued that every maker of African fantasy films has depended on Haggard for characters, settings, and actions, with the single exception of the character of Tarzan. Most straight fiction films can be traced ultimately to Haggard for the imagery they use in communicating "Africa." Weird settings, erupting volcanoes, valuable treasures, unflappable hunter-heroes, demonic black witches, lost white civilizations, warrior tribes, white goddesses—all poured from Haggard as from a spring, watering blockbusters and serials alike, wetting the edges even of documentaries, and in our own time splashing into science fiction.

She was the first Haggard title filmed, and the one filmed most often. The Edison version seems lost; the 1911 one (Thanhouser) survives. Not surprisingly, it was stage-bound and uncertain, with takes as long as forty-five seconds and scene after scene in which the actors walk into position and then stand there. Despite its exotic source, it remained mundane—an Egyptian priest prays in what looks for all the world like a small-town church, complete with benches.

Nevertheless, *She's* core is there. It is a story of obsession, reincarnation, and witchcraft, with probably unconscious resonances of racism and male sexual unease. A self-described "ugly scholar" named Holly receives, in England, a small boy and a locked box from a dying friend. The boy, Leo, grows into a handsome man; when he comes of age, the box is opened, and its contents prove that he is the latest in a line that traces back to the Pharaohs. The box also urges him to find the immortal woman who destroyed the progenitor of this line of handsome men. So ugly Holly, gorgeous Leo, and Holly's comic servant Job head off into uncharted Africa to find *She-Who-Must-Be-Obeyed*, Ayesha.

After travails along the way, they find Ayesha, now two thousand years old but still beautiful and queen of an underground world, Kor. She still keeps Leo's ancestor's mummy, but when she recognizes Leo as the reincarnation, she transfers her erotic fixation to him. A rival woman appears, Ustane; Ayesha destroys her. Wanting to make Leo immortal so that they may spend eternity together, she leads him and Holly to the magic fire that gives her life, but when she bathes in it, she burns to death and shrivels, first to a monkey, then to a cinder. Leo is freed from Ayesha's spell, and the three white men escape.

This material so gripped adult Victorians that Kipling told Haggard that "something" had spoken through him in writing it. By 1911, that something was undoubtedly dated, and the Thanhouser film did nothing to redeem it. The picture was hopelessly reductive: eroticism became allure; obsession became romance; the exotic past became civic-pageant quaintness. The beard-and-bathrobe costumes were cheesy; Ayesha's beauty was a matter of face and lots of hair, with her body covered in enough white fabric to outfit a clipper ship. The acting style was highly uncertain, with much indicating and a semaphoric use of gestures, many messages being communicated by the same outstretched arm—

Go! They went that way! See what you've done now, you fool! To the fire! Poorly painted box sets showed the movie's link to the contemporary stage. Moreover, the film was without blacks, animals, or jungle. It achieved a bizarre "Africa" by virtually eliminating the African adventure that leads up to the discovery of Ayesha's Kor; in other words, *She* was in Africa but not of it. Since 1935, film versions have moved *She* out of Africa altogether—to Mongolia, Palestine, and deep space.

Will Arda made an English version of *She* five years later (1916) but did not buy the right to do so. Haggard had sold film rights to H. Lisle Lucoque in 1913. Arda was sued and subsequently prevented from showing his film, now lost. While Arda and Lucoque were at law, another *She* was filming in America (Fox, 1917). Directed by Kenean Buel, it starred Valeska Suratt as Ayesha. "Never had an idea that Valeska Suratt could be so beautiful with a veil on," mused *Variety's* Fred. The gauze "sometimes [slips] to such an extent there is nothing left to the imagination. This alone will be reason enough to establish the box office drawing quality of the film." The male actors—Ben L. Tagart and Tom Burroughs—were "particularly weak," but *She* was a "rattling good feature" despite Suratt's emergence from the magic fire as a "hideous ape."

In London, Lucoque had begun filming "at great expense" in association with Will Barker; C. B. Cochran was also involved. Barker and Lucoque directed, with Alice Delysia as Ayesha. It marked the beginning of a productive relationship between Lucoque and Haggard. Within a year, Lucoque had bought film rights to six Haggard novels, five of them with African settings: *King Solomon's Mines, She, Allan Quatermain, Queen Sheba's Ring,* and *Dawn.* Rachel Low has cited *She* and *Dawn* as two Lucoque films that were "possibly . . . the best among the few outright adventure stories chosen for adaptation during the war."

However, the most effective *She*, and the last with an African setting, was not Lucoque's, but a virtually Anglo-American production filmed in Berlin in 1925. Directed by Leander de Cordova and produced by G. B. Samuelson, it had Betty Blythe as a stunning, disturbing Ayesha, and Tom Reynolds as a Holly who is far more interesting than the supposed male lead, Leo.

Blythe, costumed in as little as the industry's self-censorship would allow, was hardly dressed for the Berlin winter, where filming was done in an unheated zeppelin shed. Her performance gave no hint of the rough conditions, however. She had already shown her capacity for exotic sexiness in *Chu-Chin-Chow*; now, the *London Times* placed her in the vamp tradition as "a most modern and intelligent vampire." It is still a fascinating performance, with hints of world-weariness in her necrophilia, of autoeroticism in her self-absorption, as if the atmosphere of 1920s Berlin had affected her. Although Blythe was not beautiful in the manner of Garbo or Deneuve, we can believe that she is so: "Ankles more perfect than sculptor ever dreamed of," Holly says in the novel, tracking like a camera up to "the snowy argent of her breast. . . . I gazed above them at her face and—I do not romance—shrank back blinded and amazed. . . ." Somehow, Blythe makes this schmaltz believable.

Regrettably, Blythe was not matched by the other actors. Carlyle Blackwell, in tousled curls as Leo, looks as if he is playing *Charley's Aunt*—as the aunt. Mary Odette's Ustane is insignificant, a wisp of dark pancake. The various troglodytes who inhabit Kor are laughable. "The cannibals look like black-face comedians," sneered *Variety*; they lurch about in Alley Oop furs, renegades from a Three Stooges short. Reynolds's Holly is at least a figure who captures our interest, and so a fitting foil for Blythe's Ayesha. His style is all wrong, to be sure; he could easily be back in the 1911 version, waving arms and all. In his scenes with Blythe, however, we get some understanding of what Haggard was after when he made Holly intellectual but ugly. Ayesha is, of course, intellectual and gorgeous; Holly, overcome, sinks to his knees. "Women hate the sight of me," Holly says in the novel, but this woman does not: she positively *enjoys* him. Seeing this Ayesha and this Holly, you understand at last why Holly is central, how empty it would be if beautiful Leo and Ayesha were brought together without him. Ayesha-Holly is Beauty and the Beast, but it is Beauty and the Intelligent Beast—or the Beast of Intelligence. Only then, when we have seen that, do we understand what happens when Leo's beauty appears and obsesses Ayesha: Beauty and the Beauty, against all intelligence, all reason (and perhaps ultimately autoerotic because Beauty sees Beauty as a reflection). Ayesha's equal is Holly. If there were to be "love," she would love Holly. Instead, she *has to have* Leo, and we see in Blythe's performance that she has no choice. This is a character in whom eroticism is destiny.

This *She* was almost an hour long,* enough time to tell the Ayesha story but not enough to include the African adventure of finding her; again, it is in Africa but not of it. The feeling is claustrophobic: scenes open out, as in the rather wonderful party, with its rows of burning mummies for illumination, but then they close down again to patently phony caves. The route to the magic fire again opens the film up, with the crossing of a chasm and a balancing boulder done with considerable impact (clearly borrowed from the stage), but by then the film is almost over. Then Ayesha burns, a great piece of spectacle, with the contrast of apparent nudity and the fire, and the three men are left looking wonderfully relieved. They cling to a rock and let the wind blow through their hair. But where the rock is, and where the wind is blowing from, we do not know. Is this really Africa?

Haggard himself died before the 1925 *She* was released. He was given credit for the titles, however, so this has something of the status of an authorized version.

---

* Probably the cut American release; the British original ran 114 minutes (Dunham).

Haggard's real work was over by the time film became a dominant medium, so he did no other writing for it, yet he took a good deal of interest in it. "The cinema theatres are filled up with cheap lines of dumped American films," he complained in a letter to the *Times* in 1919. Censorship "might be stricter" to get rid of "mere vulgarity," to clear the way for qualities that sound like his idea of his own works: "pathos, wonders, and beauties . . . history . . . romance. . . ." Given his titles for the 1925 *She*, we can assume that he thought the film embodied those qualities.

Critical reaction, however, at least in America, indicated that *She*, and perhaps Haggard's entire vision, were outdated. "[Its] day was long ago. . . . A complete cipher . . . terrible photograhy . . . impossible story . . . just a laugh. . . ." The critic's memory was as short as his temper: *She* had never been filmed before, "nor is any previous exhibition recalled."

Yet, when you see the 1925 *She,* you understand the work's attraction. It is a great story, even if it is "impossible." It is a great starring vehicle. It offers considerable scope for spectacle. It reeks of sex, some of it more complex than boy-meets-girl. That said, you wonder why it never works better on the screen. The answer lies in good part in the Ayesha-Holly-Leo constellation; the filmmaker casts a female star, a character actor, and a pretty male. (In the 1935 version, for example, Nigel Bruce played Holly, Randolph Scott Leo, to Helen Gahagan's Ayesha; in 1965, it was Peter Cushing, John Richardson, and Ursula Andress.) The female star and the character actor interact and even, it is to be hoped, give off sparks; Leo is comatose through much of the action. Holly does everything: he deciphers the messages in the old box, leads the African expedition, saves Leo's life, has a battle of wits with Ayesha, and suffers the humiliation of being rejected by her. Such an action can work only if Holly is either sexually attractive himself or supremely repellant, a Quasimodo; Tom Reyolds managed to convey some of the latter. Most versions have settled for a middle ground—Cushing is a good example—and the films go limp.

This is too bad, because *She*'s underlying dynamics are compelling. In a real sense, because of the way that commercial movies are cast, *She* is always a movie about a powerful person, a rejected equal, and a sex object. Such a story normally has a male star, a female star, and a bimbo (female). By position, then, Leo is a bimbo. Ayesha, by position, is a powerful woman as designed by a man—a man in drag. Gender reversal is at the heart of the motion picture, with the woman (Ayesha) doing to men what men usually do to women (rejecting the worthy choice and choosing the sex object)—reason enough for punishing her by burning her back to monkeydom. (This hint of the ape within the woman, a kind of reverse Darwinism, is never suggested of any of Haggard's men.)

One of Haggard's biographers has written that the final fire "symbolizes . . . sexual lust that consumes all it touches," but a woman who has been chaste for two thousand years hardly seems consumed by lust. Rather, it is Leo (and perhaps

Holly) who is consumed by lust when under Ayesha's spell. The fire seems less like lust, then, than a release from lust. Before he becomes Ayesha's victim, Leo has a horror of her that suggests a horror of sexuality, or at least of heterosexuality. Rather than the fire's symbolizing Ayesha's lust, then, it seems to serve as punishment for being a woman, for being an object of desire, for making hetero-sex possible and then obligatory.

In another sense, *She* is a movie about youth and its preservation, and a critique of how far preservation can be carried—an obsession wherever commercial motion pictures are made. Ayesha preserves her lover through the centuries as a mummy, but of course he is dead; she preserves herself, but pays a huge price in world-weariness, accumulation of unusable knowledge, and final immolation. Leo is a reincarnation of a face and a body that seem to have come down the centuries unchanged—eternal youth through mindless repetition. Both Ayesha and Leo are immobilized by their preservation (he is literally comatose; she is the prisoner of her own immortality, living in a cave/grave). Only Holly is dynamic, intelligent, active. And he is ugly, the presumed opposite of youth and beauty. The only way out for any of the three is the fire, which is intended to admit Leo to Ayesha's eternal youth, thus allowing them to meet in sex and get out of the prisons of their beautiful bodies; Holly will presumably be wiser, at least. Instead, the fire destroys Ayesha and frees Holly and Leo—to age and die. At a popular level, this is great stuff; at another—presumably the one Kipling admired—it is tantalizing and disturbing, and it has the potential for a kind of (Victorian) profundity.

Male fear of female sexuality is at the heart of *She*. The fire is ambivalent, at best: it promises Leo immortality, but before his eyes it destroys Ayesha's beauty, leaving a shriveled monkey, then a cinder. This aged monkey also appears as the witch Gagool in *King Solomon's Mines*, suggesting a particular revulsion of Haggard's. It is as if the monkey-crone exists within the woman, a beast lurking within every female (perhaps an image of time, one that erases the appeal of youth). The fire strips away the shell, the femininity. Leo, the handsome object of obsession, is supposed to follow her but is saved by her death. There is no question but that he is *saved*; with Holly and Job, he is shown in the film as freed, in a tableau that recalls heroic paintings.

Ayesha lives in a world of caves; to find her, to have her, the men have to enter the caves; in the farthest cave is the fire. A more literal reference to the vagina and sexuality can hardly be imagined, but sexuality—fire—is seen as dangerous, even fatal: is it a reference to venereal disease?

In *Allan Quatermain*, a pillar of fire in a cave almost destroys the adventurers on a journey under the earth. When they emerge—soon to discover two white queens and a white civilization in the heart of Africa—they are attacked by giant crabs. The symbolism here is perhaps too vulgar to be believed: at almost the dirty-joke level, the fire and the crabs *both* suggest venereal disease this time. If this is far-fetched, I suggest at least that vaginal caves, male pain, and death were strongly associated in Haggard's unconscious.

After 1925, *She* abandoned Africa, but the work left an enduring archetype behind—the White Queen. She appeared again and again as various jungle princesses, white goddesses, and virgin priestesses. Not as a 100 percent Ayesha, of course: Ayesha's vampish eroticism was dropped. It is as if post-1925 movies kept the shell and discarded the peanut.

Ayesha's symbolic world went, too. Hollywood's White Queens lived above-ground, for one thing; for another, they were mortal young women, not well-preserved sex bombs with a monkey inside. Nor did they carry fire in their loins, or even crabs.

Some of them were simply glorified nature girls—pretty virgins who had grown up wild and looked cute in leather teddies, like Julie London in *Nabonga*, who had been raised by a gorilla. (She did, however, live in a cave.) Their antecedents were often quite ordinary; they were the lost offspring of dead explorers or missionaries or crash victims. Some, to be sure, were magical: Ruth Roman, in *Jungle Queen* (1944), appeared and disappeared to save her "tribe" from the Nazis. A very few were ancient and evil (as in *Jungle Moon-Men*, a Jungle Jim movie), and a few were young and beautiful and evil (the dark queen in *Allan Quatermain and the Lost City of Gold*), but most were good, or at least corrigible. And they were not hanging around waiting for a two-thousand-year-old man; rather, they were the pretty, pert objects of some young American's quest, and when they were found they fell in love at first sight and ran off with him just as fast as their now-angry tribes would allow.

"THERE IS NO woman in it," says the hero of Haggard's *King Solomon's Mines*, and there is not—not if you mean a white woman, and not until talkies arrive, anyway. The absence of a white female, however, in no way prevented this Haggard novel from creating a white archetype. Now, however, the archetype was not She, but He.

Just as the White Queen embodies racial notions of Africa, so does the White Hunter, and he, too, has his origins in Haggard. The actual term was not used by him but rather dates from a safari company's brochure of 1908, coined to assure white clients that a *white* professional would back them in the field and run the safari. The figure, however, was already perfected in Haggard's Allan Quatermain, eponymous hero of one novel and of, above all, *King Solomon's Mines*. It was to Quatermain that reference after reference was made when later hunters and explorers wrote about their own adventures in Africa: to a remarkable degree, they had read the Haggard novels as boys and saw themselves as after-images of Quatermain in their own lives. It was no accident that the first filming of *King Solomon's Mines* was dedicated to "all big and little boys in the hope that it may instill in them the love of adventure which has helped to make the British Empire what it is to-day."

Quatermain was the *gentil parfait knight* of African adventure. He was very different from the White Queen, having no magic about him, no divinity. Like the queen, however, he represented a wish fulfillment, and, as with her, the wish was a male one.

The two Quatermain novels are both quest stories; indeed, they elevate the quest to one of the major African themes. They involve the same white male characters, especially Quatermain; both have an important black African figure, as well. Both combine real African locations with fantastic objects—in one, a lost white kingdom; in the other, the source of the Biblical King Solomon's wealth. They separate, however, as those different objects radiate back to define the realism of their Africas: *Quatermain's* lost civilization of "Milosis" and its two white queens are so far off the known map that they must be reached by a fantastic underground journey, whereas King Solomon's mines are almost within the known, probable because of the real-world discoveries of Kimberley's diamonds and the Rand's gold reef. As a result, *Quatermain* is a fantasy, *King Solomon's Mines* a romance; the distinction affected their first embodiment in film. *KSM* is a myth of empire, the wealth of Africa proposed as the goal of the white hero's quest; *Quatermain* is a myth of misogynistic sexuality, like *She*. The myth of empire has had more staying power than the myth of Victorian eroticism.

Allan Quatermain and *King Solomon's Mines* were two of the titles purchased by Lucoque in 1918. The films were in fact made in South Africa by African Film Productions and serve as an introduction to the little-understood South African film industry, which had really begun in 1916. (A single film, *The Great Kimberly* [sic.] *Diamond Robbery*, had been made in 1910.) The director-producer I.W. Shlesinger became an important figure whose theatre holdings were ultimately taken over by Twentieth Century-Fox in 1955. After releasing fifteen films in 1916 alone, the South African industry continued to produce gradually dwindling numbers of pictures until 1924, when a political shift (English to Afrikaner) coincided with the end of Shlesinger's production; then there were no releases between 1925 and 1930. Although these pre-1924 pictures included the Afrikaans *De Voortrekkers* (*Winning a Continent*), a celebration of Boer history, they at first gave more weight to British culture and the English language—hence the Haggard pictures and *Symbol of Sacrifice*, a military-glory picture about the same historical events as the much later *Zulu* and *Zulu Dawn*.

At this early stage, most South African films were meant to play on both Boer and British sympathies, not least by giving them a common enemy in the native Africans. *King Solomon's Mines* and *Quatermain*, although focused on British characters and aspirations, also included symbols acceptable to Afrikaner culture—the ox-wagon, the land, the promise of wealth. Haggard himself had lived in South Africa and had set his novels there; thus, his fantasies were logical choices for two of the four epics with which that industry began.

Both films apparently were directed by Lucoque in 1918. They would now be remarkable among fictional releases if only because they were among the first to be shot on African location, but they are also remarkable for their sophistication, their scope, and their fidelity to two complex novels. *Quatermain*, regrettably, does not seem to exist any more, except as a few stills; these show white actors in rather Roman settings and costumes, Haggard's white land of Milosis. The one battle scene looks starved compared to the battles in the contemporaneous *KSM*: even in 1918, it wasn't as cheap to gather a white army as a black one.

King Solomon's Mines, however, still exists almost in toto, the only lacuna an opening sequence in Solomon's Jerusalem; the surviving still photo from it recalls the opulent sets of *Intolerance*. The rest of the film is meticulously faithful to Haggard. Lucoque's direction, however, was so nonselective that the novel's heightening of Quatermain's role—easy as pie with first-person narrative—was lost, and this bearded, unremarkable man rather fades into the film. The African character Umbopa (an exiled king in disguise) was played by a handsome, muscular black man, suggesting some of Haggard's nonracist interest in individual South Africans; the two prominent African women, however—the witch Gagool and "Foulata, Infada's Daughter"—were played by white women in blackface. This bit of racism may have been justified by Lucoque's misplaced concept of both as dancers, Gagool as a snakey slinker, Foulata as a *moderne* exponent of eurythmics. That both die recalls the two women in *She*—Gagool as the witch within Ayesha, Foulata as another Ustane, and like her in love with one of the white men: one dies for being evil, one for being good (i.e., no black woman can hate or love a white man and live). Lucoque's takes are long, his camera static. When he uses real Zulu men, he gets interesting images; when he covers Zulu women with what look like pearl-trimmed brassieres, he becomes ludicrous. His battle scenes promise much in their long shots but don't deliver in medium closeup, which shows brouhaha gone out of control. Nonetheless, there is great vigor to them (and a real sense that the white actors were in danger of getting their teeth knocked out). These scenes were something very new in London. "English film crowds . . . might learn a profitable lesson [from] a real rough and tumble at close quarters," one observor noted. One source has said that six thousand black actors were used.

The two films appeared in London a few months apart, and both were lauded. *Allan Quatermain* was judged "as good as, if not better than, *King Solomon's Mines."* Neither seems to have been released in the United States.

THE REMARKABLE SOUTH African version of *Quatermain* was to be the only one of that story until 1987. Not so with *King Solomon's Mines*, which was to see three major productions and a dizzying number of spin-offs, so that it is *KSM* that has been mostly responsible for the Quatermain/White Hunter archetype.

The second *KSM* came in 1937. When the *Times* reviewed the 1935 *She* (set in Mongolia), it warned that Haggard was now dangerous turf, and any filming of his work "would require to be made in a mood of romantic exuberance, with a large and romantic credulity." This was extraordinarily canny advice. Regrettably, it was ignored by Gaumont when it made *King Solomon's Mines* for 1937 release. Neither exuberance nor credulity was in strong supply, and largeness and innocence were markedly lacking. What the film did have was Paul Robeson.

Robeson was already a major star. However, his presence skewed the story in an unfortunate way: he aroused expectations about his role from the beginning of the film, rather than surprising with the later revelation that he is a king. As well, he had to sing, so that at times the film sounds like *Old King Solomon's River*. Nonetheless, Robeson's presence gave the film importance, whereas it easily could have fallen flat, and he made it impossible to cast white actors in blackface in other African roles. (The practice was still common.) Instead, black actors like Robert Adams and the gorgeously screen-named Ecce Homo Toto were given good roles.

The film tried to follow the novel's story. Two English adventurers, Curtis and Good, set out to find a relative, who is himself looking for the fabled mines of King Solomon. They hire Quatermain to guide them. He takes on a mysterious black, Umbopa, who wants to go in the same direction. They find their way to Kukuanaland, where Umbopa reveals himself as the rightful king and therefore the rival of the evil Twala and the witch-woman Gagool. After a titanic battle, Quatermain and his clients find the treasure, fill their pockets with diamonds, escape Gagool, and return to England rich. "No women in it," as Quatermain himself says, except Gagool, who is ageless, evil, and magical— Ayesha after the fire makes a monkey of her.

In the film, then, a female role—Kathy O'Brien (played by Anna Lee, wife of director Robert Stevenson), the stage-Irish daughter of a stage-Irish father, both of them enough to make you call for the Ulster Constabulary Force—was created from whole cloth. She glues herself to Curtis (John Loder), and love oozes all over adventure.

After "Quartermain" (that extra R will keep cropping up), played by a pipe-smoking, fiftyish, genteel Cedric Hardwicke, "meets cute" with the Irish, they head up-country, picking up Robeson along the way. They cross what seems to be the Kalahari, and Robeson sings the sort of song that whites compose for blacks to sing. They run out of water, but Robeson "smells" more and leads them to it. They come to a mountain range, and Robeson sings about climbing mountains. Everybody stands around and listens.

By this time, Kathy is preparing the food (mostly melons), as if she were a pre-feminist secretary making coffee; the black characters are calling the whites "bwana," as if they were in East Africa; and Geoffrey Barkas's location footage has been cut to the merely tepid, so that Africa does not even seem to have animals—an oddity in a film about a professional hunter. However, with the arrival in Kukuanaland, Barkas's footage gains depth and excitement. A real African village with real people working gets careful attention. So do the inevitable bare-breasted women—obligatory T & A. (Of course, Anna Lee is not shown this way.) There is some savage dancing, augmented by rather balletic work by London-based professionals.

There is the inevitable battle. The British censor before release made "a request for the toning down of violence." It has apparently been toned down to the point of disappearance; missing most of all is the savagery of the whites, which, in Haggard's novel, takes on a Viking quality, a sense of Berserker atavism. In the motion picture, their efforts seem small and very civilized.

The adventurers then find the treasure but are stopped by a volcanic eruption. Things become soggy when Kathy maunders on about Ould Ireland. All bad things must end, however, and they escape the lava; Gagool is burned to cinders; and Robeson, now king, sings again, with the massed Kukuanaland Mixed Chorus behind him.

For all its faults, the motion picture was well received and made money. Its contradictions were not noted: in particular, the contrast of diamond-rich whites and laboring South African blacks was mostly passed over, despite a pointed juxtaposition of images. "I don't approve of anyone who tears up the face of the country for greed," says "Quartermain" at the beginning—a non-Haggard interpolation—against shots of black workers in the Kimberley diggings. By film's end, he is as rich as any other diamond king, although not from Kimberley; presumably, this was a means for the film to have it both ways and for the audience to accept the fiction that the "Africa" of Haggard's Victorian imperialism was the Africa of 1937. Nonetheless, the *London Times* turned caustically Marxist in summarizing the story as "European adventurers in search of mining concessions from the pretender to whom they give support."

"Mass stuff, unashamed hokum," pronounced the American *Variety*. The *London Times* doubted that Haggard could be adapted to film any longer. But another version of *KSM* was to show just how wonderfully the old excitements could be brought to life—and with a woman in it, too. And what a woman!

Metro-Goldwyn Mayer's 1950 *King Solomon's Mines* may well be the best Hollywood sound picture ever made about "Africa." This is not to say that it was about real Africa or that it dealt with real African societies or cultures. The clichés of the 1950 *KSM* are the familiar ones of a Victorian Africa as seen from Europe, but within that limitation the motion picture is a glorious one.

Filmed on location in Kenya, Uganda, and Ruanda-Urundi, it was partly a travelogue in color that splashed "a vast panorama of Africa, its wild beasts and primitive native tribes" all over the screen. The African scenes, gorgeously photographed under the unit direction of Andre Marton, were unlike anything seen before; it was as if Hollywood, taking note of the popular black-and-white travel-adventure films of the day, had taken a deep breath and said, "Now watch what *we* can do! (now that you've showed us how.)" Money made some of the difference—multiple cameras, endless takes, a good-sized crew—but there is no denying the brilliance of photography and editing. In particular, a wildlife stampede provided footage that MGM would use over and over in later films. Yet, if *KSM*'s only virtue had been wildlife and photography, it would have been a minor work. Instead, in its bending of the Haggard story, and above all in its two principals, it reached about as high as Hollywood ever dared to grasp with the adventure film. Stewart Granger as Quatermain, and especially Deborah Kerr as a wife looking for a lost husband, were sensational.

To see the film now is to realize how undervalued Kerr was in the 1950s— how far her intelligence, sexiness, and human warmth rose above the tightly bound Hollywood notion of womanliness of that time. Utterly without coyness (in a role that could have mired the actress), playing what is frankly a type (the True-Blue White Woman), working under conditions that knocked out a number of men, she gave a performance that matched Africa's photographed beauty.

Equalling her was Stewart Granger, until recently the bad boy of Gains-borough films. Here was no Cedric Hardwicke, puffing a pipe and gazing off into the imperial distance; as Quatermain, Granger brought a snarl and an equally wonderful smile to the White Hunter. This was a passionate Quatermain, and a sexually dangerous one who gave off lock-up-your-daughters emanations like musk. The interplay with Kerr's faithful wife was spectacular: again, a stereotype had been given new life because of the performers.

Haggard's story was changed: Kerr was a True-Blue White Woman searching for a husband who had been searching for King Solomon's wealth; she was accompanied only by a dull and futile brother (Richard Carlson). She thus had a strong objective—marital fidelity—that came into collision with Granger's sexual attractiveness. He, of course, was a loner and a misogynist—"A woman on safari? Never!"—with his own inner conflict as her courage and her own sexuality drew him out.

The setting was changed from South to East and Central Africa; some anachronisms resulted (Nairobi didn't exist in 1897, the date of the action, for example), but no matter. This *KSM* does on film what Haggard did in print— creating an internal probability so powerful that, once in, you never question details. The novel was written so that its Now was the reader's Now; the motion picture, however, places its Now half a century ago—"yesterday." This is a falling-off from Haggard, as is the reduction of the epic search for the mines to a love story (i.e., a romantic search for a solution to the problem of how Quatermain and the wife can wind up with each other). These changes reflect historical changes, however: postwar Britain was about to dissolve its empire, and "yesterday" and "love" were necessary substitutions for the imperial quest.

In place of Paul Robeson, this *KSM* offered an unknown as Umbopa. This tall, slender-handed Tutsi ("Watusi") was believable as a secret king, and the subplot was more credible because of him.

An awareness of black Africans was timidly new. Kerr tells Granger that his Quatermain is "too accustomed to subservience" when he complains that Umbopa is arrogant. Hollywood's blackfaced whites have finally been got rid of, and lean, muscular, sometimes dangerous-looking Africans have replaced the often overweight American blacks who played Africans in other movies. Cultural patronizing still goes on, to be sure: the Masai of East Africa are represented as cannibals, for example. It is as if the camera has matured to the point where it can see Africans, but it cannot accept them as they are.

This separation is in the motion picture's very action, as well: in its quest structure, the whites pursue a goal and the blacks impede them. The whites exist in individualized ones and twos; the blacks exist in masses. Whites are from outside Africa and remain separate from it; blacks are of Africa. "Jungle" is everywhere, full of snakes (the film has a ridiculous number of them), insects, and crocodiles; black Africans are close to this repellant Nature. Any treasure that Africa holds is to be grasped by whites and taken away. But now, the treasure that the two principals seek is permission to love each other, which Africa gives by killing the lost husband; it is as if imperial greed is too much to be tolerated in 1950, and so what formerly was economic ("European adventurers in search of mining concessions from the pretender to whom they give their support") has been reduced to the romantic, the general to the individual.

The film's perspective is still a very male one, as might be expected. Kerr's character stumbles about in long skirts and never gets into physical condition, despite six weeks of walking. She tears her blouses, always at the shoulder. She cannot be allowed a rifle, only a revolver, with which she is expected to do in a leopard. Her hair is far too long and has to be cut off. She can't keep up with the men. Granger has to teach her, carry her, protect her.

Yet, because Deborah Kerr radiates humanity and profound competence, the sexism of the film is almost turned back on itself. (In the real-life rigors of location work, she was stalwart; Granger said that "without her courage . . . the film would never have been finished.") Her performance constituted a kind of (probably unconscious) comment on her character's supposed helplessness.

THE SUCCESS—AND the quality—of the 1950 *KSM* led to a spate of "big" African motion pictures, which combined color photography and star names (*The African Queen*, 1951; *Mogambo*, 1953; *The Snows of Kilimanjaro*, 1953; *White Witch Doctor*, 1953; *Untamed*, 1955; *Odongo*, 1955; *The Roots of Heaven*, 1958). This was happening as the old Hollywood self-destructed, and these pictures were both symptoms of the collapse and attempts to prevent it (and, in several cases, unwitting contributors to it). Some of these films were particularly bad—*The Snows of Kilimanjaro* was an especially egregious example of a film crushed by its own pretensions—but *The African Queen* has become a minor classic, and *Mogambo* (a remake of *Red Dust*, also with Clark Gable but originally set in Asia) was a cheerful, handsome motion picture with a touching performance by Ava Gardner and a quite remarkable one by the normally pinched Grace Kelly. The misogyny of Granger's Quatermain carried over into a number of the male figures, and the True-Blue White Woman was present in most, spectacularly so in Hepburn's character in *The African Queen*. By and large, these pictures were the *KSM* mixture as before.

MGM's possession of the *KSM* location footage led it to release remakes and rehashes of its great movie—and the White Hunter archetype—for more than another decade. *Mogambo* was the first, and best, beneficiary. In 1959, the company released *Watusi*, with George Montgomery playing Allan Quatermain's son (an invention). The animal stampede footage was used intact, with Granger and Kerr recognizable if you go frame by frame. The screenplay was by James Clavell, whose principal challenge seems to have been to weave a story around the *KSM* footage, a feat made more difficult by the recognizable costumes of the originals; as a result, every reused scene had to have somebody in a bush hat with leopard band, somebody in a helmet, and somebody in a calf-length skirt. In 1963, MGM released *Drums of Africa*, with Torin Thatcher as "Jack Courtemayn" (sounds like Quatermain, get it?). The stampede rode again, and in this film the game is to identify as much *KSM* footage as possible—the bath scene; the Murchison Falls scene; the Masai-at-the bridge scene, with Stewart Granger tossing straw on the flames; the battle scene; the closing shot, and more. This would be laughable if there weren't the kernel of a very good film in *Drums of Africa*—something about love, rather than romance or boy-meets-girl. As it is, the film is a ridiculous hash. And what, you may ask, was Frankie Avalon doing in Africa?

The 1950 footage went around again in *Rhino!* (1964), a film not based on *KSM*—or much of anything else—and it had another life in *Trader Horn* (1973), an even worse movie that was so sloppily made that a jet aircraft and a metal fence can be seen in one sequence.

The immediate successors to *King Solomon's Mines*, then, were a mixed lot. MGM's reuse of its footage was cynical and the result was predictable. Nevertheless, Africa was now on the Hollywood map as *the* location for spectacle, and no decade was to pass thereafter without a number of expensive and ambitious African-location films.

Perhaps unsurprisingly, films based on Haggard were not to be among them. Only in the late 1970s and the 1980s were further attempts made. By then, both Africa and movies would be very different.

HAGGARD'S NOVELS BECAME the subject of a direct attack in film reviews as early as the mid-1920s, more as a rather vague attack on style than as an overt questioning of internal probabilities or of meanings. Particularly in America, trade reviewers used terms like "hokum." By the mid-1930s, "crudities of style [and] thought" were found "unsuitable for the mature or fastidious"; the suggested corrective was to make such films in "a mood of romantic exuberance," and so on. Such comments should not be taken too literally, but they surely reflected an unease with Haggard's kind of fantasy, even in the fairly thoughtless daily review. That unease seems to have arisen from a sensed—if not understood—contradiction between the world of the film and the world of the world.

Worth noting, then, is the praise heaped on the 1950 *KSM* for the "authentic African background," which gave the film "an extremely realistic air"—as if realism were a separate "attitude" that had been achieved in the face of the Haggard archetypes and the Haggard-African fantasy, and as if a film like the 1925 *She* had not been filmed as realistically as the technology of the day would permit. The 1950 *KSM*'s cinematography was praised for, it appears, capturing the "real" Africa. Moreover, the screen images were "authentic" and thus, it seems, they authenticated the myth, although those images were highly selective and were shot with a very Euro-American bias. This raises an important question: how did the images of *KSM* authenticate what, presumably, was its otherwise archaic fiction? Why did the color photography—especially that of the wild animal stampede—confer "realism" on the motion picture? What was this concept of filmic "reality" that it was seen as distinct from action and character?

The answers apparently lie in a circularity—i.e., "I know the real because I recognize it; I recognize it because it is real." That is, by intensifying established images of "Africa" (as with color, for example) and not asking the audience to broaden its perceptions to any new images, the film achieved "realism"—despite its inaccuracies.

A somewhat different solution to the collapse of the Haggard fantasy was used by the serials and Bs of the 1940s and 1950s, which redefined the audience from adults to children and produced a huge output of Haggard-inspired cheap films about an Africa of white queens, white hunters, lost tribes, leopard men, mermaids, volcanoes, treasures, and so on and on. Here the vaguely phrased question of style was answered by moving frankly away from realism to the style of the comic book, expressed particularly in costume, in acting, and in studio settings. In this comic-book world, the "Africa" of cannibalism, savagery, jungle, and white quests outlived its adult version by several decades.

2 THE ARISTOCRAT
OF THE TREETOPS_____

Everybody this side of Mars knows that Elmo Lincoln was the first screen Tarzan, c. 1917. That said, let me suggest—perhaps insist—that the real Tarzan, the genuine article, stepped in front of the cameras in the person of Johnny Weissmuller in 1932. With Weissmuller, the Lord of the Jungle took on a peculiarly American quality that thereafter resided in the popular idea of the character—for all that it was different from its creator's idea of it. No matter, either, that during the 1930s Weissmuller was only one of three Tarzans swinging through the Hollywood jungle: he was the real thing, and furthermore he had Maureen O'Sullivan, with whose Jane his Tarzan set up a household as American and endearing as that of Blondie and Dagwood.

Tarzan was the literary creation of a man who never went to Africa, an American hack writer named Edgar Rice Burroughs. Former ad man and former steno for Sears, Roebuck, he had a sometimes unhappy combination of fevered imagination and pedestrian intellect; the results were both exotic and banal, stunning and laughable. His literary landscape ranged as far as outer space, but he placed some of his most fantastic locations in what he called "Africa"—a place that included such oddities as a valley where medieval knights still fought in armor, "Opar" and its fabulous jewels, and a land ruled by women. Tarzan was his most memorable creation, appearing first in a magazine fiction in 1912. That first Burroughs "Africa" had tigers in it, a gaffe corrected in subsequent appearances.

One of Rider Haggard's biographers has said that Haggard and Kipling (*The Jungle Book*) were Burroughs's "twin sources." However, Burroughs's imagination seems also to have fed on the sort of stuff that played to American gullibility in nineteenth-century American newspapers—Lost Tribes of Israel, hideous Mormon and Masonic rites, Cardiff Giants—the same stock-in-trade from which *Huck Finn*'s Dauphin drew. For such inventions, a little fact goes a long way: Burroughs had little impetus to learn much about the real Africa. He "had done some reading about Africa in connection with the Stanley expedition" and had "done research at the beginning of his writing career," but these efforts left him profitably ignorant. Certainly, the pop literature of the day surrounding Stanley would not have provided much that was reliable, and it was most likely the source of the howler about tigers. Rather, what he would have picked up was an "Africa" that satisfied the requirements of the explorer-colonizer: a white man's "Africa," a place of bloody deeds and rich spoils—and, for Burroughs, enough blank spots on the map to house his fantasies.

"[His] comments about blacks. . . are, if not overtly racist, certainly very patronizing," one Burroughs biographer has admitted. Patronizing blacks was not the object, of course; lauding whites was. "Burroughs implies more than once that white American and Western European (most notably British) stock is the pinnacle of evolutionary trends. . . ." His Tarzan was conceived as *Lord* Greystoke, a British peer. In Burroughs's creation, Tarzan talked like a member of the House of Lords and thought like one; he looked superb in white tie and tails and could go swinging over the rooftops of Paris in dinner dress as easily as he swung through his "Africa" in a leather diaper. His nobility of both ethos and body came from his genes—not from his life in the jungle.

It is wrong, therefore, to think of Burroughs's Tarzan as a noble savage; he is, if anything, a savage noble, an exemplar of the idea that blood will tell. In Burroughs's novels, Tarzan is the offspring of two British aristocrats marooned on the "African" coast; orphaned there as an infant, he is stolen from their hut by a female ape and raised among the apes. Hence, he is Tarzan the Ape-Man—but he is also Lord of the Jungle, not because he is the strongest and the smartest (although he is), but because he is a Lord in England. He is what he is despite his apedom, not because of it, and, contrary to what we know of children raised without human care, he instantly and greedily becomes human the moment opportunity offers, teaching himself to read and speak (quite a trick). He is, in fact, a hack's version of Nietzsche's Superman, and his story is a eugenic myth.*

Burroughs was not shy about this meaning. He might have recoiled from the word fascist, but Tarzan is a fascistic literary conception: might makes right, racial purity brings ethical purity, and authority is absolute. When, in 1939, the Burroughs-created Tarzan Clans of America were contemplated as an alternative to the Boy Scouts, their first oath was, "I will obey the Chief." There was also the usual stuff about being clean, honest, and so on, but "I will train my body to be strong and healthy" and "I will bear pain" had inevitable resonances of the contemporary *Hitlerjugend.*

---

* This is not the same as a Darwinian myth, however; it is not natural selection that has produced Tarzan/Greystoke, but selective breeding—generations of British aristocrats marrying each other. This is one of the reasons why Bazin's contention that "there is no difference between Hopalong Cassidy and Tarzan except for their costume and the arena in which they demonstrate their prowess" is ludicrous.

* * *

ELMO LINCOLN WAS a barrel-chested strongman who posed in the hollow-backed fashion of the day—chin forward, knee cocked, the posture presenting not so much a lot of chest as a lot of gut. His Jane, Enid Markey, was a wimp who adopted the worried-virgin pose favored by the Gish sisters—shoulders rounded, chin down, arms pulled up, the whole upper body trying to protect the belly. This difference in attitudes toward the abdomen about summed up the characters—and the acting abilities—of the two principals. Nonetheless, it gave them an almost emblematic visual quality: the strongman and the virgin.

The film—*Tarzan of the Apes*—did well. It was, after all, a presold property. It had a sequel (actually a conclusion of the action started in the first film) in the 1918 *Romance of Tarzan*; Lincoln also appeared in a 1920 serial version called *The Adventures of Tarzan*. Because the prolific Burroughs sold individual Tarzan titles but not the character, three other Tarzans (one actually Son of) also appeared in that same year. This early Tarzanic glut extended into 1923 with *The Jungle Trail of the Son of Tarzan*, apparently a distillation of the serial *Son of*, and the last Tarzan until the late 1920s.

Tarzan of the Apes was shot in Louisiana, with additional footage that had been shot in Brazil, probably for some other purpose (perhaps ethnological record). The Brazilian location footage seems to have been effective as a version of Africa, for all that it was a false location: "many of the views of the jungle and of animal life are admirably done." The Brazilian footage, in fact, is so uncontrived that it makes the constructed sets look puerile, and the footage of black Brazilians in a village of thatched houses is so convincing that the acting of the professionals seems forced. Such was not the perception in 1918, however, when Lincoln's arm-waving and Markey's eye-rolling were part of the dominant style; the real Brazilians' natural restraint probably served to make them seem like a different sort of landscape.

The story of *Tarzan of the Apes* is more or less Burroughs's, and therein lies much of the film's difficulty. Burroughs's plot was in fact a complicated one, especially the Lord Greystoke line, which needed a good deal of exposition and much cutting between London and "Africa." In this silent film, its realization was skimpy. (Hence the sequel to complete it.)

Titles too often replaced pictures. "Lord Greystoke was summoned by the government to suppress Arab slave trading in British Africa," so he and Lady G. sail on a ship full of mutineers, who put them ashore (title) "at the edge of the almost impenetrable jungle." The Greystokes somehow put up a house with neatly chinked joints and a complete set of furniture before dying; their baby is taken by the apes, a dead baby ape's body being put in his cradle; and the boy Tarzan—first naked, then in a pair of fur shorts—grows into the incipient Jungle Lord. One sequence has him spying on a black village (the Brazilian footage), where black women are much in evidence.

A sailor from the same ship as the Greystokes, after being delayed by Arab slavers, now stumbles on the Greystoke cabin and teaches young Tarzan to read. The sailor leaves; Tarzan grows up, as a title tells us: "Tarzan the Man—Elmo Lincoln."

Lincoln poses. He wears the one-shouldered animal skin of the circus strongman, and a lot of hair held back by a headband. Lincoln was still fairly young, but he often seems middle-aged, partly because of that enormous gut.

Title: "A group of scientists and relatives of Tarzan's parents had finally decided to investigate [the sailor's] story of the jungle waif."

Some rather naive cross-cutting tries to keep both London and Africa in mind: Tarzan fights various beasts and black men (played by black, not white, actors) and experiences the death of his ape mother; Jane (Markey) and "Jane's maid, Esmerelda"—a black woman in white apron and cap—head for Africa with the scientists, relatives, et al.

Tarzan (having taught himself to write and spell his own name) leaves a note—"This is Tarzan's house"—at the Greystoke cabin, where he could expect the London whites to show up only because it seems to be the crossroads of Africa. Esmerelda, seeing the Greystokes' skeletons, screams and points; none of the London whites blinks an eye, although the relatives show a good deal of interest in the baby ape skeleton.

An effete Londoner—we know this because he has a painted-on moustache and wears plus fours, a Norfolk jacket, and a fedora—tries to kiss Jane. When she is carried off by a black African, he shouts (title) "Help! Help! Assistance!" The other men run back and forth.

Tarzan saves Jane from the black man. The fighting is rather like YMCA wrestling, which Jane cannot resist watching. Tarzan wins.

A somewhat confused sequence of black-white battle follows, with Tarzan setting fire to the black village and then sequestering himself with Jane, at which point (title) "Every throbbing pulse-beat spurred him to take her for his own." The reason for this response is quite straightforward: (title) "The first woman he had ever known."

Jane, however, knows men, and she tells him, (title) "Tarzan is a man, and men do not force the love of women."

Tarzan sinks to his knees and kisses her hand; Jane rolls her eyes. He makes her a bed of Spanish moss. He gives her his knife.

He saves her from lions, crocodiles, leopards, pythons, and an Indian elephant.

The film ends with Jane returned to the door of the Greystoke cabin, where we see her mouth the words, "I love you, Tarzan." Esmerelda is forgotten—perhaps still out in the jungle in her apron and cap—and the matter of the baby Greystoke and the inheritance is dropped (for the sequel).

To a surprising degree, this plot will serve Tarzan films for all time. Only when too-frequent repetition stales it and producers send Tarzan into more and more fantastic adventures will the Tarzan-Jane plot not suffice, and even then Jane will often have to be saved before the movie's end. One has to conclude, then, that the Tarzan of the films (if not of Burroughs's books) is not merely the aristocratic Lord of the Jungle; he is, rather, a sexual hero. Only in the decadent later films will it be possible to have Tarzan without Jane; in the films' prime, we must have Tarzan-Jane.

Jane, therefore, is worth looking at. She is "the first woman he had ever known." But we have seen him looking at black women; we have to conclude, therefore, that they are somehow not women; they are females of some other species—some animal of "Africa." It is impossible to say how much this dehumanization derives from their being black, how much from their being of Africa: the two things are, of course, laid one over the other. But what the viewer sees is that Tarzan will not mate with either the black *or* the African.

Tarzan as both boy and man is frequently shown in the trees in this first film. He escapes to the trees when he is wounded. He watches the blacks from a tree. As an adult, he is of the trees. The film emphasizes Burroughs's own symbolism of treetop life "above it all"—reminiscent of Sorlin's analysis of *Birth of a Nation*: "The whites come from the skies . . . they fly through space in an instant," while "the blacks stick to the ground." These are, of course, the whites of the Klan. White Tarzan flies, above all, godlike, Superman. "Africa"—its people, its animals, its land—is beneath him. This, then, is also part of the early film archetype—that the Jungle Lord be in Africa but not of it, joined to a woman whose whiteness and virginity are distinctly un-African, "the first woman he has ever known." The archetype is racial and geographical and sexual all at once.

Burroughs's idea of "breeding" is perhaps less clear. The Greystoke-London-aristocracy theme is only partly developed, but it is of course completed in the sequel. The other examples given us of the aristocracy are ludicrous, the behavioral signs by which a British audience might recognize its upper class lacking.

And, as Tarzan, Lincoln's strongman image conveys raw strength without conveying (in Burroughs's sense) nobility. Might makes right, all right, but it is merely might for its own sake. This Tarzan is a fascist without a cause.

The almost contemporaneous *Son of Tarzan* made even further hash of aristocratic caste-marks but kept Burroughs's aristocratic lineage. The movie also showed the danger in too much Tarzan: with, in effect, two Tarzans (father and son) it had to have two Janes (now an aging, but still helpless, Lady Greystoke, and a lost English [upper-class] helpless virgin named Meriam) and twice as many lions, pythons, and murderous Arabs and Africans. Seen all at a gulp, the picture is a ludicrous mishmash; seen as a serial, it probably worked well enough.

Tarzan's son replicates the father's childhood by growing up wild. Tarzan himself—now Lord Greystoke, in London—comes to the jungle and takes his clothes off, rather as a later Clark Kent will enter a telephone booth, and turns back into the Jungle Lord. Everybody gets lost, then found, then lost again; black Africans and Arabs attack, seemingly on whims; and at last, all the good whites reach the same spot in the jungle and everything ends.

Son of Tarzan did little to alter the cinematic Tarzan myth but probably reinforced its racialism. Its doubling of the principals reinforced the whiteness of Tarzan and his mate; it also allowed the audience to see Tarzan as a British peer in a peer's proper London setting. (This Lord Greystoke does *not* live in Africa.) The utterly mindless attacks by blacks and "Arabs" reinforced the unreason and the menace of both.

This insistence on the evil of "Arabs" is worth noting, "Arab" and "slaver" being treated as identical (a notion accepted but not emphasized in *Tarzan of the Apes*). "Arabs" are to be recognized by their robes and headdresses and dark eye makeup, which is "un-white," as was that of the villain Paulvitch in *Tarzan of the Apes*, whose name suggested Russia but whose appearance in connection with that name probably connoted East European Jew. This stereotyping would seem to be in line with the views of eugenicists of the day (Lothrop Stoddard, for example), that a "tidal wave" of non-Northern peoples was endangering "Nordic stock," a demagogic idea of considerable appeal in America, c. 1920, because of recent immigration. To a degree, then, these first Tarzan films expressed an American racial fear as well as a white racial boast—their contribution to the archetype. They also claimed for its aristocrats the moral high ground of opposition to slavery. On the face of it, this double claim of racial superiority and opposition to slavery seems contradictory, but it is precisely the claim that many Britons and Americans were making.

TWO MORE TARZANS came and went before Hollywood reinvented the archetype. One of these was Burroughs's own hand-picked choice of 1927, "the personification of Tarzan of the Apes as I visualize him": James H. Pierce, a "college man" with a profile and muscles. Burroughs's taste was not the popular one, however, and this Tarzan of the Halls of Ivy was forgotten. Nor was Frank Merrill any more memorable in a 1928 serial. They might have been the last of the Tarzans had not MGM produced another African motion picture in 1930: *Trader Horn*, which trailed a wealth of extra African location footage.

Trader Horn was a trip to the Haggard well, with a White Queen (Edwinna Booth, née Josephine Constance Woodruff) and a White Hunter (Harry Carey). Duncan Renaldo, in more makeup than Mae West, played the usual male love interest (for Booth). Half the film was a travelogue, using location footage; the other half was the encounter with the White Queen and the love that blossomed between her and Renaldo. You have to ask why Booth, who has grown up in black Africa, isn't somebody's wife, pounding maize meal in a hollowed log. The answer appears to be that she is immune to black men because she is white; more than that, she is virginal, a "priestess" who has grown from infancy to maturity in a black tribe, speaks no English, and has never seen another white. Naturally, she "falls in love" with the first young one she sets eyes on, and turns against her African people as a result. Renaldo tells her that "white people must help each other," and so she saves the two men. Then the three run away together, and the White Queen turns into just another sweet white kid, and the Africans come after her with spears and knives, just as they come after Renaldo and Carey. Away from her African tribe, she becomes a helpless white woman, bereft of her magic: the two white men have to carry her; later, she faints. At the movie's end, Renaldo takes Booth away—you can take the girl out of the jungle, *and* you can take the jungle out of the girl, it seems—and leaves Africa, presumably because all interest in Africa is now over. Booth, whom he has taught to kiss, is set for wifedom.

Harry Carey was a very American White Hunter. His relationship with Renaldo was meant to be avuncular. Carey sometimes looks, however, as if he is going to reach across and smear the younger man's lipstick in sheer disgust. His Horn loves Africa, and at film's end he stays and lets the ex-White Queen and the greenhorn go away together: "The jungle never grows old before a man's eyes the way a woman does," says Horn. Horn's only close relationship is with his black headman (Mutia Omoolu). Of course, the black man is killed; Horn cradles him as he dies, murmuring his name. One scholar has labeled Horn an "enslaver" for this relationship. The gunbearer represented an etablished archetype, to be sure, the good black servant, now the Good African. This was, perhaps, racialism, but was it really *enslavement?*

What made *Trader Horn* remarkable was not Carey's White Hunter or the Good African, however, but the location filming done by W. S. Van Dyke—"one-take Woody"—who took the entire cast on location for months in East Africa. The venture got good press as the first Hollywood African-location feature, the more so as one company member after another got sick and, to top it all, Booth almost died (probably from bilharzia). The company staggered home to find that the animal closeups had to be re-shot; Van Dyke did this in Mexico, outside the purview of American animal-lovers, with a cruelty that is still an industry benchmark. Actual kills were filmed, and a particularly grim one shows a big cat writhing in agony like a worm on a fishhook. The movie itself was a considerable success, however, and it and Africa gained further publicity from a lawsuit started by Booth over her near-fatal illness.

At this point, the *wunderkind* of Hollywood producers, Irving Thalberg, came on the scene. He saw that Africa could be big box-office, and he knew that MGM was sitting on yards and yards of African location film left over from *Trader Horn*. Half genius, half plunger, Thalberg decided to go for a quality Tarzan film.

Two crucial choices were made: *Trader Horn*'s Woody Van Dyke as director, and the swimming star Johnny Weissmuller as Tarzan. At first glance, Weissmuller was a strange choice. He was not conventionally handsome, had no gorgeous profile, no golden curls. He had heavy brows and dark, lank hair, not at all like a British aristocrat. In fact, he looked more Native American than "Nordic." His voice was high-pitched, and his line readings were flat. He was not a strongman, and his body did not have the articulated, armor-plate musculature of an iron pumper. He was an athlete, not a beefcake.

Yet he was the perfect American Tarzan.

Burroughs, it is said, did not see it that way. He wanted a Tarzan who spoke like a peer, and here, in the first important talking Tarzan picture, he got a monosyllabic lowbrow who didn't even speak proper English. The creation had left its creator and become something different—no longer *Tarzan of the Apes* but *Tarzan the Ape Man*. The archetype had reinvented itself—with the help of Thalberg and Van Dyke (and perhaps Ivor Novello, who is said to have worked on the dialogue, such as it was).

When production started, there seems to have been no intention to make a sequel. *Tarzan the Ape Man* (1932) is therefore complete in itself, more the story of Jane's surrender to a natural world than of Tarzan or of selective breeding. Jane was played by a young, small-boned actress named Maureen O'Sullivan, who proved to be a perfect foil for Weissmuller, both in this film—where she is still the London-bred virgin of earlier pictures—and in subsequent ones, when she would lighten his male heaviness and give him a new quality. Moreover, she embodied a metamorphosis in Jane that itself became an archetype, The Wild Mate. O'Sullivan's Jane, more than any of her predecessors, was restive with her sophistication and her civilization, and she *willed* to remain in Africa. This archetype lasted for at least the first three Weissmuller-O'Sullivan films (which have as part of their plots attempts to get Jane back to England), after which O'Sullivan's role was trimmed to a pert wifeliness, which became a mere "line of business" as other actresses came and went in the role.

Tarzan the Ape Man saw another innovation: gone entirely was the Greystoke story and Tarzan's boyhood. The gain in narrative momentum was enormous.

And, despite being a sound picture, *Tarzan the Ape Man* was often silent; its dialogue was not made to carry a burden better left to images, and so it did not suffer the deadness of the silent versions, where so much action was pushed into the titles.

Tarzan comes swinging into the picture, with that chilling and now-famous yell (compounded by a sound engineer from several sounds, animal and human) only after a good deal of time has been spent setting up Jane's story: her father is a trader (C. Aubrey Smith) obsessed by "the elephant's graveyard"; she is a butterfly who arrives in Africa with six trunks and several suitcases. They go on safari and encounter thousands of tribal Africans, all dancing (some of Van Dyke's location footage), giving rise to comments from the whites like "These are our very best people," "Let me show you what our best-dressed men are wearing," and, of a man carrying an ostrich-feathered staff, "Every man his own feather-duster." Then a dying African tells them that the elephant's graveyard is beyond "the Mutea escarpment," and off they go—frequently using the whip on the reluctant porters. Jane demonstrates her female inadequacy by falling off a cliff and needing rescue. At last, they reach the top—and Tarzan.

The astonishing freshness of Weissmuller's performance is hard to account for. He was not an actor, really, but his very inadequacies became part of the role (or the role was adapted to his inadequacies; such was Thalberg's gift). His physical ease, his superb swimmer's body (better shown in a skimpy leather loincloth than any previous Tarzan's), and his rare but wonderful smile were perfect. In a day when movie actors and movie roles blended (Karloff's monster, Myrna Loy's Nora Charles, even Chester Morris's Boston Blackie—illusory tradition and stability in the perpetual flux of popular culture), Weissmuller and Tarzan became each other. When he captures Jane, then, he begins an action and a relationship that is to last for ten real-time years, and an eternity of movie myth-making. He is instantly sexual, instantly powerful, instantly compelling; and O'Sullivan's Jane is hard put to it to equal him at first, weighted with virtually all the dialogue—most of which consists of "Don't" and "No."

He perches her on a branch and looks at her. A leopard appears; he kills it, returns to looking at her. Abruptly, he grabs her and swings her up into the Tarzanic bower, his ape-style bed high in the trees. In this sequence, the threat of rape is absolutely real, and both actors carry it off—he through a projection of power and sexual dangerousness, she through a palpable terror. This is not male-romanticized rape—meaning yes but saying no—but real threat of violence and violation. It is still an unsettling scene, described by the *London Times* as having "a faint but unmistakable unpleasantness." But he relents, without any arch lecture from her on how gentlemen behave; the clear implication is that her fear disgusts him. Shoving her away, he goes outside to sleep on a large branch; Jane weeps hysterically.

The next morning, however, the most famous scene from the film—usually misremembered—occurs: he learns her name and establishes their separate identities (but never says, "Me Tarzan, you Jane"). Learning from her, he touches his own chest and says, "Tarzan." Then he touches her shoulder, just above her left breast: "Jane." Strikes his chest. "Tarzan." Strikes her shoulder. "Jane." He hits each of them harder and harder, goes faster and faster. "Tarzan—Jane—Tarzan—Jane—." It is a brilliant little sound-film sequence, combining the pictorial, pantomimic quality of silent film with the sparest possible use of sound; in it, we see him see her as a woman, as an individual—as if the whole flowering of his humanity lies in this simple act of identifying them both as individuals. Again, although Weissmuller is never thought of as an actor, his ability to carry off such a scene is impressive.

Then he lets her go, and, returned to her father, she utters the key line of the film, "He was happy." Responding to her father's objections about this ape man, she says, "I thought he was a savage, but he wasn't. . . . *He was happy.*" (To which her father says, sensibly, "He's not like us," and she replies, "He's white.")

There is the usual Tarzan carnage: a wildebeest for breakfast, two lions at one outing, the leopard; on the other hand, he rescues an elephant from a pit on the way to some other errand. He is violent when attacked, pragmatic when hungry, large-hearted when not threatened. But he is always violent toward Africans, because they are always presented as attacking him.

The mutual seduction of Tarzan and Jane is accomplished in a pool. Both are nearly naked. She is at first flirtatious, far too cute, and her lines are appalling, out of Elinor Glyn by way of Ivor Novello: "I think you're the most horrible man I ever knew." "What color are your eyes? Yes, I know—the color of the forest." "Women are such fools." "I don't think you'd better look at me like that. You're far too attractive—a man who doesn't even know what kisses are." He is bearing her through the water in his arms. The scene must have been an actor's nightmare for O'Sullivan—all the lines and no response. He simply looks and looks at her. He does not understand her words, of course, and we realize that *he* is the innocent now; she is the sophisticate, with her flippant talk of kisses and eyes. Again, it is a singularly effective sound-silent contrast, with his silence projecting innocence and sincerity. Gradually, she, too, falls silent—a final, "Oh, Tarzan, please—" and he carries her up to the bower, her head buried (speechlessly) in his neck. The eroticism of the water, their near nakedness, the balletic swimming is a quantum leap from the "I love you, Tarzan" of Enid Markey—adult erotic love in place of the romantic "falling in love."

The film ends in an orgy of violence against blacks. A grotesque tribe of black dwarves (played by whites, some of whom were probably welcoming Dorothy to Munchkinland a few years later) captures Jane and her party and throws them into a pit with a gorilla (the most maligned of the animals in Hollywood's "Africa"). Tarzan dispatches the gorilla and calls in the elephants, who crush the village, trampling the blacks, destroying them with a randomness and cruelty out of all proportion to what the whites have suffered. Tarzan then places Jane's dying father on a dying elephant, and the old man is carried to the elephant's graveyard and dies. Tarzan and Jane are left alone in his "Africa" to be *happy*.

The 1934 *Tarzan and His Mate* and the 1936 *Tarzan Escapes* reprised the same elements. Tarzan killed lions, drove away intrusive whites, and destroyed tribal blacks. Most of all, he loved Jane, and Jane loved him, and by the third film in what had become a series, they had matured from lovers to a couple—Mr. and Mrs. Tarzan. Tarzan and Jane became a Depression-era fantasy: a stable couple in which the husband was stronger than the chaotic forces of life, able to provide a home and food and security. Their dream house was aloft in a tree, equipped with an elevator and running water, courtesy of animal power. The lions and leopards were now Tarzan's "job"—a form of day at the office. The intrusive whites and the hostile blacks were the irrational and unpredictable agents of the outer chaos, and it was in dealing with them that Tarzan rose from the workaday to the heroic. In *Tarzan Escapes*, Mr. and Mrs. Tarzan's "marriage" is threatened by money and others' greed for it. (When Tarzan believes Jane has left him for a London inheritance, he wrecks the tree house.) The movie enfolds a very real Depression-era worry and a real resentment of "big money."

By 1939 (*Tarzan Finds a Son*), Mr. and Mrs. Tarzan had acquired a child (Johnnie Sheffield)—the comic chimp, Cheetah, had been a surrogate baby in the other films. Prior censorship may have been a factor, the overt eroticism of Weissmuller and O'Sullivan perhaps demanding some symbolic assurance that they were not merely enjoying sex. With Sheffield, the ideal American family was complete: Father Tarzan, Mother Jane, perfect child "Boy," and funny baby Cheetah, with a pet elephant instead of a dog. "Africa" had become suburbia.

Until 1940, the Weissmuller Tarzans were rationed to one every other year. Nonetheless, by the early 1940s, the Tarzan movies had become a run-of-the-mill series, "with *Trader Horn* footage, progressively more faded, on the back projection screen." Thalberg had died and, after a decade of restraint, the entire Tarzan package, including Weissmuller, was sold to RKO. Direction, which had passed from Van Dyke to Cedric Gibbons to Richard Thorpe, went, under RKO, to Kurt Neumann and others. More significantly, production was turned over to Sol Lesser.

It was a case of Lesser by name, lesser by nature. Because of Burroughs's prodigious output, two Tarzan titles had been bought separately and produced by Lesser in the 1930s: *Tarzan the Fearless* (1933), with the ever-grinning, ringletted Buster Crabbe; and *Tarzan's Revenge* (1938), with Glenn Morris. Neither was worth comparing with the MGM films. Now, however, in 1942, Lesser took over the Thalberg-Van Dyke creation and turned it into a sausage-making machine: six films in as many years, with the formula becoming ever more rigid, the fantasy ever more banal—the last four of Weissmuller's films being *Tarzan ands*: the Amazons, the Huntress, the Leopard Woman, the Mermaids.

O'Sullivan left the series for one picture, made one more and then left for good after the 1942 (MGM) *Tarzan's New York Adventure*, leaving Weissmuller and Sheffield with a succession of Janes—Frances Gifford, Nancy Kelly, Brenda Joyce (a cooler, very appealing Jane). In 1947, Weissmuller, now thick-waisted and middle-aged, became Jungle Jim; Sheffield got his own series as Bomba. Other Tarzans were ground up in the machine—Lex Barker, Gordon Scott, Mike Henry, on and on. Without Weissmuller and O'Sullivan, however—and without Thalberg and Van Dyke—the magic was gone, and the myth dribbled out of the films like wine from a cracked bottle. Lesser kept his grip on the series until 1958, still cranking out a picture a year; after 1960, however, frequency dropped, and after 1968 Tarzan could be found only on television.

Despite these later manifestations, the real Jungle Lord is Johnny Weissmuller, and Maureen O'Sullivan is his Wild Mate, and they are models of middle-American ideas of race and gender. They are not aristocrats—and, unlike Haggard's men, they are not colonials. Tarzan's domain is in the air; the African earth, to which he sometimes descends, is a lower world inhabited by hostile animals and plants and black Africans. As originally conceived, this was a kind of dog-in-the-manger myth, with the Tarzanic hound defending against all comers the African earth he avoids and does not want to colonize. Weissmuller added the dimension of water; it is often his chosen medium, both for travel and for sex. Swimming and swinging in the treetops both suggest a liberation from gravity and from earth: this Tarzan is, above all, free. He is also "happy"—a peculiarly American concern. For this dominant Tarzan of the 1930s and 1940s, then—the real Tarzan, Weissmuller's Tarzan—"Africa" is less a place than a dream, a reference, perhaps, to the dream of the American continent, and American domination there.

3 REAL AFRICA—
BUT NOT REALLY _____

E arly fiction films were not the only ones that dealt with Africa, and not the only ones that created film archetypes. A significant body of nonfiction films was also made, and they gave to audiences both an archetype—The Explorer (which then became the subject of most of the relatively few film comedies)—and location images of savagery, dangerous animals, and jungle. These films appeared in the same years as the Haggard and Burroughs films and provided those films with imagery; the location footage of *Trader Horn* (1930), for example, imitated earlier documentaries. The earliest nonfiction film appears to have been a brief "actuality," *Gang Making Railroad* (1898), which got the jump on fiction by a decade. It was followed by a large number of brief Boer War films, both real and staged, which played to an audience hungry for the actual— or its imitation.

In 1909, a British filmmaker named Cherry Kearton joined Theodore Roosevelt's safari to East Africa. Then almost forty, Kearton was already a successful still photographer. His pioneering film, *Theodore Roosevelt in Africa*, ran almost an hour. His pictures of Roosevelt, of the buildings of Nairobi, of massed Masai and Kikuyu, of the safari on the march and in camp were vivid and novel. The film made no attempt at narrative, hardly seemed to have been edited, and never included Kearton himself in either image or title: the camera had no persona. Kearton also filmed the American cowboy "Buffalo" Jones, who had come to East Africa in Roosevelt's wake to show that African animals could be captured with the Western lasso; this short film was released in 1911.

In 1912, a wealthy American "sportsman," Paul Rainey, released *Rainey's African Hunt*, a nonfiction picture that, with a successor in 1914, probably did more to influence American ideas of African wildlife than any pictures until the 1920s. Rainey's cinematographers, Hemment and Lydford, made pictures of animals at a waterhole that became internationally famous. Again, the cinematographers were invisible. The hunting sequences had Rainey as their protagonist, however, and they implicitly lauded him for his method of hunting lions with packs of dogs. This cruelty extended to brutal sequences of a hyena trying to escape a leg-hold trap.

World War I interrupted nonfiction filming. Kearton went into the army; Rainey produced no more films. Releases of a few "expedition" films began, however (usually the result of a camera's being taken by an amateur on a hunting trip), and by 1923 this trickle had become a flood: seven nonfiction films were released that year, followed by seven more in 1924—the two biggest years for nonfiction African films in the history of cinema. Between them, these two years contributed more than 25 percent of the 1920-1940 total.

The nonfiction filmmakers of the 1920s and 1930s proved to be of three principal types—amateurs who made a movie of a pleasure trip and released it, for better or worse; professional travelers, who typically released a "lecture film" (the traveler in person, with film-illustrated talk) and published a parallel book; and professional photographers and filmmakers. Despite their claims, none of them was an "explorer" as that word is at all carefully used, although they exploited an explorer archetype established in the nineteenth century and wore its emblematic costume—breeches and boots, sola topi or slouch hat. (The hunter looked the same but carried a gun.) The Explorer recalled a rich history of European activity: the "opening" of Africa, its seizure, the exploitation of its wildlife.

ALTHOUGH CHERRY KEARTON returned to filmmaking in the early 1920s, it was two Americans who were to become the ranking stars of the nonfiction films of the 1920s and 1930s. Their creation of personae as Explorer-adventurers, their focus on the exotic, their hyping of danger, had already served them well in the South Pacific. Might it serve as well in Africa? They had already shown an acceptance of colonial ideology: one of their South Seas films was praised in London for its imperial content: "One gets a good idea of how it is possible . . . for 12 white men to control the destinies of hundreds of natives. . . ."

Their names were Martin and Osa Johnson, from Kansas, U.S.A. He was tall, she almost tiny. He was the cinematographer and dreamer; she was the organizer and actress. They had married when she was only 16; they had been in American vaudeville before they became the world's first husband-and-wife, real-life-adventure film team. Courageous, shrewd, perceptive, skilled, disingenuous, they parlayed Martin's brilliance with a camera into international stardom. More than any other filmmakers, they gave England and America a box-office-oriented look at Africa. A generation of wildlife professionals, some still alive today, were to say that they devoted their lives to wildlife because of what the Johnsons showed them on the screen.

In 1921, Martin and Osa Johnson went to East Africa, which was to be their—and most filmmakers'—"Africa" until the end of the decade. They settled for a while in Nairobi, "in the center of a black man's country . . . a white man's town," as Martin wrote of it. They encountered white colonial fact: the *kipande*, or pass card; the black slums; the half-tribalized, half-urbanized Nairobi underclass. But these things did not get into their films; what did, instead, was wonderful animal photography and a cooked-up tale of a mysterious lake. Off they went "in search of" this lake, a journey that would occupy them into the next year. In fact, a Nairobi enthusiast had driven a car to the mysterious lake that same year; it had been on the maps since the 1890s; and it was only five miles from a government post, on a main trading route. No matter: mystery, not familiarity, was of the essence of the Johnsons' "Africa."

The Johnsons released their first Africa film, *Trailing African Wild Animals*, in New York in May 1923; in London, the next year. This record of what they called their "2-year excursion to the lost Lake Paradise" is itself now regrettably lost, although clips of it show up in some of their later films. The movie was a huge success, "received with constant outbursts of applause" in New York. The fact that most of the film was shot in high, dry country did not erase the idea of jungle, nor did the absence of tigers from Africa prevent mention of Osa's shooting a "tiger from her tent door." *Variety* did object to her "omnipresent cuteness," a problem that would plague the Johnson films more and more as she got older. A different off note was struck in London: the *Times* regretted that "the plucky couple . . . should have thought it necessary, in order to put some excitement into their film," to rouse animals to charge.

The Johnsons used *Trailing African Wild Animals* to make a leap upward. Supported by the American Museum of Natural History and such wealthy individuals as George Eastman and Daniel Pomeroy, they raised enough money to finance a more or less permanent home at their "Lake Paradise" in Northern Kenya. They were to live there, off and on, for four years, their status enhanced by the prestige of a great institution, their fame spread by popular articles and books. Both were indefatigable workers: she ran their village of a hundred and fifty workers; he filmed, then processed his own film. Together and separately, they made individual forays all over Northern Kenya. Thus, Martin Johnson was able to film animals with greater care over far longer periods than other filmmakers, and he was able also to build a backlog of film footage. Despite disastrous losses in a laboratory explosion and a fire (he was almost blinded, and his wife nursed him in their isolated "paradise"), he put together some of the most extraordinary animal cinematography ever made, the more remarkably so because of the limited equipment of the day.

Kearton, the professional traveler R.W. Ratcliffe Holmes, and the photographer-author A. Radcliffe Dugmore also released films in 1923–24. Kearton's *Wild Life Across the World* mixed new and old footage that included the old animal-roping sequences. He also released an anthropomorphic short about a chimpanzee, *Toto of the Congo*, which had a feature-length sequel, *Toto's Wife*. A new critical awareness greeted the films, however: Kearton was praised for his "showmanship," while Dugmore's lecture film was condemned for the boredom of its lecture; then another picture was praised for *not* indulging in showmanship. Clearly, different reviewers were giving the filmmakers different messages, and there was confusion over what would constitute a successful African nonfiction picture.

A pair of British rivals to the Johnsons released their first film in 1926. "Major and Stella Court Treatt" made a successful opening entry in the plucky-couple sweeps with *Cape to Cairo*. He had the virtue of being tall and handsome; she had the virtue of being young and pretty; and they had the wisdom to take T. A. Glover, a professional cameraman, along when Major Court Treatt "was the first man to drive an automobile from Cape Town to Cairo." (No credit given for the wife's driving.) The film was praised for its honesty, a quality also beginning to trouble reviewers. "Nothing is arranged, nothing sentimentalized, nothing falsified for the obtaining of effect. . . ."

Alan Cobham introduced something new to African films when he flew from London to Cape Town with a "special aluminium camera" built into his aircraft. *With Cobham to the Cape* premiered in 1926, its aerial views of Africa a welcome novelty. The "unique air views of such triumphs of British enterprise as the Assuan and Senar [sic] dams, the colonization of the heart of Africa, and the thriving communities of Rhodesia, have an Imperial meaning." This was a significant departure, for Cobham introduced both a technological gimmick, the airplane (in which the Johnsons would soon follow him), and a new subject matter, actual Africa. His was, however, an actual Africa seen from a godlike vantage point, one that allowed appreciation of British enterprise but not of the African underclass that supported it. "The modern cities of the Union of South Africa emphasize again the white man's initiative," as the *Times* saw it.

Cherry Kearton also had a film in 1926, *With Cherry Kearton in the Jungle*, a pastiche of several continents and some old footage, including yet again the rhino-lassoing from the "Buffalo" Jones film. Kearton himself appeared in the interval with a chimpanzee "who drank tea and smoked a cigarette." Such was showmanship.

The Johnsons returned to the United States from Africa in 1927; in January 1928, Daniel Pomeroy, now their producer, released what is probably the most remarkable and beautiful of all their films, perhaps of any of the black-and-white nonfiction films: *Simba, the King of Beasts: a Saga of the African Veldt*. Its excellent New York sale had a top price of $1.65 for the prestige opening.

Simba shows Martin Johnson at his best. African animals still seem new to him, and his camera is capable of astonishment and the sheer joy of looking. Many of the sequences are triumphs of those four years in the bush, apparent strokes of luck that came as the result of weeks of waiting—huge, browsing elephants; a camel that bucks off its load; a statuesque lion. The camera does not intrude into these sequences; there is no human consciousness. This is true natural history.

Not all the film is like that, however. Tacky titles and intrusive editing—both apparently the work of the producer—mar some sections. "The classic land of mystery, thrills and darksome savage drama," the opening title says a little incoherently. "You will see thrills without end. . . ." A purported elephant stampede is intercut from two different sets of footage. The elephants are "tons of impending peril—and death!" Through no apparent fault of the Johnsons, some of the titles break their arms trying to slap their own backs: "Never before in the history of African adventure. . . ." "Here was a scene without parallel in the history of animal photography."

Racial condescension is common, too: a tribal woman is a "belle," a young woman "just a little black flapper." An African in a top hat, riding a mule, is a "chief" who "always dressed up to receive us." Tribes are not differentiated. And a more pernicious racism intrudes: a black woman identified as "Osa's maid. . . got what she thought was an idea." She is shown putting on white makeup. But the camera is there, so Martin Johnson is there, and the woman can be seen looking toward him and talking uncertainly: she is being directed. This is a throwback to the comic nigger: she is being humiliated, and the sequence is shameful.

Then, reverting to animals, the film rights itself for a while with an extended, beautiful sequence of lions in the Serengeti. *Simba* ends with brilliant but disingenuously titled footage of Africans spearing lions. George Eastman's diary of this trip shows that the spearmen were hired. *Simba*, however, concocts a story line about cattle-raiding lions and a "King and Queen" of the "Lumbwa" tribe. The titles surround the pictures with fake mumbo-jumbo—"The priests went frantically to work . . . . The Lumbwa danced. . . . A prayer to their black gods. . . ."—and fake natural history: "A lion will run twice—then, angered, he will fight to the death." Johnson (and Al Klein, whom he gave credit) got good footage of the lion-spearing, and the editor then chose to show a fictional "Africa" with stupid or credulous blacks, with dances, with superstitions and "priests." Someone, probably Pomeroy (who had been in the Serengeti with the Johnsons and Eastman) had also made the choice not to tell the truth of colonial Africa, where a white man with money could pay black men to risk their lives for his entertainment.

The rest of the 1920s saw films so ordinary that jaded critics used one to whip the entire genre, exposing in the process its clichés: "To show a film of Africa the following ingredients must be incorporated: A shot of natives listening to a phonograph . . . scenes of tribal dances with subtitles comparing them to the Black

Bottom and Charleston . . . a view of several dead lions, tigers, or cheetahs. . . ." It was an ominous catalog as the 1920s came to a close, for it warned that the genre had exhausted its self-limiting imagery.

TWO SIGNIFICANT EXPERIMENTS, however, came from Great Britain in 1929–30: both Kearton and the Court Treatts released films that had narrative lines and all-African casts. In a word, they made hybrid documentary/story films. What distinguished them from other fiction films was their intention to show a genuine Africa, not with white actors, studio filming, and location work, but with African amateurs pretty much playing themselves in actual environments. Both films also included extensive wildlife footage and may, in fact, have been more than half natural history.

Kearton and his wife Ada produced *Tembi*, a "fully-fledged feature film with native cast." Fiction with much fact, it strung natural-history footage on a thin thread of plot that the *Times* summarized as "a native. . . left his tribe and wandered until he found another and became its chief." Much of the film—now effectively lost—appears to have been the wanderer's encounters with animals, including insects and a chameleon; the surviving first reel suggests that most of the film was a flashback in which the then-young protagonist was pronounced mad by his fellows because he predicted a disaster, and he then left them, taking his wife and child with him.

The Court Treatts' *Stampede*, synchronized "for music and sound effects," was also partly fiction, "an original story by Mrs. Court Treatt." Reviewers were not pleased with it. *Variety* crassly summarized it as "the tough time folks in Sudan have chasing water holes." Rachel Low, on the other hand, spoke of the "vitality of its conception." The surviving footage shows that it was a film of mixed pluses and minuses: superb wildlife and ethnographic photography; sincere presentation of African emotions and relationships, especially love and grief; but poor dramatic direction, and amateur acting that relied on European, not African, conventions. It remains, nonetheless, a far more significant film than judged at the time.

For perhaps the first time, then, documentary filmmakers seemed to have turned away from exoticism and condescension and to have tried to turn their cameras on a real—and serious—Africa. It is significant, of course, that they turned to fiction to do so, but it is also significant that they did not turn toward the hyping of the exotic, like some other filmmakers. In doing so, the Court Treatts and Kearton made a significant step away from established cinematography: they removed white context and focused instead on black Africa. The *New York Times's* contention that the result lacked "truth" is thus doubly interesting: was this an accurate observation, or was it a response to an absence of the expected stereotypes? The *London Times* objected to "so much time . . . wasted in outlining personal relationships" in the Court Treatt film, but personal relationships are the primary means of giving characters depth through inner lives. Was it, then, a waste of time to do so in the context of this film, or was the reviewer uncomfortable with black character?

Coming as they did when the silent period was effectively over, *Tembi* and *Stampede* never got the reception they may have deserved—not as oddities by documentary filmmakers, but as pioneering efforts to break a perceptual barrier that kept other nonfiction filmmakers from seeing Africans as people.

NINETEEN-THIRTY SAW the first nonfiction sound picture, and a temporary reprieve for the now-troubled genre. Paul Hoefler got in first with the all-sound *Africa Speaks*. It was so popular in America that it had immediate takeoffs in the shorts *Africa Shrieks, Africa Squawks*, and *Africa Speaks English*. The picture was the now-pat mix of interesting but limited imagery, patronizing commentary, and garbled anthropology: "a [native] beauty parlor"; "these [Ubangi women with wooden discs in their lips] are the social leaders of the tribe"; "wives are traded regularly among the Masai." Editing created a bogus reality; the use of rear projection allowed Hoefler to "appear" in scenes from which he had been absent. He also included two sequences that had become trite, a lion-spearing and a meeting with the Ituri pygmies, who dutifully showed how small they were, shot their little bows and arrows, and ate the salt the whites gave them, just as in all the other movies that had shown them since *Wild Men of Africa* in 1921.

The Johnsons revived *Simba* in 1930 with a "synchronized accompaniment" and also managed to get an all-sound film before the public. *Across the World With Mr. and Mrs. Martin Johnson* was a compilation film with no more complex story line than their careers—the South Seas, Borneo, Africa. The sound was really voice-over, but the fictional setting of "an evening at the Johnsons' home" removed the lecture-film feel. Dinner-jacketed and evening-gowned, the Johnsons and their guests sat while Martin manned the projector and talked. Martin has here the delivery of the elocution platform (probably the result of primitive recording): "I think it might in-ter-est you to know that the hip-po-pot-a-mus cannot stay under water any longer than you can." "O-see," as Martin calls her, interpolated with remarks like, "I really like the African natives. They're very loyal." When she is shown demonstrating the Charleston to some pygmies standing by a phonograph, Martin says, "Their dances don't amount to anything. There's almost no rhythm." The film included a cooked-up "adventure" of three Boy Scouts who visited the Johnsons in the Serengeti, and a golf game whose humor mostly consisted of cutting in footage of lions being hit by golf balls.

With sound, filming became still more expensive and complex. As a result, the Johnsons released their next two films through Fox, which edited for maximum box-office; the effect on the films was noticeable. *Congorilla* (1932) was a step down, in all but slickness, from *Simba*. The racialism of earlier films did not lessen, but intensified, especially in an extended pygmy sequence, which showed "swell showmanship," according to *Variety*: "The business with the pygmies attempting to light cigars was good for a marathon of laughs." It included a concocted pygmy courtship and marriage, complete with "preacher," and another cigar-smoking episode when Martin can be clearly heard saying, "I hope it makes you sick." Africa is still the Dark Continent ("a land of hardship—where Peril and death stalk amid primitive savages and primeval monsters"); the rhinoceros is "Public Enemy Number One"; elephants stampede and threaten (in old footage); the Nile is "a river of horror, teeming with slithering crocodiles."

But in 1932, the Johnsons stood at the top of the competitive nonfiction mountain. Their star status made "Mrs. Johnson Martini" a recognizable bit of parody in *So This Is Africa* (1933). *Congorilla* marked their eminence by its frank concessions to a lowest common denominator. It was more coherent, less authentic than Martin Johnson's earlier films, with "Osa" and "Martin" becoming almost characters, and the filmmaker himself—as in Hoefler's *Africa Speaks*—very much on view.

AFTER THE INITIAL impact of sound, the number of nonfiction films began again to shrink. They averaged two or three a year in 1932-1937, only one in 1938, none in 1939. Ratcliffe Holmes released his last lecture film in 1934. Cherry Kearton's retrospective *Big Game of Life* appeared in 1935; he was then 64. The Court Treatts' last film, *Struggle for Life*, appeared the same year. Aviation gave a small boost to pictures like Roy Tuckett's *Wings Over Africa* (filmed in 1931, released in 1933) and Alan Cobham's *With Cobham to Kivu*, but the African nonfiction film was dying. Some people were openly poking fun at it, too; Carveth Wells's *Law of the Jungle* (1936) "will have achieved its end if it succeeds in exposing much of the nonsense which has been talked about the hair-raising experiences of those who make films in the jungle." In Britain, objection to cruelty to animals also spilled over into objections to African films. The controversy brought to public attention the fact that many animal sequences were being faked. "Many of the scenes of animal combat [in an unspecified film] could only have taken place within iron bars," wrote E. E. Asten, late Keeper of Entomology at the British Museum, in 1934.

Baboona (1934) was the last of Martin Johnson's films. Airplanes were much used. Reviews were tepid. Much of the film was devoted to a "real land of baboons" that the Johnsons had discovered "after months of intensive search." Some excellent baboon footage ended when the "land" was "invaded," and the baboons found themselves with "leopards, cheetahs, and hyenas attacking them on every hand." The "baboon land" appears to have been an enclosure; the leopard, cheetahs, and so on, captive animals. The leopard was unable to climb a tree or fight off a warthog; it looked as if it had no claws. The leopard-warthog sequence bore out Asten's accusation of fakery and shooting inside an enclosure; to Martin Johnson's credit, this sequence was apparently not shot by him but by Fox technicians. Still, *Baboona* was a sad comedown for the man who had filmed *Simba*.

Martin Johnson was killed in a California plane crash in 1937. Osa released *I Married Adventure* in 1940, an anthology film that included scenes of her with a double as Martin. "Sadly, we must report that the Johnsons now seem a little stale," wrote Bosley Crowther. Even *Variety*, for so long an enthusiast, pronounced it "dated, tiresome, and often amateurish."

Nineteen-forty also saw Paul Hoefler's *Leopard Men of Africa*, the last gasp of the black-and-white African expedition film, "an Expose of Unrecorded Savage Rituals in the Congo." Some of the footage dated to the 1920s, but it got its title and its hook from "an unlawful secret society [of cannibals] known as the Leopard Men." This pitch to the rubes came from "field notes made in Sierra Leone by Dr. Paul L. Hoefler, F.R.G.S., M.E.C." A voice-over bellowed that "*Af-r-r-ica!*" was the "land of sorcery, witchcraft and mumbo-jumbo! Shrouded in the dark jungle—Africa! Crowded—primitive—lusty—still ruled by fang and claw!" We are told less spectacular racist titbits as well: "Africans' smells can be very distressing indeed"; "The black boys are afraid." There is the usual garbled geography—from Nairobi (hardly in Sierra Leone), down the Nile, to Abyssinia, where he finds the Masai—and a garbled chronology, with footage from his 1929 trip (the trucks clearly labeled) mixed with late 1930s footage. Hoefler contrasts the fear engendered in Africans by the "Leopard Men" with his own white courage. One is inclined to agree with the voice-over at the end: "It's unreal—ghastly—unbelievable!"

Cherry Kearton died that same year. It was the end of an era—and almost of the nonfiction film.

WORLD WAR II brought nonfiction African filming to a halt. It never really got going again: only one more nonfiction film was released in the decade, the work of a relative newcomer to the competitive nonfiction field, Armand Denis.

Denis had released his first African film, *Dark Rapture*, in 1938. Without fakery or comedy, Denis brought the kind of visual passion that Martin Johnson had shown in 1923 and 1928. The result was a temporarily revived African imagery, one presented with less corn and hype, and one accentuated by the use of color. "Certainly the most beautiful and richly documented [African film] ever to achieve general release in this country," said the *New York Times*. The *London Times* praised it, too, but hinted that it was not as new as its breathtaking color at first made it seem. Most of *Dark Rapture* seemed to promise a new beginning; bits of it suggested old wine in a new bottle. Which was it to be?

Savage Splendor, the 1949 film, gave an answer. If Martin Johnson had used color film, and his producers had toned down their racial corn, *Savage Splendor* might have been the result. It offers us again the plucky couple (but with a different Mrs. Denis this time). It tells us yet again that the giraffe has no vocal cords. An African village has "the local Chamber of Commerce . . . a village whing-ding . . . hot music . . . the local beauty shop." It denies African technology: "Somehow, from somewhere, the men of the tribe had learned the operation of an efficient bellows forge." When human beings are shown in exciting action, accomplishing things, those humans are white—Carr Hartley and family at his animal ranch. And so it went, the mixture as before, a little updated, a little cleaned up, in living color. Denis's promise, if such it had been, was vitiated in an apparent desire to grasp the Johnsons' torch—and box-office.

Denis's third film, *Below the Sahara*, came in 1953. Denis had, by his own account, worked on the 1950 *King Solomon's Mines* but had left the picture because of the treatment of animals, suggesting that he was a new kind of wildlife cinematographer—more ethical, environmentally aware. This implication of a higher ethic crept into *Below the Sahara*, with its repeated insistence that the Denises did no shooting: "Our shooting would be done with cameras, not with guns." The sense of one who protests too much, however, was increased by glimpses of what are pretty clearly baits, i.e., animals shot to attract predators. Thus, this third (and last) Denis film confirmed that, despite protestations to the contrary, he was less a precursor of a new kind of nonfiction filming than a vestige of an old one. The only significant change from the earlier films was a greatly increased emphasis on the *white* exploitation of wildlife—training cheetahs, live-trapping wild game, capturing animals with pole and rope, maintaining game ranches. What we are meant to understand is that *black* Africa is savage and violent, but white Africa is efficient and charming.

Disney's *African Lion* (1956) was an indication of where the old wildlife and travel film was going—to television. Superbly photographed, scripted, and edited, it removed the filmmaker from the film entirely and replaced him—or him and her—with a corporation. The result was more "objective" and "scientific," even while it was arguably more fictional and anthropomorphic. *Masters of the Congo Jungle* (1959) was a superb film of a different kind, more like the older ones but without the hype or the fictionalizing. Gone were the plucky couple and the corn and the garbled geography and ethnology; in their place were care and science. The loss in socko box-office was a gain in truth—in a sense, a return to the very early days of Kearton and Rainey, when images of the wild were their own reason for being. The film had no successor, however.

This more careful kind of documentary was also suggested in the few examples of the 1960s, especially in *The Flame and the Fire* (1965), which tried to look at native peoples sympathetically and honestly. The look itself, however, was implicitly false and put the film uncomfortably close to other films of the period that sensationalized exotica—*Naked Terror* (1961), *Africa Addio* (1967), *Kwaheri* (1964). This cluster of sensational movies (along with such oddities as *Africa Erotica*, 1970) probably represent the splitting of the nonfiction films into high and low, or environmental and sensational, blocs; but the sensational films themselves did not survive: they seem to have been coopted into fiction films as fiction got more violent, more openly sexual, more sensational.

Rivers of Fire and Ice (released in 1968, but apparently made some years earlier) was neither better nor worse than its models. It was "Africa" recycled, without modern realities other than those that flattered white ingenuity (another film about white animal-catchers), and with Africans who were "boys" and "natives" and "savages." *The African Elephant* (1971), by focusing on a single species, got coherence and detail in a way that the old documentaries did not, and its color photography of animals was superb. It had a treacly narration, however, damagingly anthropmorphic—perhaps the influence of fiction films like *Born Free*. It was, anyway, the last of its kind. After 1971, the African nonfiction feature film ceased to be.

This is not to say that African wildlife photography stopped. Quite the contrary—probably more, and better, footage has been made since 1960 than before. It has been shown, however, on the television screen.

THE HISTORY OF the nonfiction film of Africa is, then, one of technological improvement and ethical degradation. When Kearton and the Rainey cameramen focused on African subjects, the results were breathtaking because utterly new. The camera technique was naive, and the "gaze" was, if not unselective, at least honest about itself: there was no redefinition through editing, and no shooting in anticipation of derogatory titles or juxtaposition.

However, for the next thirty years (and beyond) most filmmakers would focus on much the same imagery, which, if photographed naively, quickly staled. A refusal—or inability—to abandon this imagery demanded that staleness be avoided by other means: editing, titling, juxtaposition, storytelling. The filmmakers maintained a falsely naive viewpoint, "discovering" and going "in search of" the already known. The resulting films, which were nominally "documentary" and "authentic," had the paradoxical effect of reinforcing inaccurate, certainly grossly exaggerated, ideas and of blinding the mass audience to much of the real Africa.

The effect became circular: the nonfiction films redefined truth. When the first location work was done for fiction films in the late 1920s—Barkas for *Palaver,* Cooper and Schoedsack for *Four Feathers,* Van Dyke for *Trader Horn*— what the directors looked for was what they and audiences had seen in the nonfiction films, not what the directors could see on site with their own eyes. Audiences got more savagery, strangeness, and danger.

That the images mostly replicated nineteenth-century ones was in their favor in attracting a mass audience. Thus, nonfiction film typically gave the illusion (reinforced by advertising) of new, more exact information while reinforcing received ideas and promising new excitements ("thrills"). In turn, those ideas were played back to the filmmakers by audiences and reviewers as "demand," and some of the filmmakers, in the name of audience appeal, increasingly falsified their work. The result was that the chronology of African nonfiction films described a parabola: from naive fascination with the moving image; through remarkable, if rare, films of beauty and significant information; to corrupt and self-imitative hackwork.

Censorship, both institutional and personal, must also have been a factor in the failure to turn the camera on contemporary Africa. Filmmakers were often the captives of white African advisers, hunters, and guides; they always had to satisfy colonial officials. Thus, while the appeal to the mass audience led them to turn their cameras on the exotic and the shocking, their reliance on colonialism led them *not* to turn their cameras on colonialism. Africa was greatly modernized in the thirty years after Kearton's first effort, but film ignored the changes; rather, it had increasingly to seek out the primitive and the exotic, ultimately paying Africans to stage events and ceremonies and to wear costumes.

An alternative can be seen in the story films of Kearton and the Court Treatts. Here, at least, were Europeans turning the camera on Africans as individuals with inner lives. The results may have been no more authentic—and no less patronizing—than the analogous efforts of Edward Curtis among Native Americans, but they were a significant broadening of the extraordinarily limited vision of the other filmmakers. That their efforts had no imitators says much for the grip that the received imagery had on nonfiction filmmakers—and their audience.

PART 2

To the Eve of Independence

4 PILLARS OF EMPIRE_____

While the Johnsons were making their last films and Weissmuller's Tarzan was ruling an Americanized Africa in Hollywood, a very different Africa—and a very different kind of hero—flourished in London. Jeffrey Richards has called these British films "a flourishing cinema of Empire . . . powerfully advocating a view of the British Empire as beneficent and necessary. . . ." In fact, these films had begun before 1930 and continued past World War II, but it is as representatives of the same era as Weissmuller's Tarzan that they are remembered—albeit curiously different ones.

This "imperial" cinema is particularly associated with Alexander Korda and Michael Balcon, each of whom produced three otherwise unrelated films about the Empire, each cluster now misnamed a "trilogy." Their films and others like them took "imperial" men for their heroes and promoted the triumphs of imperial soldiers, imperial administrators, and imperial conquerors. Not quite propaganda, they nonetheless ignored any warts their subjects might display.

BRITISH CINEMA OF the 1930s was not encouraged to embark on critique. Films were marked by "the almost total absence of the reality of contemporary British life," partly because of censorship by such entities as the British Board of Film Censors (1912) and the Colonial Films Committee (1930). Censorship, which often manages to be both paranoid and authoritarian at the same time, played to the most cautious and entrenched ideas. By the 1930s, it was trying to forbid "adverse reflection" on the British army or whites, offense to other nations, the "inflaming" of native populations, and miscegenation. Rachel Low has noted the unquestioning acceptance by the British Board of Film Censors of "the social and political assumptions of the extreme right wing, which seemed to them normal, neutral, desirable and non-controversial."*

Other bodies were exerting pressure for "positive" pictures. In 1928, a British Film Services Board was formed "to influence the use of films for the dissemination of true national culture and ideals." The Empire was thought particularly vulnerable to the effects of motion pictures: concern for the effects on

_____

* By contrast, the censorship exercised by former colonies at the moment of independence (1955-1965) turned this attitude on its ear, and films were rejected in the former British colonies because of their insensitivity to nonwhite peoples.

colonial audiences caused Great Britain to create the Colonial Film Unit, which both produced films favoring Britain's interests and censored supposedly negative ones, including Chaplin comedies thought harmful to white prestige because they showed policemen and clergymen in "undignified" ways. In 1930, the Colonial Office formed the Colonial Films Committee "to promote the better distribution of British films in the Colonies and to consider how to ensure a supply of British films of a nature calculated to be of educational [i.e., pro-British] value to the native races." Depression-era and wartime bodies like the Bantu Educational Kinema Experiment, the Colonial Film Unit of the Ministry of Information, the Colonial Marketing Board, and the Crown Film Unit of the slightly later Central Office of Information all used film as propaganda.

Some pressure was unofficial, but no less real. Perceived threats to the dignity of white women became a frequent subject of letters to the *London Times* in the 1920s and 1930s, with American films being found particularly offensive. A clutch of lords and ladies appealed for expressions of opinion on films "showing only what is desirable in the social and economic life of the Empire. . . ." Movie producers (who sometimes hankered after titles themselves) were not deaf to such appeals.

The result of all these pressures, among makers of feature films, was an understandable tendency to err on the side of caution: the enshrining of conservative "good taste" (a political agenda masquerading as an aesthetic one) and acquiescence in the view that "the social hierarchy must not be questioned."

Effects on American movies were much the same. In America, formal censors included the National Board of Review (1908), the National Association of Motion Picture Industries (1916), and the Motion Picture Producers and Distributors Association (the "Hays Office," 1922). As well, American companies filming in Britain or the colonies needed the same "full-hearted cooperation of the army and the colonial authorities" as did British companies. Prior censorship became inevitable, including submission of proposed Hollywood films for British review; this prior censorship included—especially in Hollywood—creation of film ideas that constituted imperial propaganda, as a way of appeasing criticism. A spurious Britishism was waved like a flag in such 1930s films as *Gunga Din* and *Lives of a Bengal Lancer.*

"THE NOVELS OF A. E. W. Mason have always been a useful source of material for the stage and screen," noted the *London Times* in 1954, when yet another remake of Mason's *The Four Feathers* was being contemplated. Indeed, Mason was a voice for Edwardian imperialism, and a mother lode of imperial films.

Four Feathers was one of the most frequently filmed novels set in Africa, after Haggard's and Burroughs's books. Lucoque seems to have made a version in

1915; Dyreda Art Film Corporation also released a version that year. Stoll released its example in 1921, with some Egyptian location work. None of these three exploited the novel's cinematic potential, however, which lay, not in Mason's dubious tale, but in its spectacle.

Four Feathers is nominally about cowardice and courage. Like much of Haggard and Burroughs, it is an adult novel that became a "boy's book"; unlike the books of Haggard and Burroughs, however, it is now little read. Time has done its own deconstruction on it, and its values now seem upside-down: what was once courage now seems like social cowardice, peer-induced conformity; and what was cowardice to Mason now seems sensible and even admirable action. Mason wrote from an unquestioning bully's pulpit, and British filmmakers used generally to take his position; however, with World War II (real war, as opposed to Mason's boy's idea of war), praise for the cinematic versions has focused on cinematography and backed away from flag-waving. Mason's story follows a young officer, Faversham, who is ordered to go with his regiment to Egypt for the expedition that will revenge Gordon at the Battle of Omdurman. Faversham, the son of a fire-eating general, resigns because he fears that he will not prove a hero. His three best friends, and then his sweetheart, Esmee, send him white feathers, the symbol of cowardice. Faversham then, to prove himself, goes to Egypt, disguises himself as a mute Egyptian laborer, and saves the three friends one by one, returning to each the white feather that he had sent; his final gesture is made at the Battle of Omdurman, contributing to the British victory. Restored to manliness, he is then able to return to England and again claim Esmee.

In 1929, Hollywood tried its hand at this concoction. This was a substantial production—Richard Arlen, Fay Wray, Clive Brook—with location work by Merian Cooper and Ernest Schoedsack. Already known for nonfiction filming (*Chang* and *Grass*), Cooper and Schoedsack took a crew to Egypt and Sudan and shot extensive footage there (running into the party of photo magnate George Eastman and wildlife photographer Martin Johnson far down the Nile—Africa was becoming crowded with filmmakers). The results, however, did not pay off in the finished movie. Shots of hippos and crocodiles had little to do with the action; unlike *Trader Horn*, whose first half is a kind of travelogue, this *Four Feathers* has little place for scenery or animals.

Seen now, the wonder of it is that this *Four Feathers* wasn't laughed off the screen. It is painfully slow and archaically photographed, with many two-person shots framed from the waist up, as if it were 1915. The acting is all indicating, and the constructed sets are unconvincing and stylistically wrong (one desert fort looking like the Ballet Russe set for *Prince Igor*). The Cooper-Shoedsack location footage is, by contrast, crisp and convincing, but it is often imposed on the action, as when a grass fire has to be set so that shots of baboons fleeing from a fire can be used. The emotions—sentiment in place of love, pathos in place of grief—are as much Mason's fault as Hollywood's, but nothing has been done to mitigate their trivialization. Cliché piles on cliché—of course the slavers are Arabs; of course the black soldiers "will not hold" without a white officer; of course the "dervishes" give up when Arlen/Faversham kills their chief—until the accumulation is even worse than Mason's novel, a "boy's film" of gross effects and the narrowest possible vision of human behavior. As Faversham, Arlen seems to succeed through sheer (white) will, expressed as an unwavering stare and a frowning brow. When, casting off his disguise and replacing one of the feather-givers as commander of a desert fort, he cries, "Has a British officer ever failed you?" to the near-mutinous black troops, none of them asks the obvious question, "Who are you, white man?" Certainly, he is no longer a British officer, having resigned his commission. But this sort of quibble does not bother this preadolescent view of manhood and war. The film has the mentality of a serial, and nothing now gives it distinction except the unfortunately skimpy location footage.

Ten years later, the Mason novel was given its definitive cinematic reading, produced by Alexander Korda, directed by Zoltan Korda, and scripted by R. C. Sheriff. Ironically, it was one of the films whose showing was interrupted when theatres were closed after the declaration of real war in September 1939; that declaration could not, however, prevent its winning the Venice Biennale's cup in December. Without question, that award was given for the spectacular scenes in color directed by Zoltan Korda.

"[Alexander] allowed [Zoltan] to shoot *Four Feathers* in the Sudan. Let loose on location, Zoli not only created a splendidly rousing film . . . but shot so much footage that he was able to supply location scenes for dozens of Hollywood pictures over the next thirty years. . . ." These location sequences—correctly decribed by Rachel Low as "magnificent"—were, unlike the location footage of the 1929 version, so completely integrated into the picture as to reverse the usual balance of first- and second-unit work: they *were* the picture, and the Victorian interiors, the talk, the acting (some of it very good) merely extended them, rather than the other way round. Michael Korda later saw evidence of "disagreements" between the two Kordas, resulting in "uneasy compromises between Zoli's love of the natives and their way of life, and [Alexander's] desire to produce pro-Empire motion pictures." However, it is not "natives" or a way of life that enchants Zoltan Korda's cinematography, but African spectacle, not merely in the superb battle scenes but also in panoramas of the Nile and in shots of black men working, straining to pull the British boats upstream. It is as if Zoltan has espoused the spectacle of Africa as his riposte to his brother's dated parable of Empire; the director's vision again and again draws the viewer away from the producer's lesson. The story of Faversham and the feathers shrinks as the spectacle expands, almost disappearing in the waves of galloping camels and black fighters.

John Clements is a very young, vulnerable Faversham; June Duprez is an inevitably vapid Esmee (the role itself is misogynistically conceived). The actor whom one remembers, however, is Ralph Richardson as a feather-giver who goes blind in the Egyptian desert and is saved, nursed, and returned to safety by Faversham. Richardson was an actor whose performances always walked the edge of the comic, and this is no exception: losing his helmet in the blinding sun and going almost instantly blind, he is uncannily near farce; the scene is absurd, and he lets us know he knows. But he soldiers on to play the noble blind man who first wins Esmee, then relinquishes her when he discovers that the unknown native who saved him was in fact Faversham. Self-sacrifice here is a form of love, much more real than the "love" between Faversham and Esmee; it is also a form of abasement, in a film that reeks of it. Faversham's whole action is a form of abasement (the feathers, the resignation, the disguise, the endless *serving* of the men who have humiliated him), even masochism, which becomes the real measure of one man's feeling for another. It is the willing self-degradation of the Eton School "fag" for the older "sixth-former," boyish idolatry mixed up with adolescent sex.

At film's end, Esmee, Faversham, and the others (minus Richardson) meet for dinner with her boring old father. It might be a scene from *Peter Pan*: Peter and the boys after a terrific day of playing war, with dear Wendy at one end of the table and Captain Hook at the other. It is a boy's idea of triumph, this sitting at dinner with the General and the Beauty. Or at dinner with the headmaster of Hegemony Hall, top boy at last: all he ever wanted to be—or could be.

The *Times* was not dazzled. Noting that Faversham as a boy read Shelley, it said that "the hero's study of the poets should have given him the moral courage to ignore the feathers or to hand them back with a withering repartee." That said—and that was a lot—it praised the spectacle but quibbled at the "extravagant" country houses, finding a T'ang vase "an unlikely object" to be in one—a way of putting the social-climbing Alexander Korda in his Central European place. Too late, however; he got his knighthood, anyway. (And someone who should know assures me that a T'ang vase would not have been out of place.)

Four Feathers hit in America, rousing Bosley Crowther to dub Alexander Korda "the Kipling of Kinema." When, however, it was revived in London in 1943, the *Times* attacked its "glib imperialism and . . . juvenile attitude to war"; it seemed "to belong to another age." But it was "a remarkable [cinematic] achievement"—a tribute to the Korda who saw Africa rather than the Korda who saw Empire.

It was the former Korda, the undervalued Zoltan, who made a second version of *Four Feathers*, this time producing, with Terence Young directing. First titled *None But the Brave*, it was released as *Storm Over the Nile* in 1955, a scant year before the Suez crisis and thus a colossal anachronism. The Faversham this time was Anthony Steel, already everybody's favorite postwar colonial and already too old for the role. Mary Ure was cursed with Esmee. In place of Richardson was Laurence Harvey, who would have been better cast as Faversham. The real reason for the remake appears to have been Korda's possession of that marvelous Technicolor location footage, here used again but expanded for a wide-screen process, so that in the night scenes the moon is ovoid, and the effect on animals led to its being called the "stretch-camel *Four Feathers.*" Nothing is gained otherwise in the remake, and the losses of Richardson and even Clements are not compensated for: both Steel and Harvey are too much of the 1950s for this antique, Harvey's febrile anti-heroism particularly seeming out of place. A further remake in the 1970s (for television) was unremarkable, proving only that Mason's time was long past.

HE "HAS BEEN programmed with (a) homoeroticism, (b) self-pity, (c) self-righteousness, (d) sweat, and (e) an insatiable need to be crucified over and over." The film in which he appears is full of "narcissistic jingoism" and "comic-strip patrotism." This is Pauline Kael, talking not about Faversham but about Rambo. *Plus ça change....*

IN 1935, ANOTHER imperial white male was brought to the screen as "a tribute to the 'keepers of the king's peace.'" The film sought to bring an equally definitive African male to the screen, as well; for that "comic role," the author of the work on which the film was based wanted Charles Laughton—in blackface.

The film was *Sanders of the River.* The white male, Sanders, was played by Leslie Banks. The black male was not played by Laughton, however; the producer-director team was the Korda brothers, in their initial African outing, and for Bosambo they cast the charismatic black American, Paul Robeson.

Whether or not this casting was the first example of Zoltan Korda's undercutting of his brother's imperialism cannot be known; certainly, Michael Korda later wrote that the film was a compromise, "with Zoli fighting to give his 'native' performers a forum to show the dignity, the heroic traditions and the enduring strength of their own tribal institutions." It may have been Zoltan Korda's support, as well, that convinced Robeson that his role could say positive things about Africans—a view he seems to have accepted until the film's opening, when he walked out of the premiere.

Sanders is a laudatory treatment of the professional life of a British district commissioner in West Africa. It makes no bones about admiring the eponymous hero. The opening title says, "Africa. Tens of millions of natives live under British rule, each tribe with its own chieftain, governed and protected by a handful of white men whose everyday work is an unsung saga of courage and efficiency. One of them was Commissioner Sanders." It is "we happy few" time again—a "handful of white men," an utter lack of white women. Banks as Sanders is a pipe-smoking prig, oblivious (as the film is) to his own arrogance. In an opening scene quite without irony, he sits drinking with his assistant as they discuss illegal gin-drinking among "the tribes." Then, with a group of "chiefs," he calmly accepts flattery that would have embarrassed Louis XIV: "He is our father and we are his children"; to all the "black children" (some of whom have gray hairs) he is "Lord Sanders." He is also a closet fascist: we learn that Lord Sanders has spies everywhere and a "pigeon house in every village" for messages.

The bulk of the film is devoted to a plot that will have Sanders saving the good and childlike chief, Bosambo (Robeson), from various tribes and chiefs that have gone bad. Bosambo's goodness is, of course, defined by his fidelity to Sanders, the others' badness by their infidelity. It is a classic good nigger/bad nigger dichotomy that can have been invisible to Robeson only because of the shooting schedule. It put Robeson squarely into the Good African archetype—"good" as defined by whites; he joined there assorted servants, gunbearers, and Toms.

Much of the film was shot on location—but not with Robeson, who never left London. When first announced (with the title *Kongo Raid*), *Sanders* was to have had two units, one in the Congo for "scenes of native warfare" and one in Dar es Salaam for "big game." Zoltan Korda took the Congo unit out in November 1933 and completed his filming the following January. This location footage, along with closeups of Robeson and the remarkable sequence when Nina Mae McKinney sings "Little Black Dove," was Zoltan's mostly visual riposte to his brother's pro-white, pro-British drum-beating.

Filming in London used "almost anyone with black skin, including Johnstone (later Jomo) Kenyatta." It evidently did not put Robeson on the set when the most embarrassing sequences were shot, or else subsequent editing greatly altered what he thought the film was about. Whatever the cause, he was an unconscious collaborator in the perpetuation of two damaging archetypes, the Imperial Man and the Good African. He was not, however, comic. The idea of the lip-smacking Laughton in the role rather boggles the mind.

The premiere was attended by Queen Victoria Eugenie, the Brazilian ambassador, Sir Cedric Hardwicke, Basil Dean, Victor Saville, Anna Neagle, and Anthony Asquith, among others; nobody other than Robeson is reported to have walked out. "If it is shown abroad, it will bring no discredit on Imperial authority," the *Times* opined; not so, however—the Commissioner for Nigeria in London "protested that it brought disgrace and disrepute to his country." He seemed not to have liked the statements that all Africans wore skins and feathers, that they were childlike and amoral, and that only one white man with a machine gun stood between them and savage bloodshed. Still, it was enough of a hit in England to be brought back in 1938. It was less successful in America, but even there it was taken as further proof (after Korda's earlier *Henry VIII*) that a new spirit was moving in British film, one that could spend money to good purpose and create films with "values."

Some American critics (who presumably watched Zoltan's cinematography rather than listening to Alexander's imperialism) saw Robeson more positively than he had seen himself; *Variety* found it "more the triumph of Bosambo than Sanders," Robeson acting "with authority and dignity." To British audiences, and to the patrons of Alexander Korda, however, the triumph was Sanders's, and the dignity and authority were the Empire's.

The Sanders figure—restrained but arrogant, condescending—was the perfect Imperial Man. He was youngish but not a boy. He had no sex. He was socially of the privileged class (or so his accent told us). His manner was sophisticated and urbane. This Imperial Man archetype was connected to but less boyish than, certainly less unsure than, the romancer of *Four Feathers*. *Sanders* is about control, *Feathers* about ritual qualification. Self-sacrifice is common to both, although the sacrifice in Sanders is more reported than seen—an offscreen sweetheart left behind, the foregone pleasures of "civilization"—and a cynic might question the sacrifice involved in having one's own gunboat, a kingdom of thousands of square miles, and power, power, power.

BRITISH FILM ATTEMPTED to reassert the Imperial Man in the waning days of World War II, this time semiofficially (there was some governmental involvement in its inception, via the Ministry of Information). The result, *Men of Two Worlds*, was an even more schizophrenic film than *Sanders* (as its title suggests), with an even more attenuated and priggish district commissioner in Eric Portman. The Good African was the Robeson lookalike Robert Adams. Called Kisenga, this Good African was a British-educated composer who returns to Africa as a new archetype, the Educated African—belated admission that Africans were now earning university degrees and doctorates, several hundred years ahead of schedule. Consciously or otherwise, the role was clearly intended for Robeson, who would have sung instead of playing classical piano. However, not even Robeson could have saved *Men of Two Worlds*, which wore its good intentions on its sleeve but constantly gave itself away with lines like, "What are [years of schooling in England] against ten thousand years of Africa in my blood?" The direction was no better than the script (supposedly by the novelist Joyce Cary), the camera constantly looking *down* on Adams, straight at Portman.

Portman pushed "restrained authority" beyond acceptability and became reminiscent of those British actors who played Nazis in American war films; what was probably meant as restraint and patience communicated as arrogance. This actor's mistake may have been a sincere one, arising from an awareness of ambivalences in the role—the projection of an ambivalence in British colonialism. Portman's D.C. was also very much of the privileged class in manner and accent, as was a doctor played by Phyllis Calvert; both could have stepped through any set of French doors into a drawing-room comedy without missing a beat. The Calvert role was utterly bloodless and utterly genderless. (There was *nothing* between her and Portman; it is as if the filmmakers wanted to emphasize the Imperial Man's indifference to sex.)

In a much smaller role, Cathleen Nesbitt played a female writer, all manner and froth, whose evident silliness (we are to understand) undercut her argument that African traditional ways were to be respected. Unlike Calvert, she was presented as feminine—and hence not to be taken seriously. Her speaking out on a serious subject recalled the old sexist rhyme:

> Whistling girls and crowing hens
> Always come to some bad end.

For this Crowing Hen (a new, if minor archetype), the bad end was to be presented as a fool.

Men of Two Worlds inspired an unusual number of letters to the *Times*, most of them negative. Educated Africans particularly objected to the use of what one called the projection of "the European concept of witchcraft into Africa"; a white objected to the lack of "day-to-day" African activities, the emphasis on witchcraft, and Phyllis Calvert's "unnatural neatness," which seemed designed to emphasize the Africans' backwardness. Director Thorold Dickinson replied astonishingly that "this is not a film about 'Africa'. . . ."

Men of Two Worlds was intended to cast a good light on British admin-istration in East Africa. Instead, it illuminated the inherent contradictions in a colonial administration that had, for example, conscripted hundreds of thousands of black soldiers but paid the black farmers left behind—often women—less for the same products than they paid whites. It exploited the most ancient of white bogeymen, the witch-doctor, and relied on the oldest of white-settler clichés—that Africans could never be "really" educated—to try to give new luster to its Imperial Man. In fact, it revealed its own racism and its own outdated notions, and in the Crowing Hen and the Imperial Man it exploited a sexism so deeply structural as never even to be challenged. It did attempt to grapple with problems of a mature colonialism, above all the appearance of the Educated African, but the attempt was doomed by its own prejudices.

* * *

BIOGRAPHIES COMPRISED A separate group of imperial films. M. A. Wetherell was a South African actor and sometime director who made a number of African pictures, the most notable his *Livingstone* (1925). When his "expedition" met for a sendoff luncheon in 1923—fittingly, at the Hotel Victoria—imperial enthusiasm ran high. The "warm support" of the London Missionary Society, the bishop of London, the moderator of the Church of Scotland, and assorted peers, KCBEs, and clergymen was reported. Livingstone was toasted as "one of the best makers of the British Empire."

Wetherell spent seven months in Africa making *Livingstone*. He had had earlier experience in South Africa; the example of pictures like *Winning a Continent* (in which he had appeared) may have been before him as he embarked on a program of location shooting, trying to film the scenes of the missionary-explorer's life where they had actually happened. Wetherell both directed and played Livingstone. Reports that he had traveled twelve thousand miles on foot were a bit exaggerated (that amount would have required sixty miles a day, every day), but there is no question that the trip, in 1923-24, was arduous.

Livingstone opened with a private showing at Albert Hall in January 1925, with the Lord Mayor and the Royal Geographical Society in attendance. Wetherell followed the example of the tonier African documentaries in launching his motion picture this way and in speaking before each showing. The event was set up to emphasize a quasi-official approval: the Under-Secretary for Colonies praised it as "a call to the youth of the country," which showed "something of the wonderful heritage which now lay before the British Empire in Eastern and Central Africa . . . one million square miles of the most fruitful land in the world, which were still practically undeveloped." The "twelve million native inhabitants, in all stages of development," did not seem to be a problem. Livingstone himself was depicted as "a real man," and the speaker hoped that similar films would show other British "pioneers and explorers."

When the picture was released in the United States as *Livingstone in Africa* in 1929, however, the *New York Times* thought it "creaked with age"; it was "filmed with touching sincerity," but the direction was "sadly unimaginative." New York had no imperial-colored glasses; it was attuned to production values (always the bugbear of British films until Alexander Korda came along). Undeterred, Wetherell re-edited his film for British re-release in 1931, with synchronized sound. British reception, at least as shown by the *Times*, was respectful, but no further American release is recorded. The historical Livingstone would continue to attract filmmakers, however: first with the negligible *David Livingstone* (1936) and then with Hollywood's entry, the values-laden *Stanley and Livingstone* of 1939.

First, however, Michael Balcon would produce a biography as part of *his* "imperial trilogy." *Rhodes of Africa* was a pious effort welcomed by both the Boy

Scouts and the Southern Rhodesian government. Directed by Berthold Viertel, it is full of sit-down-and-talk scenes of a numbing boredom, relieved from time to time by location shots made by Geoffrey Barkas. The script contains such clangers as, "Sooner or later, the two great white races of this continent must work together" (said, apparently, of the British and the Boers); "I always think of the native people as children" (Rhodes); and, when the Matabele go to war, "Black children . . . must be punished."

Rhodes was played by the American actor Walter Huston, a good actor who was not here required to act; rather, he had to appear middle-aged (apparently from birth) and sincere. Given much of the script, this was a formidable task. Oscar Homolka was far more interesting as Paul Kruger, and the entire film picked up whenever he appeared. The only woman of consequence (other than Mrs. Kruger, who walked through a couple of scenes) was a journalist played by Peggy Ashcroft. She was another Crowing Hen—a straw woman given asinine lines to silence any real criticism of the central male. Given that Ashcroft had incredibly stupid lines, her performance was nonetheless remarkable for its badness from a usually superb actress, here replacing character with manner, singing her words, posing like a nineteenth-century Delsartian.

Rhodes is a film without an action, about a man whose life was intense with action. It is a drab pageant, with events sketched rather than dramatized and pronouncements of will replacing action. Rhodes himself is nothing but will and voice, making pronouncements: I will, I must. Given this view of history, so pleasing to successful film producers and politicians—i.e., that history is the record of the appetites and satisfactions of "great men"—there could be no real suspense.

This is the way children see adults, as unexplained power. Thus, Rhodes is an Imperial Man of a sort very different from Sanders or Faversham; there is still "no woman in it," but he is parental, not boyish, and if he is homocentric, he is so because he is egocentric, not because of some triviality like sexual preference.

Like Wetherell's *Livingstone,* the film touched an official chord. A special showing was given in 1936 in London to scout and guide officers, "arranged with the approval of Lord Baden-Powell, the Chief Scout." At the end of the Oxford term, the film was shown to the Rhodes scholars, and it was "selected by the National Film Library to be handed down to posterity."

These were Hollywood's biographical years, too (Alexander Graham Bell, Dreyfuss, Lincoln, Jesse James, et al.), so it is little wonder that Stanley and Livingstone got swept up. Cedric Hardwicke, every American's idea of an English gentleman, played Livingstone in Hollywood's 1939 contribution to imperial hagiography, *Stanley and Livingstone.* Spencer Tracy played Stanley. Osa Johnson, recently widowed, was technical adviser on the three months of location shooting, from which she cabled such observations as, "I think there is not a native in Africa who would not rather dance than eat," and "All this [dressing up and dancing] is part of the call of the jungle."

Dare one say that Spencer Tracy was fat? Dare one suggest that he was not much of an actor? Dare one assert that this was a dreadful film? Yes, yes, and yes. This was Hollywood biography at its worst, utterly cut off from the facts of its subject, keeping only the tenuous connection of the subject's name. It relied on the crudest of identifications for time and place: this Africa was "a vast jungle in which you could lose half of America." It relied on sheer fabrication to give its subject stature: "The man who finds Livingstone will be doing a great service to the world." It relied on the historically impossible to jump over tedious realities: "The American consul in Bagamoyo is taking care of [hiring porters]." It relied on racist clichés for titillation: "Listen! War drums!" It relied on racist sentimentality for justification: Stanley marches across the map of Africa as "Onward, Christian Soldiers" plays.

There *is* a woman in it (Nancy Kelly), but she is of course in Zanzibar, so she doesn't get in the way on safari. This Stanley is one of the nicest men in the world—he never, for example, takes the whip to his employees, as the real Stanley so liked to do—so that Evelyn Waugh would never have said of him, as he did of the real thing, that his "last expedition was tragic and villainous, tempered only by force." He is distinctly American, and what is most American about him is his idealism and his niceness.

And this is a Stanley who can say when he is lost in the midst of what would soon be called Tanganyika—as if he had pulled into the only filling-station for a hundred miles—"Ask if they know the way to Tanganyika." And check my porters' oil.

This Stanley is no fascist, living by the will; rather, this is a well-meaning, thoroughly swell guy who really wants to find Doctor Livingstone because this Stanley is a two-fisted Yankee newspaperman, and his editor has told him to find the Doc.

Which brings us back to Cedric Hardwicke, who tells Stanley that in fact he's "neither lost nor hiding," so one wonders what all the searching and suffering were about. (The real Livingstone was not lost, either, although he was in bad shape; he was actually being fed and nursed by the Arabs of Ujiji, a truth too unfashionable for Hollywood to swallow.) Hardwicke's Livingstone, of course, is very well spoken and gentlemanly and English, and he fits well the British definition of the great Imperial Man—older than Stanley, well educated at a good university, parental. It is not surprising, then, that he gives the now adoring Stanley a long speech about mapping Africa so that whites won't be afraid of it any more and will come to settle in droves, "bringing civilization to people who have never heard a word of kindness."

Onward, Christian soldiers!

Reinvented as Stanley the Explorer, the former reporter now marches across the blank map of Africa as names spring up under his feet like weeds: Stanleyville, the Belgian Congo. The martial music, the moving bodies, a flag suggest the soldiers of the hymn; it is with this military image that the movie ends. The personal quality of the search for Livingstone has been subsumed under a larger cultural, probably racial march; will—which the real Stanley had by the bucket— is at last very much in evidence. What had been a job ("Find Livingstone; get that story!") has become a cause. Stanley has become an Imperial Man in the mold of Huston's Rhodes. We do not see Tracy *act* this new Stanley; rather, we see his stand-in at a distance. Tracy's democratic style would not have allowed him to project this new and implacable will. As with Weissmuller's Tarzan, the intensely American quality overrules a lurking fascism; thus, it is only in its conclusion that *Stanley and Livingstone* can be said to resemble *Rhodes of Africa*.

ONE FURTHER FILM on imperial themes remains, from the 1950s, but most fans will refuse to see it as one: the widely admired *The African Queen* (1951). Starring Humphrey Bogart and Katherine Hepburn, and directed by John Huston, it is a nexus of their three Hollywood-star myths, and thus inevitably a "great" motion picture—whatever its subtext. Insistent upon being a piece of romantic realism, it is in fact an imperial fantasy that could be deconstructed by a bright chimp.

Bogart is Charlie, a belching, scratching, hard-drinking captain of a derelict African riverboat; Hepburn is Rosie, the spinster sister of an epicene missionary (Robert Morley as inept Imperial Man). At the beginning of World War I, these three come together on an African river; the missionary dies; and the sister determines to take the boat down the river to put a little bit of England on the great lake at its end, where a German gunboat waits. The blue-collar captain objects and misbehaves, but all's well: they fall in love, he stops boozing, she becomes softer, they get to the lake and, through happy accident, blow up the gunboat and end blissfully floating hand-in-hand on the lake. It is not an entirely typical imperial film, for it has a woman in it, and both its Imperial Men are failures, but it accepts the imperial idea of Africa. The only black Africans to be seen are the missionary's converts in the first reel.

Huston was a master manipulator of stereotypes, including those of Hollywood acting. His acceptance of a star's personality was part of this talent; direction became to some extent the encouragement of the star personality to explore and open itself as the film progressed—a substitution for the Stanislavskian idea of through-line. As a commercial film technique, it was brilliant: audiences got to see their stars become more like themselves. This idea of star acting appears to have been linked to that form of American romantic realism based in "life study," which was itself a reliance on stereotypes, carefully selected and observed: a spinster holds herself this way; a lower-class man scratches himself so; a whore carries herself like this. The urge is toward the general rather than the particular, a defensible one that tends toward the larger-than-life. Acting is, then, a careful nurturing of highly selected behaviors, which have semiotic value for the audience; "truth" is outer rather than inner. Such an attack enables star personality by not requiring erasure of the actor's self; on the contrary, it is the style that typified the great period of stage stars. It certainly works here for Bogart and Hepburn.

Huston also accepted and mined certain assumptions that he seems to have believed and that he relied on in his audience: Africa is a European possession, to be legitimately fought over by Brits and Krauts; hard drinking and masculinity are linked; what a spinster is really looking for is a (white) penis; if a man and a woman—or at least two Hollywood stars—are isolated together, they will "fall in love"; "love" ennobles and changes character; and so on. In *The African Queen*, these ideas undergird the characters and explain the delight audiences take in this fable of two people overcoming individual weaknesses with each other's help; this is coupled with a delight in romantic love between two unlikely but satisfying partners. That these ideas do not in fact correspond to observed reality is clearly irrelevant.

The film, then, is a brilliant manipulation of stereotypes and star personalities. The illusion of Hepburn's and Bogart's playing against type is wonderfully rigged (Hepburn *sweats*! Bogart *belches*!). Their isolation together for most of the picture, fighting a raging river, diving to repair the boat, fighting their way through swamps, gives them heroic stature. What everyone remembers from the picture are the moments when this stature is humanized by oh-so-forgivable weakness: Bogart panicked by leeches, Hepburn panicked by bugs. It is immensely enjoyable.

Some of us would now say, however, that the basic assumptions are untrue: alcoholic men are not converted by love but, instead, pollute love; single women are often perfectly happy that way, thank you very much; a man and a woman isolated together need no more fall in love than any other isolated pair. As well, we would point out the extent to which this piece of supposed realism relies on accident: the death of the brother, the encounter of Hepburn with Bogart, the blowing up of the gunboat. And, most of all, we churls would point out that the film accepts an unstated assumption about colonialism that is repulsive: the one that says that Germans and English have a right to contest for ownership of an African lake. This assumption is the essential imperial one, already archaic in 1950 but accepted by Huston and therefore by his audience, and thus comforting to that audience as a result: see, the film says, Africa is really white!

And the result is that this is another "African" film that is not about any real Africa, after all. Its African humans are part of the scenery in the first reel, needed only to tell us quickly that this is a missionary station. Africa thereafter is the old dangerous verdure, beautiful but filled with disgusting things like those leeches. It is the obstacle against which Rosie and Charlie struggle to reach their (white, European) goal. Its people are easily manipulated extras who disappear when the going gets tough. Interaction between whites and Africans is top-down, impersonal, ephemeral.

In a slightly less fantastic departure from reality, the film would be more believable if the last shot opened out and showed thousands of Africans cheering onshore as the floating Rosie and Charlie are gulped down by a crocodile.

A COMMON THEME of maleness runs through the imperial movies, divided between mature and youthful, or paternal and filial. *Four Feathers, Stanley and Livingstone, Sanders of the River*, even *Rhodes of Africa* show this older-younger male relationship. The central figures themselves can be divided into the boyish (*Four Feathers*), the old-boyish (*Sanders, Men of Two Worlds*), and the paternal (*Rhodes of Africa*). The absence of women and the emphasis on manhood and such "masculine" qualities as will and courage suggest that the films speak from the pulpit of patriarchy, that they are male speaking to male. Except for the American *Four Feathers* of 1929 and *Stanley and Livingstone* (and, to be sure, *The African Queen*, atypical in many ways), they seem to take their model for this relationship from the English public school. So, too, do they take their morality and their definition of *man*: their (often submerged) homocentrism is the sentimentalized old man's yearning for youth— and, perhaps, youths: Housman's "To an Athlete Dying Young."

The films have their pernicious side, as well—a boy's world's view of girls. Women are excluded from this society and are shown only as feeble china dolls (Esmee) or as offensive and intrusive Crowing Hens—women who are foolish precisely because they are women and precisely because they are vocal. They are used to discredit a perceived oppposition by putting a straw argument in their mouths, where any argument, we are to believe, would be absurd *because the speakers are women.*

By comparison, the Haggard White Hunter films, which also have older/younger male pairings—Carey/Renaldo, Hardwicke/Loder, Granger/Carlson—escape the imperial films' claustrophobic homocentrism by the very active presence of women who are objects of desire and action: Booth, Lee, Kerr. None has the fully developed coupling of the Weissmuller-O'Sullivan Tarzans, but the White Hunter movies at least suggest that society coalesces around men *and* women, not men alone.

One effect of the imperial films, then, was to suggest that imperial men do not have sexual selves—that they are eunuchs of empire. Indeed, so severe is their sexism that the *absence* of women can be taken as an identifying mark of the imperial film. In others of the films, the eunuchs of empire are less imperial men than imperial boys. This view of the imperial civil servant and soldier sees manhood as merely a projection of boyhood, the man all the better imperialist for preserving the boy's naivete, racial prejudice, and misogyny.

Whether eunuch or boyish misogynist, the Imperial Man of film is demonstrably untrue to the imperial men of life, who had wives, raised families, started schools, and had family picnics in faraway places. Given that the film version is so obviously different from the reality, one has to conclude that film-makers wanted it that way.

5 BLACK EVE, WHITE GRAVE ____

The best movie ever made in America about "Africa" was silent and black-and-white. It used all the African clichés and stereotypes that undergirded the imperial and fantastic films, and nonetheless rose above them to greatness. It was Tod Browning's *West of Zanzibar* (1928), which tells you from the first frame that you are seeing the work of a master. It made its Africa a place of slithering horror, one that was an externalization of its characters' inner lives; in that sense, the "Africa" of *West of Zanzibar* was no more real than Browning's Transylvania in *Dracula*. Both places were, rather, metaphors with strong visualizations, to be exploited by this poetic director. This is not to say that Browning's genius or his poetry excuses that exploitation, but only that the particularization within the work transcends the clichés.

Lon Chaney played the central role. He was so good that he seemed to be working in a different medium from other silent actors; here, on the cusp of the change to sound, Chaney created a role that cannot conceivably have been bettered by sound or color or any technological enhancement. The story is an absurd melodrama, but Chaney makes it a life, as believable as any. Browning's imagination leaps beyond the real, into styles well removed from realism (especially expressionism), and Chaney's passion and conviction grasp what so easily could seem excesses or mannerisms and knit them into the fabric of his performance. Director and actor complement each other, correct each other; the result is greatness.

Chaney plays a vaudeville magician whose wife runs off with another man (Lionel Barrymore). The film begins on a stage, with Chaney performing: we see closeups of his made-up, mask-like face, then of a skeleton that is part of his act. He transforms the skeleton into a beautiful woman; a few frames later, he is embracing her. The film has hardly started, and the visual cross-references are already dazzling: mask-skull-woman-magic-love, at the very least. The woman—his wife—breaks from his embrace and goes to the dressing-room, and there she prepares to go away with Barrymore. He is not, here, the lovable old man in the wheelchair we know from "Doctor Kildare" and *You Can't Take It With You*; this is a middle-aged, sardonic Barrymore on two good legs, rather handsome, his triangular face a little diabolical. Barrymore tells Chaney that he is taking his wife away. They are backstage, and an elephant act is coming to its end and a comedy act is beginning on the stage, of which we see and hear fragments; Browning is extending his reference, daring to go to comic grotesque even with this deeply serious moment of mature, and destroyed, love. "She loves *me*!" Barrymore snarls, triumphant. "Do you hear? And I'm taking her to Africa."

The comedy plays on, onstage; the audience laughs.

Barrymore pushes Chaney, who falls backward over a railing and is so badly injured that he loses the use of his legs. The film leaps forward. The stage is gone—exactly as it is gone from Chaney's life—and in the next scene, two years later, he moves around by pushing himself on a wheeled dolly, his legs tucked under him. Both Browning and Chaney are relentless with the character. Like the comic stage act, he has become a grotesque; the glamor of the stage (magic, mask) has vanished as surely as his wife has.

But the wife, rejected by Barrymore, comes back, and, from a church, she sends a message to Chaney. He propels himself along indifferent streets; powering himself with his hands, he seems a speck in the city, which is photographed as rather blank stone walls. His wife dies in the church; she gives him the baby she has borne. Chaney looks up at a statue of the Virgin (an exceedingly ironic shot, the man so close to the ground, the stone woman so elevated) and promises, "I'll find him! I'll make him pay! He and his brat will pay!"

And then, with the flash of a title, we are in Africa, and it is eighteen years later.

Now Chaney's shaven head dominates the screen. Little about him is attractive, as if even love, if held to too tightly and too long, turns into something ugly. He swings about on his hands, goes up and down a rope like an acrobat, his body held straight so that the rigid legs suggest a crocodile's tail—a comparison made visual at several points in the film. Chaney is now the master of a small African trading post. His second-in-command is played by Warner Baxter, who calls him "Dead-Legs" and refers to the Africans around them as "black-birds." The paraphernalia of Chaney's magic show, particularly the cabinet with the skeleton, mingle with the visual clichés of "Africa"—masks, feathers, weapons. Chaney rules through this bizarre meeting of cultures; his "magic" is used to impress the local people; he eats fire. Around him, the other white men of this grubby outpost are a parody of "civilization" and "higher culture": they are sweaty, unshaven, dirty, dressed in undershirts and filthy trousers. They are seldom far from a drink.

Lionel Barrymore, whom we now see again, looks like these others, not at all the gentleman in the dinner jacket who stole Chaney's wife: his hair is filthy and tangled; he needs a shave. He is trying to send ivory to the coast and doesn't know that the "spirit" that frightens the porters away is, in fact, one of Chaney's underlings; nor does he know who Chaney is. At this point, we think we see how Chaney will revenge himself: he will destroy Barrymore's ivory trade, ruin him.

Even as we conclude this, Browning is telling us visually that both men are already "ruined"—i.e., no longer human. Chaney is now a monster; we have barely guessed at his corruption, however. "He made me this thing that crawls. . . . *Now I'm ready to bite!*" Shots of crawling insects and lizards, a crocodile, then something like a scorpion that seems to be drowning in the rain. And then, in Zanzibar, Mary Nolan as the now-grown child of Chaney's dead wife. Chaney has had her raised there as a prostitute; now, ready to have his revenge on Barrymore, he sends a henchman to get her.

Waiting for her to arrive, Warner Baxter and another henchman get drunk in "Dead-Legs's" house. Two black women are with them; they dance. This association of booze and black women is played against scenes of Nolan in the bar in Zanzibar, her very young blondness against the women's blackness. This lingering on her gives us time to entertain the possibility that she will redeem Chaney: because she is blond and young and beautiful (such is the convention of film), perhaps her arrival will cause him a change of heart.

Not a chance.

Her blond but corrupted innocence is played against Chaney's darkness and cannot touch it; Chaney projects an inner savagery that makes the savagery of "Africa" seem as unreal as the masks of the film's early scenes. When the girl arrives, she immediately despises the drunks around Chaney (including Baxter) but pities Chaney's lost legs. He rejects her pity, hates her pity. He puts on a skull mask and crawls out to an idol, where drums and skulls are waiting. It is a funeral, he tells her: "It's a lovely custom. When a man dies, they always burn his wife or daughter with him." And, as the flames rise, there is an incredible closeup of Nolan, as riveting as the same screen-filling shot of Joan Bennett in *The Macomber Affair* and used for a very similar end: the usually flattering shot of the screen beauty made to emphasize horror.

Chaney treats the girl as an animal; he won't drink from a glass she has used, makes her eat on the floor. He gives all her clothes to the Africans; we see black women dancing in them. She is offered alcohol but refuses, repeats her contempt for the drunken men she served in Zanzibar. But Chaney keeps up his pressure on her.

Now Chaney springs his real trap. He sends a message to Barrymore to come to him. When Barrymore arrives, Chaney repeats the magic trick with which the film opened, this time replacing the skeleton, not with his wife, but with the girl. She is soddenly drunk—Chaney's pressure has worked. It is clear that she has become an alcoholic; he torments her with drinks that are held just out of her reach.

The magic trick has caused Barrymore to remember him (it is part of the film's cynicism that he had forgotten both Chaney and the wife), and Barrymore makes jokes about the blond "beauty" whom Chaney has "made a wreck of." Warner Baxter, enraged at the two of them, carries the girl away, saying he is in love with her. Baxter, it seems, has been redeemed, not so much by her innocence, as by her degradation.

Now—only now, springing his trap—Chaney tells Barrymore that the girl is his, Barrymore's, daughter, by the wife he stole and then rejected. Barrymore is stunned; he lowers his face into his hands; he weeps as Chaney tells him how he corrupted the girl: "I had her raised in the lowest dive in Zanzibar so *you* could be proud of her."

And then Barrymore raises his face, and we see that he has not been weeping at all—he has been laughing. With a terrible glee, he tells Chaney that the child is his own, not Barrymore's. Chaney has corrupted and destroyed his own daughter. He has made his magic, and out of the cabinet, he has brought, not a woman, but a skull.

Then the rest of Chaney's revenge runs on under its own terrible power: Barrymore is killed by Chaney's Africans, and they prepare to burn Nolan alive because Chaney has told them she is Barrymore's daughter. Chaney, repentant, manages to save her by again using the magic box, this time causing her to vanish and the skeleton to appear. She and Baxter escape. Chaney, however—wearing a mask, "dancing" with his arms—is burned alive by the black men he has tricked.

You can find everything wrong with this story and almost nothing wrong with the film. Even the stage-bound action (it was made from a play) is overcome by Browning with such cuts as those to the swamp creatures, wriggling in the rain. And the lurid excess of the plot becomes a vision of human foulness in Chaney's and Browning's hands.

The "Africa" that we are given is one of unalloyed degradation for whites. (No consideration at all is given to what it might have been for blacks; in this film, Africa exists only as a white hell.) The poetic reference—crawling, teeth, skulls, fire, evil magic, sweat, drunkenness, corruption—draws on the African clichés of the nineteenth century. Africans themselves are presented as purely savage. Africa is a place without love or even satisfying sex (nothing is made of Nolan as sex object); it is a place without even satisfactory revenge (Chaney's eighteen-year plot rebounds on itself); it is a place without redemption or the hope of redemption (the beautiful girl who hates booze becomes a drunk). It is not a real place at all, but an imagined home of horrors. Unlike all the other films where the white characters have a "civilized" home to which to return, *West of Zanzibar* offers its characters only variations on the idea of universal savagery.

West of Zanzibar is properly understood as a Gothic film. In its vision, innocence exists only to be corrupted, love only to be betrayed; there is no redemption, and suffering brings neither wisdom nor forgiveness. Although melodrama is the dominant genre, dark comedy is not far away, so that tricks and quasi-comic reversals are possible. That moment when Barrymore raises his face and shows that he is laughing, not weeping, is stunning—pure evil fun.

The film's Africa is an intensification of the Africa of the clichés—more insects, more slitherings, more wetness. Africa is not singled out, however; it is merely a different embodiment of Browning's somber vision, which also includes the grotesqueness of the stage, the stony indifference of city streets, and the ironic coldness of the church.

WHITE CARGO also dug the White Man's Grave, and it did so by using many of the same stereotypes as West of Zanzibar. However, it used them for their contrast with "home"—i.e., England, the Land of Whiteness. Derived from a novel (Hell's Playground) by way of a play, it was stagebound in both its movie versions. It briefly gave popular culture a gag line—"Me Tondelayo, me good girl"—and Tondelayo herself, the West African sexpot, initiated the only African female archetype of any importance until the 1980s: the Black Eve.

White Cargo was first filmed in 1929 and was released in both a silent and a sound version. Gypsy Rhouma was Tondelayo; Leslie Faber was Witzel, the veteran colonial; Maurice Evans was a young newcomer. The perfectly Victorian plot could be summarized as "the seduction of a nice young man by amoral Africa as represented by a hot-blooded black woman," but behind the plot were generations of white sexual fear.

It is not entirely negligible that the novel on which the play and film were based was written by a woman. The fear of "miscegenation" (white men and black women), also known as "going native," was in part white women's fear of losing white men; this, in turn, was in part a fear of the destruction of the white family. Many films send British men off to Africa, leaving women behind, but those films never allow sexual contacts while out of England. They allow a sublimated homoeroticism (the all-male world of the Imperial Man); they allow any amount of action; but they do not allow black female sex objects even to exist. Yet the reality of the colonies was that white men took black sex partners all over Africa: "concubinage" was a major scandal of the early days of East Africa, and one English officer said that "everybody" bought one, sometimes two, Masai girls as soon as he arrived. Rider Haggard probably had his first heterosexual experience in Africa. Real-life white hunters were sometimes pestered by clients who wanted them to pimp for them, along with everything else.

The reality of colonial life was, then, the opposite of popular myth. The myth was perpetuated not only by the absence of black women from movies and other forms, but by the presentation of black women in many films as ugly and comic, by their inclusion in the dehumanization worked on blacks generally, and by widespread tales of venereal disease. The myth of imperial life, on the other hand, enshrined male chastity.

The myth's sexual unreality (meant as sexual idealism) served the British government's need to recruit colonists and colonial administrators. If England had believed that its men aggressively and successfully made black liaisons, English mothers and clergymen and schoolmasters might soon have dried up the supply of young manhood. Thus, while it might have been well known in certain all-male venues that interracial sex was one of the perks of colonialism, the official and mythic line was that interracial sex did not exist. Black women, the myth said, were not attractive to white men.

By the late 1920s, however, the myth and the reality appear to have collided. *White Cargo* and a few other films showed their uneasy suspicion that black women *were* attractive, after all, by introducing the Black Eve. She was African (or thought to be African); she was aggressive; and—an isolated but horrifying instance—she was beautiful. As embodied by Tondelayo, she was the heart of a cautionary tale that was apparently meant to warn young men of one of the perils of the jungle that they hadn't read about in Kipling. And the warning was a strong one: if the young man gave in and allowed himself to be wrapped by Tondelayo's coils, he would wind up as WHITE CARGO!—that is, the man who has to be sent home, worn out, disgraced, and ruined.

"The true-blue British hero repulses the advances of a sultry half-caste maiden . . . with a strangled 'Now listen—I'm white!'" Rachel Low noted. He was expressing the piety of the colonial myth: No sex, please—we're white. But Tondelayo is a girl to whom you can't say no, and he, poor fool, goes to hell in a handbasket. Nonetheless, this 1929 version of the film did not make Tondelayo's charms *too* glorious. "More torpid than torrid," was *Variety*'s assessment.

When Tondelayo again slithered to the screen in 1942, she was played by Hedy Lamarr, a very beautiful actress with a reputation for sex. (Nobody was allowed to forget that she had been filmed nude at fifteen in *Ecstasy*.) A Viennese accent was not thought to be a detriment to the role of Tondelayo, the more so as she was costumed and directed as a sort of Elinor Glyn sexpot. The stalwart Witzel this time was Walter Pidgeon; Frank Morgan was an alcoholic doctor; and Richard Carlson was the young man whose lusts would reduce him to White Cargo. Otherwise, it was the mixture as before, with Leon Gordon, author of the stage version, given screenwriting credit. Perhaps his presence accounts for the extremely dated feel of the picture, the body of which is a flashback to 1910.

Pidgeon's Witzel is rude and unpleasant, perhaps a welcome change for the actor who usually played genteel Brits (*Rogue Male, Mrs. Miniver*). He hates

Africa, hates the other whites who come there. His brusque advice to the newly arrived Langford (Carlson) is, "Do your work and don't get involved with the natives. Never let the men see you're afraid and don't mammy-palaver—don't talk to the women." To which the handsome young white man replies, "Women! That's ridiculous! As if I'd be interested—." But Pidgeon is a cynic: he predicts "damp rot," a process of degeneration that sounds like Harold Hill's catalogue of the sins that begin with pool—"First you stop shaving every day—then you'll stagnate—in the end—*mammy-palaver*." Carlson's failure to go immediately into this decline makes Pidgeon contemptuous, and he begins to call the young man "Little Lord Fauntleroy." After Tondelayo makes her entrance, however (so clearly an act one curtain that you expect the house lights to go up), the young man rapidly goes to hell; and shortly we see him, unshaven and with a bottle in front of him, contemplating marriage to her. "I don't care what any of you think, Tondelayo's the only thing that matters to me now!" he whines. "That's damp rot!" Pidgeon bellows.

The local clergyman balks at marrying a white man to a "native," but he changes his mind when he is convinced that "Tondelayo is not of Accra blood. Her father is Egyptian, her mother is low-caste Arab." The young man is delighted: "I'm marrying one of us!" (He and the padre both seem to define whiteness as the absence of blackness.) Five months later, however, his delight has changed to despair; Tondelayo, bored with playing white man's wife, whips a black servant more or less for amusement and then tries to get something going with Witzel. Things pick up for her when Carlson falls sick; she sells his rifle (a capital crime, we have already been told) and buys poison, then pours out her husband's medicine and pours the poison into the bottle. The omniscient Witzel, however, knows what she has done, and he forces her to drink from the bottle; she staggers offstage (that is, out of the house) and dies. Witzel consigns the white cargo—what is left of Carlson—to the riverboat.

This is all fairly awful stuff, but what is most remarkable about it is that it was made in America in 1942. Its racial content is essentially that of the eugenics craze of the first years of the century, notions already rejected by the Weissmuller Tarzan films. That it was selected for production in the United States at this late date seems remarkable. That it was not an aberration, however, is clear from the 1941 release of *Sundown*, in which the beautiful but terminally wooden Gene Tierney played a supposedly half-white, half-Somali woman who was able to marry her white man (Bruce Cabot) only when she revealed that she was, in fact, 100 percent white. *Sundown* was a pro-British Hollywood war movie, made before Pearl Harbor; an opening title paid tribute to "a few men [who] by their courage and faith are serving many." That "faith" meant Christianity is made clear by George Sanders's words as a dying Imperial Man, "The church and the army are the basis of civilization." Then Cedric Hardwicke preaches a sermon in a bombed-out London church about "men who have died in these outposts of freedom." Remembering the padre's refusal to marry a white man to Tondelayo until he knew she was "one of us," it seems more or less clear that these films of 1941-42 saw Christianity and white purity as allied, if not, in fact, identical—an odd response to Hitler. They tended to see white civilization and the British upper class as allied, as well; Hardwicke looks and sounds as if he ought to be Archbishop of Canterbury, if not God Himself.

The other noteworthy aspect of *White Cargo* is its cinematography, which is lackluster until it takes Hedy Lamarr for its subject. Most of the movie is shot in two- and three-person medium shots, virtually all in stagey interiors. Lamarr, however, is often seen in tight closeups, or in fairly tight shots that show her breasts and shoulders; she becomes so much the object of "the gaze" that, in the context of the film, the closeup itself becomes the signal of her badness. As her face fills the screen, its meaning shifts from "movie star" to "destructive Eve," celebrating her and hating her at the same time. Because she is the lone representative of nonwhite femaleness, the camera's equation of beauty and evil seems patently misogynistic—the more so when the absurdity of her pedigree is trotted out, and we are told by one mouth (the padre's) that she is "white" and by another (Witzel's) that she is "native." There is a sense here of both being correct—the film certainly means to have the thing both ways—so that we are caused to think that not only *nonwhite* women are evil, but also that *all* women are evil. Thus, it may be that one explanation of this otherwise archaic work's appearance in 1942 lies in its misogyny. The camera moves in and in; Lamarr's face grows bigger and bigger; context announces, "*This* is the White Man's Grave." The same negative use of extreme closeup in *West of Zanzibar* and *The Macomber Affair* has already been noted. It rather stands on its ear the idea that the screen-filling female face is "a shining sign signifying . . . a transcendent power of Great Love."

But if you think that *White Cargo* holds film's most ridiculous moments, then you have not seen a supposedly black woman lean against an imitation tree and sing "My Bwana," a waltz supported by a chorus of white men in bush jackets and pith helmets. This happens in *Golden Dawn*, the operetta whisked to the screen in 1929. Hardly pausing for breath in its translation from the stage, it had Vivienne Segal as Dawn, "Muta's daughter," who is about to be married to a wooden idol; Walter Woolf as Tom Johnson, the white bwana to whom she sings; and Noah Beery, Sr., as Shep, a slaver who sings a love song to his whip—"In this whole hell-hole down in Africa, I am de boss man of all"—and says things like, "I knows what I knows." It also has a comic (Lupino Lane), of the sort standard in musicals before 1940, who sings, "To share a jungle bungalow [with] your dusky jungle queen"; a funny American; a funny duke; and a chorus of supposedly black women who sing rather Viennese numbers like "Where are the golden days?" (i.e., before the whites arrived). No concessions are made to real life, except for putting the "black" people (all played by whites) in dark makeup; otherwise, the chorus wear skirts of obviously cloth leaves; Segal wears a sparkly costume of sequined fabric; and Tom parades himself in impeccable white breeches, helmet, and bush shirt. The camera, apparently having bought itself a seat in the front row, center, sits and watches.

This is supposed to be East Africa after "the great war . . . [where] victors and vanquished held together to keep the natives in peaceful subjection." *Subjection* is rather a more honest word than the characters themselves care to use, however: the district commissioner says, "Listen, men of Africa! England is your friend!" Friendship doesn't include miscegenation, however, and it appears that Tom and Dawn are star-crossed. We get a tipoff to a way out, however, when a "witch-doctor" sings about "the blue of [Dawn's] eyes, and her red-tipped lips"; we are not surprised, then, when Tom—a little smarter than the average bear—says, "Did it ever occur to you —Dawn—that your father—might have been—*a white man?*" Then Tom has to go back to England, and Shep lusts after Dawn, and the "witch-doctor" gets ready to marry her to the idol in the "temple." Tom comes back and goes to Mombasa to get Muta to prove that Dawn is white, and the disctrict commissioner fears that peaceful subjection may not be working— "My small guard would be no match against a frenzied multitude of superstitious natives." They put Dawn on the "altar," and Tom rushes in and cries, "The British government will not tolerate this sacrifice of a white woman!" so they throw Shep on the fire instead, and the British army marches in, singing, and everybody sings "Dawn," and it starts to rain.

Golden Dawn is truly awful, but it came from the period of the truly awful musical; what is shameful about it is its overt racism, without which it could not exist. Its "Africa" is a stupid melange of South Seas and "jungle" clichés, over which both racial and "African" cliches have been laid. At its heart, however, it is no worse than *White Cargo* and *Sundown,* using the same device to weasel out of the contradiction of a white man's loving a black woman.*

Taken together, these motion pictures about the White Man's Grave suggest a negative "Africa" very different from the exotic, if dangerous, place of Haggard and Burroughs. However, to lump them obscures some differences among them,

---

* It is perhaps significant that *Show Boat*, in which miscegenation was also a concern, had come to Broadway only a couple of years before (and to silent film in the late 1920s), although *Show Boat* dealt with the matter a little less cavalierly.

the most obvious being that between Africa as place and Africa as the locus of black (or apparently black) women. This is roughly the division, too, between *West of Zanzibar* and the others, although *West of Zanzibar* suggests in one scene (that in which Warner Baxter and the other men get drunk and dance with African women) that recourse to black women is the last degradation for the white man. In fact, the "damp rot" defined in *White Cargo* is pretty much accepted by all of these films: a symbolism of dress (undershirts, dirty clothes) and toilet (the unshaven face), followed by drunkenness, and ending with sexual connection with a black woman. Another film of 1930 is worth noting in this connection: *Mamba*, in which Jean Hersholt plays August Bolte, a fat-gutted, unshaven boor in German East Africa. Most of this film is now lost, so it is impossible to see how much it resembled the others; however, the presence of a black vamp in Bolte's house suggests that here, too, a black woman was the symbol of degradation.

Africa as place is most important in *West of Zanzibar*—the clichés of wetness, heat, and the reptilian—and also gets some attention in *White Cargo* (primarily as heat and dampness). It is irrelevant to *Golden Dawn*, in good part because of the musical's nonrealistic style; its "hell-hole down in Africa" is the White Man's Grave only because the characters tell us so, with only the scene of Tom's visit to the dives of Mombasa suggesting the hell of *West of Zanzibar* and the "damp rot" of *White Cargo*. *Sundown* does not exploit any negative quality in African place at all; its visual reference—especially Tierney's costume—is "desert," Maria Montez-land, although it is supposed to take place in Northern Kenya.

African place and the signs of "damp rot" are, of course, connected, heat and damp encouraging the shucking of neckties and shirts, at the very least. The fatal first step in *White Cargo*, however, is *not shaving*. Shaving is submission to the general will. It is only in the last ten years or so, in fact—perhaps only since "Miami Vice"—that a few days' growth of beard has become fashionable. Before that, stubble represented uncouthness, sometimes menace (Bluto in *Popeye*); often low social status, especially when combined with an undershirt; even alcoholism and social ostracism. *Not shaving*, then, seems to symbolize in Africa a giving in to local conditions and a rejection of "home" and its social rules, with the result that the guilty man descends in class and may reach outcast status. This imagery is exploited brilliantly in *West of Zanzibar* (the movement from the dinner jackets of the early scenes to the roughness of the African ones) and in the surviving frames of *Mamba*, and it is specific in *White Cargo*.

However, the bottom of the White Man's Grave is not a beard and a bottle, but an African woman. This is only touched on in *West of Zanzibar*, a film in which social fall has meaning mostly as it symbolizes moral fall, whose bottom is represented by the crocodile and the scorpion. The symbolism of the black woman is exploited in *Mamba* to show how corrupt the man is. A black woman is, of course, at the heart of *White Cargo* in both versions, and her threat underlies the boy-loses-girl part of *Golden Dawn* and *Sundown*. In the latter two, the urge toward a black woman is cast as "love" that is returned, but without sex; in *White Cargo*, it is "love" that is not returned but that gets sexual satisfaction; in *Mamba*, it is apparently purely sexual. In all cases, the films are anti-female, several using cinematography to derogate rather than elevate women.

These films are quite unclear as to whether "love" justifies the device of turning the black woman white or whether "love" happens because she is really white and the male character recognizes her. Certainly, the latter seems to be true of *Golden Dawn*, which may partake of the musical's sappy convention of love as a kind of recognition ("Some Enchanted Evening," etc.). Otherwise, however, love seems to profit from accident (the woman just happens to be white, after all). In either case, the films cannot face the question of what happens if love fastens on a wrong—i.e., black—object that does not turn white. They thus tell their audiences either that interracial love is impossible or that interracial relationships are unthinkable.

Behind these meanings lies another, perhaps. The social degradation that begins with not shaving is a "giving in" to Africa and a rejection of the values of "home." "Giving in" to Africa is presented as a priori wrong; the alternative is not considered. That alternative is, of course, the creation of a new set of rules, a new "home," one that would have new sumptuary laws and new behavioral rules that would allow both appropriate clothes and interracial relationships. The inability to consider this alternative leaves the colonist no choice but to transport the home society and that society's rules to the colony, no matter how absurd—which is precisely what the colonial powers did in Africa. In actual practice, they bent the sumptuary rules (although English women were still wearing serge skirts on safari in 1910), but the racial rules were much more rigid. Where "home" was most rigidly maintained, the colonials got South African (and Kenyan) apartheid.

These films about the White Man's Grave (made between 1928 and 1942), then, may have been a response to the maturing of the African colonies—a kind of filmic attempt to glance at a very large tiger out of the corner of the eye and conclude that it was an unattractive polecat. They are the flip side of the imperial films: both forbid white women, one ascending into asceticism, the other crashing toward miscegenation.

6 THAT'S AFRICA FOR YOU!: COMEDY BEFORE 1950_____

O n the face of it, pre-independence Africa would seem to have been a ripe subject for comedy. It offered recognizable icons for mockery; it had fit subjects for deflation, from the pomposities of colonial bureaucrats to the posturings of big game hunters; its racialism, its contradictions, its hypocrisies were begging for satirical attack. In the event, however, it proved a less rich subject than it seemed. The number of African comedies has been small, their quality low. Yet some are worth noting.

Rastus in Zululand was an early (1911) short (about a comic Coon, according to Bogle), and there were a few other short comedies. There was, however, little extended comic treatment of Africa until the now-lost *Hold That Lion* of 1926, about which it is hard to say more than that it was only partly about South Africa and that some of its comedy revolved around a hunt. It was followed by Syd Chaplin's feature-length silent, *The Missing Link* (1927).

Much of the humor in *The Missing Link* comes from animal jokes, some of the rest from racial ones. Early on in *The Missing Link* a number of lions chase a "native" (a white in blackface); two "blacks" show supposedly comic fright when Chaplin, in a laundry sack, is taken for a ghost: "A spook am rockin' de boat!" is the title. Later, a "black" exclaims in a title, "If dat ape grabs me—it'll be bye-bye blackbird!"

The Missing Link's comic premise, however, is not one of race but of mistaken identity: that the epicene Chaplin will prove better than seasoned hunters at capturing the "missing link" (the fabulous animal who was supposed to be the Darwinian connection between humans and apes). Chaplin accidentally gets on a ship bound for Africa and then, after a series of misadventures, is hired by a woman-hating peer to impersonate him in Africa because the peer knows he will have to be with a woman there. The woman is Beatrice Breeden (played insipidly by Ruth Hiatt), a young white "on a brief vacation from college life in Cape Town." Her father's estate, located in "the African jungle—where many a scientist lost his life, trying to prove that man at one time hung by his tail," is prime missing-link habitat.

The funniest part of the picture actually deals with events before Chaplin ever gets to Africa. Chaplin, a skilled mime, was able to do a lot with misplaced luggage on a dock, slapstick encounters there, and a chase scene that spilled over from the dock to the shipboard sequences. By contrast, the African sequences (about half the film) seem forced. The missing link proves to be represented by a man in an ape suit, neither comically conceived nor comically executed; far funnier is a real chimpanzee, which unfortunately had to wear fur pants, apparently for reasons of censorship. Chaplin and Hiatt have an insufferably cute scene in which the chimp does things to Chaplin that he thinks the woman is doing, so he thinks she is "fresh," and so on. The man-woman comedy is not helped by Chaplin's obvious age or his mannerisms; the scene really looks like one between a rather pretentious young woman and her middle-aged hairdresser. When Chaplin is performing alone, however, he is far better. Alone with a trunk or a leopard or the Link, he is funny and his scenes have point, and the climactic sequence—he and a lion, locked into a house together—is excellent. Syd Chaplin lacked Charlie's ability to create character, however, and so *The Missing Link* is a series of comic bits strung on a not very interesting narrative line. Its choice of Africa for a location merely exploits the supposed danger from animals to put Chaplin into the same kind of comic threat again and again, with predictably diminishing returns. Africa also gives the opportunity for racial jokes, mostly verbal, but hardly enough to carry the film, even in the racialist 1920s.

The Cohens and the Kellys in Africa (1930) was a continuation of a comic series that took its eponymous heroes here and there (Atlantic City, Paris, Scotland). Charlie Murray and George Sidney played a pair of ethnically mixed partners, one Jewish, one Irish, whose popularity was also that of works like *Abie's Irish Rose* and radio's "Pretty Kitty Kelly." One was tall and thin, the other short and fat; partners in a piano-making firm, they fought about everything. In this picture, they go to Africa to find ivory for piano keys; the resulting plot is thin and episodic, but it hardly matters because what we are supposed to find funny is the two central characters. Sometimes, indeed, they are so, but what is at bottom a vaudeville routine makes for very static filming, not in the least helped by direction and camera work that is content to keep the pair in three-quarters (knees and up) framing while they mug and talk. There is a reliance on stock jokes and sayings. Cohen's stock putdown is "Phooey on you!" (which in fact came into popular everyday use in the 1930s). The film has occasional visual laughs—the two and their wives supposedly in rickshaws, until a change of camera angle shows that Cohen is actually between the shafts, running right behind the man pulling his—but is mostly verbal: of a black policeman, "He is very tan"; "He was born in the dark." Much of the humor is patronizing—from Nairobi, they go to "Gumbo-gumbo"—and it relies on the hoariest of cliches: they are captured by "man-eating cannibals" who are about to put them into a boiling pot. Occasionally, however, there is a flash of something funnier: in a village, they meet a "chief" named Nathan Ginsberg, from Brooklyn, also there to buy ivory; the three play miniature golf to determine who will corner the ivory market, Ginsberg represented by the "club professional." Abruptly, the film shifts its focus as Kelly's and Cohen's wives are kidnapped by "Arabs," and Africa turns into the same quasi-Arabia as that of *Sundown*. It ends with a genuinely comic visual sequence: Kelly and Cohen trade their old pianos for new ivory, and the jungle is filled with people and animals, including an elephant, playing pianos. Despite a few good moments, however, *The Cohens and the Kellys in Africa* is mostly a standup comedy routine with "African" backgrounds.

So This Is Africa (1933), on the other hand, was a comic but bizarre picture that relied on gender reversal for much of its humor, with results that were as unnerving as they were funny. It is the only comic African film to show an almost Aristophanic playfulness, with gender most of all, to the point that that playfulness sometimes seems almost perverse. The overall effect is of a film that is undeniably comic but not very funny, a contradiction that may be explained by the limited talents of the principal funny men, Bert Wheeler and Robert Woolsey.

The comic premise is that these two, playing failed vaudevilleans with an animal act, are saved from suicide by "Mrs. Johnson Martini," an explorer who is afraid of animals. She is a clue to the direction of the film's humor: it will get much of its fun from movies about Africa (here, the Martin Johnson films) rather than any actual Africa. The mere use of the words "Africa speaks," for example, (title of the 1930 hit) becomes a song cue. (We learn from the resulting song and dance that the stars can neither sing nor dance.) The hoary film lesson that bears do not exist in Africa (mentioned in a number of earlier documentaries) is stood on its ear: there are bears all over this film's Africa. Nor are African movies alone the comic target; one scene is a parody of Eugene O'Neill's *Strange Interlude* (recently, at that time, filmed).

It is, however, in gender reversal that *So This Is Africa* finds itself: Wheeler spends most of the film in evening clothes, Woolsey in a nightshirt that looks like a dress; thus, they seem like a man and a woman. Mrs. Johnson Martini, however, is attracted to Wheeler and offers to set him up in a little apartment, as if she were a man and he a woman; after ogling her for most of the film, he resists her. At almost the same time, Woolsey, walking in his sleep, is captured by a female Tarzan, who tries to steal him as Weissmuller had stolen Maureen O'Sullivan the year before. When that complication is resolved, Wheeler and Woolsey are captured by a tribe of Amazons and are told that "to be loved by them means death." The two flee, disguised as Amazons, but are captured when a marching chorus of Tarzans—who enter to a football song—capture the Amazons in a mass rape. "One year later," a title tells us, and we see Wheeler and Woolsey, still in their female disguises, doing laundry—and then they turn around, and reveal that each has a new baby strapped to his back. "That's Africa for you, that's Africa for you," we are told as the movie ends.

What *So This Is Africa* most closely resembles is the zany *Hellzapoppin*, at least in its anarchic playfulness, which utterly detaches itself from reality in the two men's final childbearing. This is a wonderfully comic moment, and so is the macho entry of the massed Tarzans. The gender contradictions that precede these, however, suggest less comedy than uncertainty: the role reversals that put the male comics in passive sexual positions work, but the conventional ogling and the conventional male innuendoes do not. They are boys in men's—and sometimes women's—clothes: in this film, they tell us, they are at a stage of sexual development from which they can become either males or females. The closing statement that "that's Africa for you," therefore, would seem to want to remind us of Haggard's Africa, that place of fantasy and of exotic sexuality, rather than of the Africa of lions and crocodiles and savages.

That *So This Is Africa* makes other movies its comic object (rather than Africa itself) is no bad thing, as those movies had much to answer for: the bit about bears, at least, was aimed at one of the sins of the documentaries, and Mrs. Johnson Martini satirized the pretensions of some of the self-styled explorers. Otherwise, *So This Is Africa* used "Africa" as an enabling locale for the suspension of reality, just like Haggard and Burroughs.

OLD BONES OF THE RIVER (1939) was Britain's lone addition to the list of African comedies; it featured Will Hay and Graham Moffatt, who had made other successful film comedies but who struck out with this one. A spinoff of *Sanders of the River*, and based on stories by the same author, it was distinguished only by the appearance of Robert Adams (later of *Men of Two Worlds*) as Bosambo. Looking remarkably like Paul Robeson, Adams managed to invest an exceedingly Uncle Tomish role with dignity, if not with Robeson's charisma; a mostly workmanlike Bosambo, he slogs through an embarrassing scene in which Bosambo's brother, M'Bapu, contests for the leadership of the tribe and wins— M'Bapu being that horror of the white mentality (and a new archetype), the Educated African. "Educated natives always bring trouble into the country," says the district commissioner. Shortly, however, he gets sick, and Will Hay, as Professor Tibbetts, takes over. Until then, Hay has been performing extraordinarily limp comic scenes in which he, for example, wears cap and gown with bush shorts, carries a flit gun at shoulder arms, and tries to teach a class of African children. As acting D. C., he goes upriver to collect taxes, has to take payment in goats, and finds that they smell. At last he runs crosswise of M'Bapu, who has led the tribe into human sacrifice (the inevitable result of education, apparently) and winds up being saved by Bosambo in a battle scene that never strays from the obvious in trying for laughs.

Old Bones of the River is, like *Sanders*, sexless. There are no women in it, and no ogling, no gender reversal, perhaps no gender. The comic premise is a shopworn one: the fool will take charge and save the day. But Hay is most unfunny; all that can be said is that he is, in fact, a fool. At heart, the film wants to be serious about the same things *Sanders* was, and comic about only those things that a right-thinking Imperial Man would find comic: professors and education for Africans. The opening title lays this out quite baldly: "*Darkest Africa.* Where . . . a handful of Englishmen rule half a million natives—teaching the black man to play the white man." Thus, Hay's professor is doomed to become an object lesson in how not to deal with Africans, just as actor Jack London's M'Bapu is an object lesson in how Africans must not be allowed to behave: he wears a suit, drinks whiskey, and talks to whites while sitting down. Any hope of laughter from anybody who is not anti-intellectual and racist is lost; but the hope of laughter is slim, anyway, in this film that was made without any of the imagination or zest that went into *So This Is Africa.* Its "Africa" was not a place where reality was suspended, but a place where reality was colonialism.

Congo Maisie (1940) continued the only series that brought a female protagonist to Africa. Although a modest little picture, it had Ann Sothern as Maisie, a 1930s female capable of wisecracks and toughness—one of the few that African film would see, a late example coming in Ava Gardner's "chorus girl" in *Mogambo* (itself a remake of a 1930s film). Equally of the thirties were the roles taken by Bob Hope, Bing Crosby, and Dorothy Lamour in *The Road to Zanzibar* (1941), in which they played the same fast-talking, brash, optimistic Yanks of the other *Road* pictures, roles that they slid into with the same greased ease as Sothern into Maisie. The road pictures have taken on their own myth, and *The Road to Zanzibar* is one of the better of the series. It has a breezy cynicism and a counterbalancing niceness, and Hope in 1941 was still a very talented comedian. His ability to play comic terror probably had no equal in film, particularly when he was trying to cover that terror so as to impress somebody, usually a woman. Here, Hope plays Fearless Frazier, the Living Bullet, whom Crosby pretends to shoot out of a cannon as part of a traveling circus. But they are always on the run, always inventing new scams and stratagems—this was made when the Depression was still very real—and when Eric Blore, as an eccentric millionaire, sells them a lost diamond mine, they are off to find it. Along the way, they find Lamour and Una Merkel as two tough-minded women who are pretending to be the captives of Arab slavers so that they can con white men into "buying them back," after which they split the money with the Arabs. They persuade Hope and Crosby to take them across Africa; Lamour supposedly has a millionaire waiting for her on the other side.

Lamour and Crosby travel in palanquins carried by overweight blacks; Hope and Merkel walk. Crosby sings, "Lions may roar, savages may shout." Hope tries to carry Merkel across a river; she winds up carrying him. Hope is, of course, attracted to Lamour, but whenever he gets close to her, he gets frightened. That neither Hope nor Crosby will be attracted to Merkel is a given: Merkel plays a witty woman, and witty women, the subtext tells us, do not attract men. It is Merkel who has invented the slaver-kidnap scam, and it is Merkel who wants Lamour to get to the millionaire. She is smart and tough—but not pretty. (Ann Sothern's Maisie is pretty, so she has to be dumb-smart and soft-tough, and she attracts men.)

When a leopard rips up Lamour's clothes while she is swimming, Crosby and Hope think she has been devoured. "What hogs these leopards are," Hope says. They bury the clothes in a parody of a funeral scene, and this sequence, which must be at least as old as *commedia dell'arte*, works. Lamour and Merkel take off with the safari, and Hope and Crosby stumble on alone, at last coming to a deserted village with a structure full of skeletons and drums. They begin to play; blacks in paint and feathers appear, capture them, threaten to eat them, put Hope into a cage with a gorilla; they escape by doing the patty-cake routine familiar from the other road movies.

Thus, *The Road to Zanzibar* was another funny movie that exploited an "Africa" that had long since passed into history. Its lost diamond mine, its cannibals, were of the nineteenth century. Its characters, on the other hand, were of the moment, Depression-era survivors. What was most comic about them was their ability to surmount obstacles: despite Hope's being a coward, he was, of course, a hero, wrestling with the gorilla, performing for cannibals. There is, in retrospect, a slightly nasty quality to both Crosby's and Lamour's characters, a hint of exploitation and dependency. Lamour, however, had a wholesomeness and a humor that saved her. What saved Crosby was that in him, in 1941, exploitation was merely Depression mannerism, toughness, breeziness—the coping skill of a survivor.

Nonetheless, it is Hope who is funny and endearing in *The Road to Zanzibar*. He makes a fool of himself over Lamour, and she uses him; yet, when Crosby gets her, he is generous. Hope at this time could be a very attractive performer who could balance laughter and suffering—his singing of "Thanks for the Memory" in *The Big Broadcast of 1938* was memorable—and he was at his best in the road pictures, as the road pictures were almost at their best in this visit to Africa.

AFRICA BECAME THE subject of another of Hollywood's comedy teams when Abbott and Costello appeared in *Africa Screams* in 1949. The title itself, however, suggested the movie's archaism: it looked back to *Africa Speaks* (1930) for its point. Most of the humor of the film looked back even further.

Sadly, the two comics, who could touch a very American nerve when they were on (*Buck Privates*, the "Who's on first?" routine), were a little off here. In part, there is a feeling that *Africa Screams* is a juvenile film, and much of it is childish (hardly new for these two); it is not the childishness of the jokes that hurts it, however, but the acceptance of the utterly bankrupt stereotype of "Africa," the one that was by this time relegated to "the juves," as *Variety* put it. It is the Africa of overweight "savages," of confused geography, of cannibalism and boiling pots and lost white princesses—while in the real world, World War II is over, and colonialism is tottering.

It would have been refreshing to have comics as talented as Abbott and Costello go after these stereotypes, but they did not: by and large, whatever humor is got out of "Africa" is got out of the same old clichés—"funny" language ("Walla-walla-koo," the Africans sing; "Ngowa," they say, on all occasions); mixed geography (the Tarabongo and Okavango rivers); black grotesques (the "Bangi" tribe wear bones in their noses). This is also the "Africa" of dangerous animals, including the usual multitude of crocodiles in every bit of water bigger than a puddle. This overworked crocodile footage cried out to be parodied, but the chance was let slip; there is a not very funny sequence, instead, in which Abbott bathes in a pool with a crocodile—the same motor-driven log that had appeared in every jungle movie since the introduction of sound. It, too, cried out for comic treatment but didn't get it.

This is not to say that the movie utterly lacked laughs. Abbott's infantile persona could squeeze laughs from almost anything; here, he is a man named Stanley Livingstone with a pathological fear of cats. At the film's opening, we see him trying to "tame" a kitten with the lion-tamer's whip and chair; he is even dressed in pith helmet, Sam Browne belt, and breeches. (The joke is essentially the same as that surrounding "Mrs. Johnson Martini" in *So This Is Africa*.) A nonsensical plot about a treasure map is introduced, and it all seems promising enough. So, too, do minor moments, as when Costello, lounging in the stern of a dugout canoe while Abbott wears himself out paddling up front, sees a crocodile behind him, and he whips out an eggbeater and uses it as a motor to shoot the canoe forward. Even better—in fact, a genuinely comic performance that is worth seeing for itself—is Shemp Howard's playing of Gunner Jensen, "the best follow-upper in Africa," i.e., the skilled White Hunter who fires the followup shots that protect the amateur. Howard plays him as a virtually blind bumbler in thick eyeglasses, squinting everywhere but at his target, threatening everybody around him whenever he picks up a gun.

But these things were not enough. Regrettably, the movie was weighted by the leaden presence of Clyde Beatty, a "lion-tamer" (i.e., animal tormentor). Much of the movie has to do with building a cage in the jungle where Beatty can "fight" the lions. Earlier, Frank Buck made a cameo appearance. (Buck, no longer well known, was the hero of a number of 1930s movies about Southeast Asia, cooked "documentaries" that were mostly filmed in enclosures, using starved or even dead animals—Buck once "wrestled" with a tiger that had in fact drowned the night before.) Both Beatty and Buck were prewar figures who were aging and half-forgotten by 1949; more importantly, the attitudes they represented were obsolescent. They were from the end of that time that had begun on film with *Paul Rainey's African Hunt*, when animals were mere objects, and when "catching" and "taming" animals went unquestioned. Their attitudes were essentially those of the carnival and the cheap circus, and the postwar world was rapidly outgrowing them. Their presence was another sign of the film's archaism.

Africa Screams should have been made in 1931.

IT IS A TRUISM that comedy is often reactionary. Movie comedy can be particularly so, given the perpetuation of images and careers that is worked by, for example, the use of stock footage and the studio system's creation of series. With both location scenes and series replicating themselves for two decades or more, it is not surprising that these movie comedies often had an outdated look to them.

Most belonged to series—the only exceptions are *So This Is Africa* and *The Missing Link*. But, typically, the African comedies came late, when it is to be expected that a series would be living on past performance. *The Road to Zanzibar* was an exception, coming at the peak of the *Road* pictures; otherwise, these comedies were mostly reworks, and they mostly show it.

This artistic fatigue does not entirely explain the comedies' generally low quality, however. Some of this may be a matter of economics: films like *Congo Maisie* were ground out cheaply and sometimes carelessly. Some failure, too, may be more apparent than real, the result of looking at them from this distance. Comedy seldom travels well, over either distance or time; it is only comic genius—Laurel and Hardy, the Marx brothers—that makes the leap. The rest seem flat, even incomprehensible; certainly, this is the case with *Old Bones of the River*, in which three comedians whose other work was very highly praised now seem like tedious old men.

Nonetheless, these comedies do not seem to be very good as a group, even when we look at them with something like contemporary eyes. When they are set against other work by the same people, they suffer: *Africa Screams* won't bear comparison with *Buck Privates*, for example. When they are set against work by other people, they suffer even more: nothing in any of the films, with the possible exception of Howard's "Gunner Jensen," will bear comparison with Groucho Marx's sendup of an explorer in *Animal Crackers*.

Is it that something in Africa itself militated against comedy? This defies logic. Rather, it may be that something in the London-Hollywood idea of Africa militated against genuine comedy—if, by "comedy," we mean a form that subverts by undercutting our expectations for what we call "reality," by which we mean an agreed-upon version of the usual. We have to separate the comic from the cheerful or the merely pleasant to examine this notion, however.

Do any of these films give us reasons to place them in that line of genuine, subversive comedy that zigzags back to Aristophanes? Intermittently, some do show such caste marks as classic comic situations (mistaken identity, imposture); suspension of "rules" of probability or "reality" (the laws of matter or internal probabilities that are created and then shattered—e.g., a miniature golf course in the jungle—or such "laws" as sexual identity and consistency); attacks on figures or institutions (through parody, imitation, exaggeration); the adoption of a radical persona by the comic center (infantilism, divine idiocy).

By and large, however, these films refuse to apply these classic comic devices to much that is adult or important. *Old Bones of the River* goes as far as exaggeration (the professor's clothes, the flit gun) and impersonation (the profesor takes over the district commissioner's duties), and it goes to a suspension of probability in the final battle scene; but it will not turn its mockery on racism or colonialism, on white pretension or the imperial posture of the all-male society it finds in Africa. *The Cohens and the Kellys in Africa* suspends probabilities of space and time and gets comic benefits from suspending cultural probability, as well (the miniature golf course), and it can utterly suspend "reality" for its final sequence of piano-playing elephants; but it will not subvert the clichés of "Africa" or of racism. *Africa Screams* benefits from a comically infantile hero (Costello) in an imposter's situation, and it often productively suspends probabilities (the eggbeater that works like a motor, a lion that befriends Costello), but it will not subvert Beatty and Buck and their outdated ethic, nor will it look comically at either the clichés of "Africa," the "Africa" of film, or the Africa of reality.

In fact, these films seem to have drawn a line around certain subjects and declared them off limits. Those subjects can be roughly lumped as the real—that is, contemporary—Africa: matters of race and colonialism, including a number of colonial persons, such as the missionary, the bureaucrat, the soldier, and the colonial family. Indeed, it can be said that for comedy generally (excluding *Old Bones*), "Africa" is hardly either colonized or governed; few if any whites live there, the exception being the odd trader or guide-cum-white hunter. In other words, the "Africa" of pre-1950 film comedy is implicitly *pre*-colonial Africa, and by being so it defines itself right out of genuine comedy. That is, you can't get many laughs from something that has already been disempowered.

Because these ignored subjects roughly coincide with the subjects prohibited by censorship, it is likely that they were ignored quite consciously. Censorship was specific about mockery or denigration of such racial/colonial icons as the clergy, the army, white women, and colonial government. It is to be remembered, too, that "bringing the white race into disrepute" brought angry letters in the 1920s and 1930s. It is likely, therefore, that the comedic failure in these areas was the result of deliberate, probably prior, censorship.

The result was to emasculate African comedy generally. Only one of the films can be said to have carried through with a consistent comedic attack, and it did so by taking the clichés of film, rather than the clichés of race or colonialism, as its object: *So This Is Africa*. But its real comic subject was something not at all specific to Africa, gender.

The other comedies, because they declared quite large areas of their supposed subject off-limits, now seem out-of-date and unimaginative. They picked up one of the world's greatest weapons for demolishing the smug and the false—comedy—and they waved it in the air without ever letting it strike a blow.

7 THE AFRICAN RETURNER

When *King Solomon's Mines* appeared in 1937, it carried above the title the name of the first black actor to become a major international star. Paid £8,000 for the role, Paul Robeson seemed to have arrived at an eminence that transcended race. Yet—as his quasi-exile in London showed—his was the bitter eminence of the superbly overqualified, separated from his own country by its prejudice and his undeniable talents. He had already been through the jolting experience of *Sanders of the River*, and thereafter, somewhat wiser, he was making in England films that would explore his own sense of what it meant to be African by descent and international by achievement. The secret king he played in *King Solomon's Mines* was only one variation on a personal myth, embedded in his British films, in which he would create a new black archetype: the Westernized black man of the world who goes to Africa—the African Returner.

UNTIL ROBESON, BLACK actors had played roles almost entirely dictated by white sensibility, the Good African and the undifferentiated "black horde" of the jungle movies. Black women had been restricted to virtual invisibility, except for Black Eve (often played by white women in blackface).

In *Sanders of the River*, Robeson's Bosambo was a Good African, his role vis-à-vis Sanders essentially that of servant to master: Sanders conferred chiefdom upon him with a medal, scolded him, rescued him; in a palaver scene, Bosambo sat at Sanders's feet. The archetype was further defined by an essential adolescence that Robeson gave the role, nudging it toward the childishness often noted by scholars as an attribute assigned to Africans by whites (epitomized by the word "boy"). This was not, of course, Robeson's intention; rather, he appears to have solved an actor's problem (Bosambo's optimism and cooperativeness) by going for a youthful bounciness, playing it against Sanders's older-and-wiser man and using it as a level from which to grow at the film's end. It is an interesting case of the actor's (and perhaps the director's) seeing the problem in nonracial terms: that is, the solution (Imperial Man-younger apprentice) would have worked perfectly well for a white actor (Carey-Renaldo) but was a trap for a black one—or at least for Robeson. As his later African films suggest, Robeson was always in a delicate balancing act between the color blindness of his sophisticated private self and the color symbolism of his public self.

Shooting *King Solomon's Mines,* 1918—one of the outstanding productions of the early South African film industry; the set is for Solomon's court in a scene before the main action begins. *(Courtesy Toron Screen Corporation. Photo from South African National Film, Video and Sound Archive.)*

Allan Quatermain, quintessential White Hunter (left), in the 1918 *King Solomon's Mines. (Courtesy Toron Screen Corporation. Photo from South African National Film, Video and Sound Archive.)*

The *She* production unit, Berlin, 1925: seated, right, producer G. B. Samuelson and his wife, Marjorie, who played a small role; Carlyle Blackwood, standing, left, with Mary Odette; framed by the tripod legs is Tom Reynolds. *(Courtesy of Sidney Samuelson.)*

She-Who-Must-Be-Obeyed, Ayesha—the first and greatest of the white queens, goddesses, and jungle princesses, here played by Betty Blythe in 1925: eroticism as destiny. *(Courtesy of Sidney Samuelson; photo from British Film Institute Stills, Posters and Designs.)*

One of the great Hollywood entertainment films—the 1950 *King Solomon's Mines*, with, from left, Richard Carlson, Deborah Kerr, and Stewart Granger. *(© 1950 Turner Entertainment Co. All Rights Reserved.)*

Edwinna Booth and Duncan Reynaldo in *Trader Horn*—jungle princess meets white male. *(© 1931 Turner Entertainment Co. All Rights Reserved.)*

In 1929–30, British filmmaker Cherry Kearton made *Tembi*, a blend of fiction and documentary that broke ground with an all-African cast and a story that treated Africans as real human beings. *(Photo from British Film Institute Stills, Posters and Designs.)*

The only real Mr. and Mrs. Tarzan—Johnny Weissmuller and Maureen O'Sullivan in *Tarzan and His Mate. (© 1934 Turner Entertainment Co. All Rights Reserved.)*

Nonfiction filmmakers on African location: at this accidental 1928 meeting on the Nile, Martin Johnson (to right of camera in pith helmet) and Osa Johnson (woman in light dress), with photography magnate George Eastman (dark suit, center), crossed paths with Merian C. Cooper (behind camera) and Ernest Shoedsack (with pipe), who were shooting location footage for *Four Feathers*. *(Courtesy George Eastman House and the Osa and Martin Johnson Safari Museum.)*

Lon Chaney in the stunning *West of Zanzibar*, 1928, directed by Tod Browning—Africa as horror-movie set: the white man's grave. *(© 1928 Turner Entertainment Co. All Rights Reserved.)*

America's idea of the African woman—when she's bad, she's very, very bad—here played by Hedy Lamarr in tanface: *White Cargo*, 1942. *(© 1942 Turner Entertainment Co. All Rights Reserved.)*

Even for black filmmakers, Africa was the source of horrors like this ape-man in the 1940 *Son of Ingagi* (Zack Williams, Laura Bowman). *(Courtesy of the Academy of Motion Picture Arts and Sciences)*

The best Hemingway ever brought to the screen was *The Macomber Affair* (1947), with, from left, Gregory Peck, Joan Bennett, and Robert Preston. *(Courtesy of Willis and Geiger, New York.)*

The heritage of black motion-picture actors before Robeson was a difficult one. In America, an accepted racialism made such early films as *The Negro Kiss* (1898) and *A Nigger in the Woodpile* (1904) racial jokes. Until at least the midteens, most black roles were played by whites in blackface, Sennett's *Colored Villainy* (1915) using whites exclusively. *Birth of a Nation* (1915) had only one black actor, an elderly woman, despite several major black roles (played by whites in blackface). Ustane in the 1925 *She* was played by a white; the villainous pygmies of *Tarzan the Ape Man* (1932) were blackfaced whites; as late as 1942, Tondelayo was played by Hedy Lamarr.

Within this blackface period, some films suggest an ambivalence toward black Africans that appears to have been subsequently resolved in favor of the savage stereotype. D.W. Griffith's early *The Zulu's Heart* (1908) shows an "African" (a white in blackface) as grieving over a dead child, as reluctant to leave his wife to go to war, and as sympathetic to a white woman whose child it is in his power to kill. Such emotions were antithetical to the savage stereotype, which assumed that the savage black felt both physical and emotional pain less than whites (and was thus not truly human).*

A very different situation pertained in his *Birth of a Nation*, which pretty well set out the racial agenda for the rest of the silent era. This famous Griffith film about the Civil War dealt specifically with American notions of race. It is worth remembering Pierre Sorlin's analysis of the film. Sorlin notes that in the film's prewar scenes, blacks "are almost invisible"; invisibility, then, was the normal condition. When seen, they are often dancing. The Civil War, however, makes blacks visible because it gives them legal and social status: they then become menacing. The whites form the Ku Klux Klan, and Sorlin finds an almost medieval psychomachia in the earthbound blacks and the angelic, "flying" whites. Rape of white women by black men becomes the epitome of white fear, and the menace of bad black men is expressed in terms of sexual threat and brutality.

This threat easily attached itself to the African-savage stereotype, and sexual threat explains the wealth of threatened white women in the first half-century of movies about Africa. In *The Slaver* (1927), for example, a white woman is sold to an African "king" by a gang of mutineers; she is undressed (shirt, jodhpurs) and is put into a leopard-skin teddy by African women (blackface whites), who grin and dance when the fat, top-hatted "king" comes in. She is saved from a fate worse than death by a white man and a Good African, Gumbo, who is killed in the

---

* Griffith may have been influenced by the Haggard association of "Zulu" with nobility. As well, Griffith's "Zulus" had visual affinities with American plains Indians, and there may have been a neoromantic sense of "noble savage."

subsequent jungle chase. "Gumbo is dead—but he didn't die in vain," the hero says. Thank you, massa.

Not noted by Sorlin, because irrelevant to his subject, is the extension of this sexual threat to the big apes, with "ape" and "black man" becoming mutually reflecting mirrors, and "ape" and "savage" having a kind of identity (i.e., blacks are part animal). In the faked documentary *Ingagi* (1930), apes rape black women, "proof" of the closeness to animals of black Africans. The half-ape, half-human creature became a horror-movie staple (*The Missing Link, Son of Ingagi, Konga*).

Thus, in American films the savage/sexual stereotypes seem not to have been universal before about World War I but became so thereafter. The change (which may have been less a change than an elimination of anomalies) may reflect the fears aroused by immigration, and particularly by the "tide of color" forecast by the eugenics movement. If so, it was a response to an American condition, not an African one. Ironically, it was paralleled by an increasing visibility of black actors on the screen.

Despite the use of whites in blackface, some black actors' names began showing up in film credits in the 1920s and early 1930s—James B. Lowe, Clarence Muse, Eddie Anderson, Hattie McDaniel, Everett Brown, and, above all, Noble Johnson, who had appeared in the credits for *Leopard Woman* as early as 1920. In Britain, Ecce Homo Toto and Robert Adams were playing significant roles in the early 1930s, and the American Nina Mae McKinney had her name below the title of *Sanders*. As well, a small black film industry made movies for black audiences in the United States; an early film with an African setting was the now-lost *A Daughter of the Congo* (1930), produced and directed by Oscar Micheaux, with Katherine Noisette, Lorenzo Tucker, Roland Irving, and Clarence Redd. It was a romantic melodrama about black American soldiers in West Africa. According to the press book, it was "The story of Lupelta, a beautiful mulatto girl, who has been stolen as a baby and brought up among the savages of the jungle." Lupelta is captured by slavers, and "Captain Paul Dale, colored, United States Army, assisted by his First Lieutenant, Ronald Brown, who have been sent to the little black republic [of Moravia] to [word missing] a constabulary," save her. Lupelta is taken to a mission school, "where she succumbs to learning readily" and becomes "the most popular maid of Moravia" despite temptations to "revert to the wild life of the jungle." The film seems to have been a variation on the White Queen or jungle princess myth, with "mulatto" given privileged status vis-à-vis the jungle and the Africans among whom the woman has been raised. The film's implied attitudes toward the jungle are those of white American films: jungle is bad, civilization is good; light is good, dark is bad; civilized American male is good, African male is bad.

It is hardly surprising that, in films made for white audiences, the Good African was often a servant: an "acceptance of servility" was made the necessary "characteristic of the black race" as it was seen on film. For the masses of Africans—particularly female Africans—however, invisibility was still the filmic norm, with few films showing Africans in their proper numbers in everyday activities; rather, like the blacks in *Birth of a Nation*, Africans were shown again and again in frenzied, atypical "savage dancing." Otherwise, as another scholar has noted, Africans were either "scenery props (picturesque crowds with spears) or curiously unintelligent menials."

These types, nonetheless, were not monolithic. The replacement of white actors in blackface with black actors suggests that the industry was capable of change, albeit sluggishly. Such change, however, did not happen across the entire industry at the same time: it is clear that the cheaper and cruder movies—the Hollywood Bs and serials—perpetuated the "jungle" stereotypes for two decades after certain other films had begun to discard them.

PAUL ROBESON WAS only the third black man to attend Rutgers University. Isolated by his race (he was not allowed to live in a dormitory), the future international singing star was "not invited to join the Rutgers Glee Club because of the social events that followed their concerts." Robeson fought such imposed invisibility by being astronomically better than those who isolated him: an All-American football player, a member of Phi Beta Kappa, a recipient of a law degree from Columbia University, a stage actor, and a world-class concert artist.

Robeson early made himself famous as a singer of folk songs, and singing remained the axis of his career. In the mid-1920s, however, he played the leading role in Eugene O'Neill's *The Emperor Jones*, later repeating it on film in 1933. By 1927, he was an international concert artist with a lucrative career, settling in London because he found the racial climate better: "For me, London was infinitely better than Chicago for Negroes from Mississippi."

In London, Robeson "discovered" Africa and "came to consider that I was an African." His acquaintances included Kwame Nkrumah, Jomo Kenyatta, and Nnamdi Azikiwe. His Africanism was not part of any back-to-Africa movement, however, but was, like his art, a personal matter. (For all his gorgeous smile and his warmth, Robeson was a "star," a self-created entity, perhaps not capable of submerging himself in movements.)

Between 1935 and 1937, five British films were released with Robeson either in an African role or—in one—providing an introduction to African footage. The first film (*Sanders*) put his personal Africanism to the test and mocked it;

then, as he seized control, the later films became the medium for a redefinition of the filmic Africa and the creation of a new African archetype.

"I hate the picture," Robeson is quoted as having said of *Sanders* "years later." As a recent scholar has noted, *Sanders* "put [Robeson] to the task of convincing the world that Africa needed the British," which can hardly have been the actor's goal, no matter how tolerant he found the English. He may have believed he was too big a star to be exploited, although you wonder now how he can have got round the name Bosambo when he first read the script. However, his performance was not itself a sellout, not Uncle Tom in Africa; particularly toward the film's end, he was magnificent. Robeson found a shape in the role, a movement from adolescence to manhood, and what he as actor would have seen as the payoff—the mature Bosambo—may be, for the audience, submerged in the entirety of the picture. And, although it was not Robeson's doing, *Sanders* had a glorious moment when Nina Mae McKinney, as Bosambo's wife, sang a lullaby, "Little Black Dove." The song may be un-African, but the sequence is a moving one whose dramatization of the love of a black woman for a black child obliterated the "savage" stereotype. It also extended the inner life of Bosambo in a way that most previous films had not allowed African characters, at least since the crudities of *The Zulu's Heart*: it gave him an emotional and social life and marked a rare archetype, one that was both African and female, the Black Wife.

Song of Freedom, released in late 1936, is a better film than commentators have suggested. One found it an "artificial but well-handled musical drama"; Rachel Low thought it "misguided" and "unintentionally far from flattering." Robeson himself, however, took out an ad in *Film Weekly* to push it, and he has been quoted as calling it "the first film to give a true picture of many aspects of the life of the colored man in the west . . . a real man."

Robeson's name appeared above the title. Other black actors in featured roles were Ecce Homo Toto and Elizabeth Welch, an American singer who also lived in England. *Song of Freedom*'s story was simple and fast-moving. The film begins with a flashback to an image of savagery: the African island of Kasanga in the eighteenth century, where a drunken black queen is abusing her subjects, two of whom escape. Then it leaps forward to the present, to a London dock worker named John Zinga (Robeson). He lives in a London that knows no color bar: he drinks in the pub, jokes with his mates, lives among them, and sings them all to sleep.

But the docker has a dream—Africa. "Africa, it's always Africa, isn't it, John?" his wife (Welch) says. "That's my home," Zinga replies, although he has never been there. "It's where we come from. But—our people—I have a feeling they're grand people, too—the people we belong to." He confesses to her that "I always feel out of place" in London. His magnificent voice is overheard by an impresario (Esme Percy) who cries, "What an amazing voice! It is unique! That colored man—a voice like that can be great anywhere." With this nod to Robeson's own beliefs (art knows no color), *Song of Freedom* moves quickly to make the docker an international concert star.

Soon he is zipping about the world, giving concerts. A little song he has learned in infancy becomes his encore piece; an anthropologist who hears it recognizes it, and a medallion that Zinga has inherited, as coming from "Kasanga, an island off the west coast of Africa."

"Kasanga!" John Zinga cries. "Our home—our people!" In the recognition is a collapsing of time: not merely the time to the flashback with which the movie opens, but the lost time of the African diaspora, the temporal hole of slavery. This recognition seems to have been lost on white reviewers at the film's release; it should not be overlooked now. This is a film in which very careful and informed choices were made; you have to suspect that Robeson's input was large.

The anthropologist warns Zinga that "the witch-doctors have gained ascendancy over the island" and the people are "backward, uncivilized, impoverished." (It was this statement, and its demonstration, that probably caused Low to see the film as "far from flattering.")

Zinga and his wife go to the island. He is downcast to find it is exactly as the anthropologist said. "It's all so primitive!" he moans, striding about in a white suit and white pith helmet. (This ironic appropriation of colonial symbolism must have been deliberate; it is far too consistent and clear to have been "misguided.") Then he cries, "It's got to be changed!"

His attempts to bring change of course create conflict with the "witch-doctors," and the film climaxes with Zinga's wife about to be thrown into the fire as Zinga is held by grimacing "savages." Zinga has shown them his medallion, however, which proves him to be the rightful king of Kasanga. They put him to a test: if he is really their king, he must know the King's Song. Can he sing it? The answer ought to be No (he doesn't know the Kasangan language), but the answer is of course Yes, as the encore piece he learned in childhood pours out of him in the correct, now-recovered Kasangan. The film ends with the "witch-doctors" deposed, Zinga in concert, and the island the recipient of all his earnings. "Every season he returns [to Europe] to sing," the impresario says. "Tomorrow, he goes back again [to his island]."

This is a neat myth: the gifted black man is an artist in white culture, a king in black. Through his efforts in the white world, he will reclaim the degraded society of the black. It is also a neatly constructed film. Early on, Robeson sings in an opera called *The Black Emperor*, obviously a variation of *The Emperor Jones*; it ends with his shooting himself with a pistol. On the island, however, when offered a gun, he pushes it away, saying, "No, that's not the way—these are my own people." In London, he sings "River of Dreams" to his wife and his neighbors; on the island, his wife sings it to him to comfort him after they have been captured. Elements from white jungle movies are exploited: a comic black servant for the now-wealthy Zinga, savage dancing (wonderfully athletic dancers from Sierra Leone), the final tied-to-the-stake scene. The language of clothes is used ironically: both Zinga and his wife wear complete white outfits on the island, like two tourists just off a cruise ship; yet, at film's end, in concert, Robeson is seminude to sing "Lonely Road."

This was not a film that was "unintentionally far from flattering." It exploited stereotypes as part of a strategy to dramatize Robeson's myth. It acknowledged "savagery" but did not use it as a stick with which to beat black Africans, suggesting rather that problems could be corrected without white presence. It sees a high place for returned blacks in Africa. It asserts that the real triumph is not the fame and wealth to be found in white culture, but the productive life to be found in black culture: "Tomorrow, he goes back again." It takes the African stereotypes of commercial motion pictures and stands them on their heads.

Song of Freedom is not a first-class film, mostly because of its obviously low budget. It was indifferently directed and indifferently shot; no advantage was taken of the beauty of Africa—or of London, for that matter. The cinematography was perfunctory. Most of the film's strength is in its verbal text and the performances of Robeson and Welch, with some (often rather sly) support in such visual details as costume. It remains, however, a film whose strong points are those of the theatre rather than of the cinema. Nonetheless, as a film about Africa, it is an eye-opener for those who have eyes to see.

There seems to have been talk of a sequel. It was not made.

MY SONG GOES FORTH (*Africa Sings*) was a "strange film" of early 1937 for which Robeson provided only an introduction and a song. His part of the film seems to have been quickly made: he stands by a piano, sings, reads his words, looking solemn and rather heavy in a double-breasted suit. The rest of the film is a pastiche of documentary clips with a rather self-congratulatory and obviously white voice-over (*not* Robeson) explaining conditions and the advances made in South Africa. Originally titled *Africa Looks Up*, it may have had its title changed when Robeson came on board. The *London Times* saw the resulting picture as showing "the ambitions to be achieved and the work already accomplished by the African Negro," although the footage appears to be exclusively South African. It showed "how Johannesburg has grown" and "the changes in the traditions and customs of native life. . . . The progress is remarkable, but during the film it is difficult not to wonder sometimes whether all has been gain." Seen now, after apartheid, after Soweto and Sharpesville and Boitesphong, it is a painful picture, and Robeson's participation in it seems hard to explain. What attracted him was probably the focus on black African modernization: Zinga's cry, "It's all so primitive!" surely reflected the sophisticated Robeson's own view, and Zinga's desire to change things was surely Robeson's. The film's shots of black industrial workers, then, of black city streets, and of black crowds in European dress must have seemed embodiments of that change. The *Times*'s doubt that "all has been gain" was a romantic white one, to be sure, based on some fuzzy notion of a black Never-Never Land where the noble savage lay down with the lion. Nonetheless, *My Song Goes Forth* was a poor example of Robeson's ideal of Africa, perhaps seen by him through the same naiveté that took him into the role of Bosambo.

Three months later, Robeson was on the London screen again in *King Solomon's Mines* in another role in which he progressed from obscurity to African kingship, the device this time not a medallion but a tattoo. He came out of *KSM* well, praised for his performance and without any attacks this time from Africans.

Then, before 1937 was out, he appeared yet again. The picture was *Jericho* (*Dark Sands* in America), a "heroic sentimental story" to one reviewer, although the consensus was that Robeson could have done better. Again, white reviewers seem not to have understood what Robeson was about, although this time, it is true, the script and the direction were very poor. Again, a number of black actors were brought to the screen with Robeson—Ike Hatch, Lawrence Brown, Rufus Fennell, and others.

The story was again one of a black man who moves from obscurity (and, this time, a crime) in the white world to leadership in Africa. Much of the filming was done in Egypt—ironically, because this was Robeson's last African film, the first time he set foot on the continent. Director Thornton Freeland made good use of location footage of a desert caravan, so that some of the visual impact of Africa was gained, but his direction of many studio scenes was flat and stage-bound.

The story, like *Song of Freedom*'s, was broken into pieces—one in Europe, one in Africa—without any device like Zinga's career to integrate them. The result was a sense of two movies glued end-to-end. *Jericho* begins on an American troop ship in World War I. The officers are white, the troops black. Robeson is "Jericho" Jackson, a soldier who accidentally kills a sergeant during the panic following a submarine sighting. He is arrested for murder. Then, at a Christmas celebration, he is allowed out of jail by his captain (Henry Wilcoxon) to "sing with the boys." Jericho chooses life over the firing squad and escapes, unwittingly ruining Wilcoxon's military career (for trusting him) and sending him to prison for several years.

Jericho joins up with comic deserter Wally Ford, steals a boat, and sails to the African coast. He becomes a man of importance, marrying, using medical skills acquired in America to help his village. Ultimately made the village headman, he leads the annual salt-trading caravan and saves it in a defensive raid against bandits.

Wilcoxon's character, released from military prison, sets out on a vendetta to return Jericho to military justice. By chance, he sees a film of the great salt caravan and recognizes Jericho; off he goes to Africa, arriving at Jericho's oasis in a light airplane that he somehow knows how to fly.

At this point, both script and direction are at their worst: Jericho sings "Mama's Little Baby Loves Shortnin' Bread" to his child; Wilcoxon confronts him with the line, "You ruined me! The army was my life!" and Robeson responds, "That's terrible."

Then Robeson introduces his wife and his child, and Wilcoxon about-faces to self-sacrifice: now he *won't* take Jericho back, and Jericho, inspired also to sacrifice, insists that he be taken back. It is all very silly, very white, very British— very *Four Feathers*, in fact. Wilcoxon practices Oxbridge one-upmanship by telling Jericho/Robeson he will take him back, then flying off without him, winning the gold medal for self-abnegation.

As released in America, the picture had a falsely ironic ending: some of Jericho's villagers ran out with their jezails and shot Wilcoxon out of the sky, killing him; Jericho then gave him a formal burial and sang over the grave. This was at least an ending. For some releases this sequence seems to have been cut (too little poetic justice to suit British audiences?), leaving a hole and making for a very weak ending—Robeson putting his son to bed and smiling at his wife.

Jericho was the worst of the four fiction films Robeson made, largely because of the poor script. The direction of key scenes was hardly better, the Robeson-Wilcoxon confrontation at the end being as lifeless as a scene about choosing rooms at a country house party. As well, the film's moral world was out of whack: Jericho really does kill one man, if accidentally, and perhaps a second when he pushes a drunken fisherman overboard to steal his boat; he really does leave the Wilcoxon character to face the music; he really does desert from the army. To be sure, these lapses can be seen as moral slaps in the face of the white world—the only ways out for a black man. If such ideas were intended, however, they were not followed through, and in fact they seem the product of indifference rather than intention. The sharpness of *Song of Freedom* was entirely lacking.

Jericho brought out the racialism in its reviewers. The *London Times* described the black troops as "playing their interminable dice games, singing, chattering, laughing." *Variety* found the same scenes "the genuine stuff. Their crosstalk and remarks during a game of craps couldn't possibly be duplicated by white folks." It was a "sock pic" for its "unusual story and absorbing African scenes which provide popular entertainment for all classes." Bosley Crowther was less flattering: "Some of the most ludicrous dramatics to be seen this side of 'The Sheik.'"

It was not, indeed, very good. But it was another mainstream movie in which Robeson presented the new archetype, the black man who finds eminence in Africa. The picture turned its back on white culture, although it accepted white science (Jericho's medical skill). Its black characters were not invisible; they were not "scenery props" or "curiously unintelligent menials." It reversed filmic stereotypes: the comic sidekick/servant was a white man (Ford).

As in *Song of Freedom*, Robeson played a man with a full emotional and sexual life, one presented as normal and nonthreatening. And, although the Wilcoxon character came out of the sky, he did not do so as one of Griffith's "heavenly militia"; indeed, as originally made, the film had him shot down. Divine retribution did not pursue the protagonist to Africa, and the film seemed to say (perhaps despite itself) that in Africa the Returner shed all the shackles of whiteness, even white justice.

PAUL ROBESON'S AFRICAN myth left movies pretty much when he did. He returned to the United States in 1939; his later films did not touch on Africa. He left behind him, however, the image of a charismatic black actor in a new kind of role. That role was better remembered in England than in America, if only poorly understood, and when British producers came to try to reshape their idea of African character, it was to Robeson and his archetype that they turned. It is impossible that *Men of Two Worlds* was conceived without Robeson in mind or without *Song of Freedom* as a model. Unhappily, the producers didn't understand that model well enough, and in reshaping it to flatter the white Imperial Man, they corrupted it. Necessarily so: Robeson's theme of the African Returner's self-sufficiency could not be made to serve the needs of Sanders.

Robeson's idealism, however, did not seize the imagination of either film-makers or other blacks outside Britain. His idea of a benign return to Africa faded, for reasons not clear, although the radical changes in the world after World War II certainly contributed—the end of the Depression, white resistance to the transfer of power, the seeming need for demonstrations of black power—all of which may have rendered Robeson's romantic ideas moot. Robeson himself suffered personal eclipse, but it is likely, as well, that the Euro-centered culture in which he believed and of which he was a star was ultimately unacceptable to blacks in Africa and America (less true, I believe, in Britain). Donald Bogle has implied that this Euro-centrism was a form of Uncle Tomism: he asserted that the Robeson figure in *Song of Freedom* "has been trained by whites and adheres to their value system" and "takes his British manners and mores and civilizes the savage natives." This appears to me a misreading of the film, in that it seems to suggest both that to succeed in Africa a black man must not be "trained by whites," and that "civilization"—which, in the case of *Song of Freedom* means the infusion of money, plus education and release from (noncolonial) oppression—is bad if associated with white society. Bogle's ideas are always to be respected, but in this case I think more recent African history has shown that infusions of money and non-African technology have been what the continent itself wants, although I acknowledge the likelihood of neocolonialism's traveling in the baggage of good works.

At any rate, in going from Bosambo to John Zinga, Robeson made a quantum leap. Almost certainly, no other black performer could have made it as he did, at the time he did. His later American movies pretty much ignored the leap; his later treatment by political enemies punished him for it. Yet the fact of the leap represents an important change in the way film (especially, at that moment, British film) viewed the black actor. After exploiting him (*Sanders*), it bent to his vision. That this happened in Britain rather than America suggests a yielding to pressure other than the locally racial. That pressure was probably the evolving sense (mostly on the British Left?) of something very wrong in colonialism, a counterpoise to the pressure that produced the imperial films of the same period. The smallness of the African Returner films and the bigness of the imperial films suggests where the power lay at that moment. An exchange of power was still two decades away; Robeson, having helped to bring it about, would not profit from it, either as actor or as man.

PART 3

From Independence to the Nineties

8 THE DANGEROUS AFRICANS

Without question, the most influential black actor to appear in Britain or America after World War II was Sidney Poitier, whose performances in two motion pictures—*Cry, the Beloved Country* and *Something of Value*—replaced Robeson and brought a new vividness to audiences' understanding of Africa. A number of other actors, particularly Orlando Martins and Earl Cameron in Great Britain, and later Ken Gampu in South Africa, also brought talent and excitement to a new kind of film African. These men were actors: they did not have Robeson's history of overqualification in several other fields or his reputation as a singer. They were more flexible, too; in a sense, they were better actors, although, like the young whites of this period (Marlon Brando, Laurence Harvey), they partook of a new style that perhaps makes them now more accessible. Robeson had been cast because he was Robeson, bringing the dignity and status of the concert stage to the screen; the third-generation black stars brought less in advance, although Poitier immediately accrued star qualities. Lacking Robeson's golden baggage, they did not portray African Returners but Dangerous Africans, often as fighters, sometimes as killers.

No female actor emerged to match them. As there was no female Robeson, so there was no female Poitier. The problem was not a lack of actors, but a lack of roles. In the 1940s, the two films with leading black roles for women (*White Cargo* and *Sundown*) were both cast with whites. The 1950s were almost ended before a black woman made a name in a film set in Africa—Miriam Makeba in *Come Back, Africa*—but Makeba was a singer and it was as a singer that she became an international star. The 1960s were no better, only *Voice of the Hurricane* providing a black woman with a major role, an opportunity not again offered to her.

What a scholar has said of South African society is also true of films about Africa: patriarchy is the only thing that cuts across all racial lines.

A HIATUS OF more than a decade lay between Robeson's and Poitier's African roles. It was not a period of outstanding African films, but one in particular is worth examining. The 1940s saw a reduction in filmmaking, especially in Great Britain, with the war dominating the early years of the decade. Films about

Africa multiplied at the low end: eight Tarzans, six other films with "jungle" in the title, four serials. Only *Men of Two Worlds* and *The Macomber Affair* tried to deal seriously with African materials. *Men of Two Worlds* failed, as we have seen, but provided a major role for Robert Adams. *The Macomber Affair* was concerned mostly with white Africa (safari hunting) but, under Zoltan Korda's direction, was the best Hemingway ever brought to the screen and a fine, small *film noir africain*. *Africa Screams*, as we have seen, was archaic. Only one other film of the forties stands out: *Son of Ingagi*, a picture never seen by white audiences.

A cheaply made horror-comedy with an all-black cast, *Son of Ingagi* took off where the 1930 *Ingagi* had ended—with the rape of African women by big apes. (There was no other connection between the two films.)

So carelessly made that certain plot points change as the movie runs (the place where a newly married couple are supposed to honeymoon, for example), *Son of Ingagi* exists for the ape-rape menace of its resident monster—a half-ape "jungle-man" (Zack Williams) brought back from Africa by a female "doctor" (Laura Bowman)—and the comic antics of Spencer Williams's dumb cop. Most of it is limited to cheap interiors, without significant lighting and with merely perfunctory camera work; it looks as if it was shot in single takes, the flaws be damned. It would be merely a run-of-the-mill example from the black film industry except for one thing: its disturbing idea of Africa.

Africa is the source of the film's horror. The doctor, the only character who has been there, is weird: she keeps a skull on her desk and mixes potions in her cellar, where she has the jungle-man locked in a cell. He escapes and carries off the newly married heroine (Daisy Bufford), but he is burned to death in the doctor's house before he can do whatever it is that monsters do to heroines. The movie's urban blacks watch this African evil being burned out of them with all the delight of the Transylvanians watching Karloff go up in smoke. Where, in 1940, is Paul Robeson and his belief that Africans were "grand people—our people"? Africa in *Son of Ingagi* is the source of horror, particularly the horror of brute sexuality; its only symbols are the skull, witchcraft, and the jungle-man. Normality, the film tells us, is black people living in an American city, falling in love, marrying, dancing; abnormality is Africa. "African-American" would not be the term of choice.

Laura Bowman's doctor does suggest an ambivalence, however. Despite her oddness, she is attractive as a character, perhaps because Bowman was a skilled actress; she has a woman-to-woman closeness with the young heroine, even while she is harboring the threat to the heroine. Perhaps the link to Africa is itself ambivalently seen—a source of some warmth as well as guilt and fear. *Son of*

Ingagi should not be pushed too far—it is only a commercial quickie—but it suggests that in America in 1940 the Africanism that Robeson had defined for himself was still to be resolved. Like the other black film about Africa—*A Daughter of the Congo*—it uses a set of conventions and stereotypes that are American and white rather than African and black.

CRY, THE BELOVED COUNTRY was made from a novel that itself had brought white racism in South Africa to international attention. Alan Paton's wrenching books educated a white postwar generation about a real Africa they hardly knew existed—the Africa of pass cards and hostels and shanty towns, of absolute color bars and minority rule. Even as South African intellectuals were putting together the theories that would undergird legal apartheid, Paton was telling the world of their horror. His work perhaps found greater sympathy because of the recently revealed horrors of the Holocaust, itself justified by theories to which those of the South Africans seemed dangerously similar. But other forces were shaking up the white world's racial smugness, as well. Hollywood was making tepid movies about "tolerance" (*Pinky, Home of the Brave*), and even Broadway found racial injustice a workable subject (*Finian's Rainbow*). Black American writers were venting their rage in mainstream books (*Native Son, Invisible Man*). South Africa, heretofore identified with diamonds and the romanticized Boer War, emerged as a place of racial oppression, given international attention by Paton's novels. In 1950, as well, London saw a 16mm sound film, *Civilization on Trial in South Africa*, which showed townships and locations and "organized fights" among black workers, at which "European police [stood by] with whips to prevent the natives from fighting in groups." Audiences were being taught to see a new Africa.

Zoltan Korda had, by 1950, directed three African films: *Sanders of the River, The Four Feathers*, and *The Macomber Affair*. The first two had been made under his brother Alexander's oversight; differences between the two brothers, as already suggested, led to a perhaps unconscious critique by Zoltan Korda, expressed in his direction. With *Cry, the Beloved Country*, however, he became his own producer, and the resulting film was both tougher and more serious than anything he did with his brother. Filmed in black and white, it eschewed the glories of *Four Feathers*, as if they were too easy, perhaps too gaudy; its spectacle was of a different kind—that of the best of the 1930s documentaries and studio photographs. It is hard-edged, lustrous, often deep in contrast; and the footage of South Africa's cityscape and its industry and its beautiful countryside recalls a lot of Depression-era, socially conscious shorts.

Alan Paton wrote the screenplay from his novel and coproduced. For this profoundly sad and serious story of a black clergyman whose son has committed murder in Johannesburg, Korda and Paton cast the veteran actor Canada Lee. For a young Johannesburg priest who helps the old man, they cast Sidney Poitier. We can quibble because the two do not sound the way South Africans sound, but we cannot argue with the pain that their skilled performances evoke from an audience. *Cry, the Beloved Country* is a film of character and of relationships, which twist and reflect and shift, and it demands fine acting or it is nothing. It is Canada Lee particularly who carries this burden. Parts of the film are almost too painful to watch because of him, but other actors are superb in small moments, too. Much of the credit has to go to Zoltan Korda.

Cry, the Beloved Country looked into the racial abyss of South Africa and found unbounded suffering. The father suffers the loss of his son, indeed of his whole family: his sister is a prostitute in Johannesburg, his brother a greedy self-server there, his son a thief; a white father suffers the loss of his son, murdered by the clergyman's; a white social worker suffers the loss of his self-respect because he cannot help sons or fathers; it is all loss, tangle, sadness. Yet, like all serious work that succeeds, it is a joy to experience, despite its pain. Paton, in making the old man a countryman (in Zululand), seized on the essential myth of black South Africa and of much of Africa: the movement from the land of belonging to the city of the whites, and the dream of return. Korda gave this visual life with black-and-white film of train journeys that seem epic in their length, hideous with industrial noise. His camera makes visual beauty out of a pile of mine tailings, an industrial moonscape. Zululand is by contrast beautiful for its serenity, for its very lack of movement. It is, the pictures tell us, the center, the heart; the city is frenzy. In the city, whites and blacks are separate, and they meet only in violence; it is only on the land that they can meet (as at the film's end) for something like reconciliation.

Because of its novelistic origins, *Cry, the Beloved Country* has too many static scenes and too much dialogue; on the other hand, it is those scenes that create the intricate network of character that is the film's strength. It is a very slow film, particularly by recent standards, but nonetheless a film, not a filmed play. There is really no other like it, and probably no other film about Africa to equal it either for seriousness or for the interplay of text, direction, and actors' performances. Its myth is the myth of dispossession, its hero the dispossessed who cannot find wholeness ever again ("This is a country of the old," the film begins, showing Zululand, "the soil cannot keep [the young] any more"). It is an inescapably sad myth because it is about a loss that cannot be fixed. Yet this is a true African myth—the insight was Paton's—truer than anything the screen had shown before.* Poitier, playing a secondary character on the periphery of it, nonetheless partook of it, both giving and taking stature as a visible, vital black man. Whether a film created by two white men and featuring non-South African actors could perfectly capture the South African reality is open to debate; but if the result is imperfect, it is with an imperfection that most other films can only envy.

Another film in this period also used documentary footage to try to show the cruelty of South Africa. This was *Come Back, Africa* (1959), whose opening titles announced that it "was made secretly" with amateur actors to show the suffering of a man "forced off the land and into the gold mines." It is an odd combination of stunning documentary cinematography and stolid dramatic direction and acting; its limp script, apparently improvised, barely makes sense because it has so little internal causality. Dull and unconvincing fictional scenes thus alternate with brilliant real-life footage of the Johannesburg streets, black workers, street musicians, and the misery of the "locations." Deeply serious, it probably belongs in the tradition of heart-in-the-right-place populist films and plays of the thirties, and it is for this unquestionable moral seriousness that it survives in video. A cameo appearance by the young Miriam Makeba—who appears out of nowhere, sings, and disappears—also gives it importance. As a film, it cannot compare with *Cry, the Beloved Country*, but as a document, as a cry of anguish, it is perhaps more rending. Significantly, it contains a brief rejection of Paton's "liberalism" and his black protagonist in one of its rambling talk scenes. Yet, with *Cry, the Beloved Country* and perhaps *My Song Goes Forth*, it presents vivid evidence of the depth of racial oppression in South Africa, where even architecture and the rhythm of the early morning have racial meaning.

IN 1952, THE uprising called "Mau Mau" began in Kenya. Largely confined to the Kikuyu community, it was part revolution, part cultural manifestation, part

---

* The myth of the dispossessed was a staple—some would say a cliché—of South African work; as Albert Gerard has noted, "The Jim-goes-to-Jo'burg theme was a stock situation [in Xhosa fiction]." [Gerard, *Literatures*, p. 198] In film, it had already appeared in *Song of Africa* (194?), a South African black picture with a loose story structure that provided opportunities for musical numbers. The picture was mostly variety numbers, strung on the story of a young Zulu who makes it as a musician in Johannesburg. Its principal interest now is its evidence of a vigorous black musical culture with strong American ties; there are, as well, several sequences of all-male worksite performances (mostly group dancing) that are remarkable in their originality. This musical culture in part produced the people who created such other black South African works as Gibson Kente's *King Kong* (a stage musical that used the myth of the dispossessed, in this case a black boxer) and *Come Back, Africa*.

pathology. Marxists would later claim it as a people's war; rightists would see it as a Communist plot. It was put down in 1956 with the help of the RAF, but it nonetheless marked the beginning of the end of the British presence in East Africa. By the 1960s, Great Britain had given up all of her African colonies except Rhodesia, whose white minority clung to power for another decade, becoming a renegade from the British Commonwealth in the process. The same thing was happening in most of Africa: France suffered the loss of Algeria; Belgium gave up its central African colonies after great bloodshed; Portugal hung on, and then pulled out so suddenly that it left Angola and Mozambique in chaos.

Mau Mau terrified Britons in both the colonies and England. It seemed to threaten whites with the very horrors that had dominated the imagery of Africa: whites overcome by the sheer numbers of blacks; whites hacked to pieces by blacks armed with primitive weapons; whites destroyed by a culture based in "magic." Tales of Mau Mau initiation ceremonies spread—night-time rites involving goats, blood, witchcraft. Killings were often done with an appalling savagery. The killers struck by night, anywhere; they could be anybody with black skin—a trusted house servant, a farm worker, a teacher. Or so whites believed, and they turned that belief into a state of siege.

The legend that was created was of a primitive cult bound by oaths and ceremonies, so binding on its members that they responded unquestioningly to commands to kill whites. The legend had whites being driven from East Africa or murdered, until none was left. The legend made anyone with black skin untrustworthy, murderous, deceitful.

In actual fact, thirty-two white colonials died as a result of Mau Mau. (Some sources cite as many as eighty, apparently including military.) More than seven *thousand* blacks died. Yet the myth of Mau Mau was a myth of mass white death, and so it came into popular white culture. It may have received particular attention in film because Kenya had become such a common location for African filming; film people had contacts there, learned their prejudices there. And Mau Mau had a presold sensationalism that made white prejudice almost an obligation. The result was four films: two focussed on the whites; one pretended to be fair to both black and white; and one tried to present the black side in a mostly white context.

Simba begins with an arresting sequence in which a white man, lying wounded beside a dirt road, is approached by a black man on a bicycle. The black man sees the white and gets off his bicycle. The scene is a visual reference to the parable of the Good Samaritan. The black man approaches the bleeding white, bends over him, and then attacks him with a knife, killing him. The act is made particularly savage by both the Good Samaritan reference and the purely coincidental relationship between killer and victim. It is partly ambiguous—we know nothing about them—but the fact of race is the most obvious one.

Dirk Bogarde is then seen arriving at the Nairobi airport as a young ex-colonial—imperial top boy with introspective intellect—visiting his brother. Everybody at the airport is white, except for one uniformed guard, a briefly glimpsed soldier, and Bogarde's porter. Virginia McKenna is there to meet Bogarde; a prior relationship is hinted at, but the real subject is Kenya and Mau Mau. McKenna, although young, is already the True-Blue White Woman: she says, "I was born here; Africa is my home." Bogarde's uneven face twitches as if Mau Mau is an unpleasantness of which he would rather not be reminded.

However, when he arrives at his brother's farm to find that his brother has been murdered, that signature twitch becomes the outward sign of Bogarde's torment. Always an actor who communicated neurosis, Bogarde is like the young men of the imperial films gone all neurasthenic. Now he plays his suffering off the restraint of Donald Sinden's policeman: "Were any of our own boys killed? Nobody stood by him?" "Nobody." "He trusted them." "Too much." Later, McKenna's mother says, "After all we've done for the Africans. No one could have done more for his boys."

The film resolves itself into a two-track story: the search for the leader of the Mau Mau murderers, a mysterious figure known as "Simba" (Swahili for lion), and the relationship between Bogarde and McKenna. A black doctor, played by Earl Cameron, becomes the prime suspect. "I'm always a bit wary of educated natives," Sinden says, playing the familiar card of the Educated African. The whites have an emergency meeting, at which "both sides" of the issue are supposedly presented, but the all-white crowd and the assumptions underlying the presentation of the African case make fairness impossible. More effective than this verbalizing, however, is the showing of a Mau Mau initiation ceremony, which pulls out all the racist stops: drums, bare black skin, feathers, paint, chanting, animal teeth and skins—all the imagery of "savage Africa."

Bogarde withdraws deeper into his white neuroticism. "You're beginning to hate Africans, aren't you?" McKenna says. The issue divides them.

Then McKenna's parents are murdered. Bogarde weeps and sweats but never wrinkles his clothes; Cameron's doctor betrays his own father to the police as Simba; and Cameron, Bogarde, and McKenna come together when the Mau Mau assault Bogarde's farm. Bogarde kills Simba (Cameron's father); the Mau Mau kill Cameron; and the army arrives, giving rise to scenes of carnage. The film ends with a close-up of an African child.

Simba was an ambivalent motion picture that kept muddying the waters in which it tried to see itself. Its attempts at "fairness" involved presenting one side or the other of an issue in words, while often betraying that fairness with visual images (the Mau Mau ceremony, for example). On the other hand, the white side ("I was born here," and so on) is undercut by scenes of Africans in rags and whites in clean, pressed, fashionable clothes; of Africans with sticks and whites with guns; of blacks always on foot and whites always in cars or on horseback. The scene in which colonial police burst into Simba's house is not unlike the scenes in which Mau Mau burst into white farms.

At the same time, the pretense of fairness is itself exposed by the utter failure to show the most painful moral and emotional struggle of the picture—the doctor's betrayal of his father. The Educated African might here have been dramatized in a really probing way. One can conceive of a film about this black doctor's struggle, but it would be one in which the white love story would drop into the background; or one can conceive of a film in which both stories might be told, but in which the white love story would have to be seen more darkly, less trivially; or one can conceive of a film in which McKenna's suffering after the death of her parents might be played against the suffering of the doctor as he wrestles with destroying a parent. Instead, the film that was made is about a white man's suffering as he strives to forgive Africans so as to win a white woman. This was a heavily weighted choice, one in which "fairness" was impossible; but it was likely that what was aimed at was not real fairness but its appearance. Real fairness would have required some fidelity to the ratio of black and white deaths, rather than the dishonest pretense that four white deaths were representative, when they would have comprised one-eighth of Kenya's real total.

Contrasts with the imperial films can be made—how violent, for example, Simba is for a British film: the opening murder, the Mau Mau killings, the final carnage. Sinden's police officer, as if in response to this change, is very different from the Imperial Men—always in uniform, armed. Cameron's Educated African has been allowed to make an advance on the Kisenga of Men of Two Worlds: he is not moved by witchcraft; he is a healer; he makes a terrible moral decision. Yet Simba needs to be seen in the context of the imperial films, from which it seems to be trying to extricate itself even while using their frame of reference. The young Imperial Men of those pictures are here replaced with the unsure Bogarde, on the one hand, and the militant Sinden, on the other. A woman has been placed in Africa and is very different from the insipid Esmee of Four Feathers, although she is foregrounded only as love interest and moral persuader, and she has no independent existence; and belonging-as-birthright ("I was born here") has become part of the colonial claim, so that male-female couplings have a resonance of both reproduction and imperialism. (The emphasis on family, especially parentage, is hardly accidental.) Class, as represented by accent and manners, is still a somewhat hidden factor, in that a generalized sense of "upper" typifies the whites, who sound far more like upper-middle-class Londoners than like white Kenyans.

Simba was a film, then, that was torn into several chunks by its own contradictions. It was confident only about the horrors of Mau Mau, for which it could imagine only a Dangerous African who was a Killer African and whom it could not bear to individualize. (The doctor's father—Simba— is barely seen.) It wanted to be confident about the white birthright to Africa, but it wanted also to qualify that birthright with "liking" Africans—but without giving them dramatic size. It could conceive of the Educated African, but it demanded stupendous sacrifice from him, and then killed him, thus in a sense reducing him to the Good African. It had no confidence in white privilege, pointing its camera again and again at the inequalities of white and black while seeming to accept a class-based image of whites. Its closing shot suggested that the future belonged to black Africa—correct enough, but surely in conflict with its notion of white birthright.

A far more self-confident film about Killer Africans appeared one year later. *Safari* used the White Hunter archetype and cast Victor Mature in the role. Paired with him was Janet Leigh as an "ex-chorus girl" traveling with ("engaged to") Roland Culver as a very rich nutcase. (This triangular plot is apparently a remake of a 1940 fim with the same name but much less ambition.) The film made no pretense of being thoughtful, a posture that made it far easier to be confident—and violent.

Mature was an indifferent actor who could project enormous charm; he got better as he got older, and his thick-lipped, Mediterranean face could suggest the charisma of an aging *don*. Very much of the streets, very American, he was a curious choice for a White Hunter; but in *Safari* there is a conflation with some American action figure like the soldier or the cop (not, for once, the cowboy), and so he seemed well enough suited to it. He was called on at the beginning of the film to play a very difficult action, a father's grief for a murdered child, and his expressive face was good for this, as Mature was always good in communicating two feelings with his face, brute suffering and rage. Other than that, he had only to be a beefcake and action hero.

Safari begins with the murder of the child. The violence is done by the White Hunter's most trusted house servant, who deliberately kills the boy with shot after shot; the house is wrecked, and the horror of the act is emphasized by the presence of a hyena, the hated scavenger, in the aftermath. Mature, like Bogarde, comes into this scene as the police are sorting it out. (Coincidence is okay; this is melodrama.) Unlike Bogarde, he is not thrown into existential doubt; instead, he is set off on a rampage of revenge.

Leigh and Culver fit into his plans because they are going in the right direction and want a guide, but there is no essential connection between them and revenge and Mau Mau. That Leigh and Mature will be attracted to each other is a given of this sort of film, but she is present only for this function. In fact, *Safari* looks as if it could have been made without Mau Mau and revenge—a standard triangle, with Culver odd man out because he is rich and older—but it is as if it found a further dimension and a bang-up ending in the coincidence of the Mau Mau violence (i.e., it is the 1940 *Safari* with Mau Mau laid over it). A good deal of the picture is thus devoted to the triangle: such stereotypical scenes as Leigh in a bath, Leigh and a snake, Leigh on a crocodile-infested river in a rubber raft; and Mature saving her from the river, hanging from a vine like Tarzan, and so on. Culver begins as an autocrat and ends as a maniac, supposedly because of sexual jealousy, secretly unloading Mature's rifle before they go after a lion. "He's always been [mentally] sick—only out here you can see it much plainer," Leigh says of him, leading us to question why she has come with him. The answer has to be his money; thus, there is a vaguely disquieting undertone to the Leigh-Culver relationship. Leigh is pert, like most American women in films of the 1950s, and she is markedly "female" in the way that Molly Haskell noted that American sex objects (e.g., Marilyn Monroe) are, "in drag," parodies of the feminine. Her clothes are too tight, her breasts too pointed, her mouth too shaped, too often open, as if offering fellatio. But Mature is in male drag, also a parody; there are scenes in which it is a question which of them has the deeper cleavage. Theirs is not a "love story"; it is not about reproduction, even though Mature has lost an only son; it is about images of sexuality, signaling to each other. Framing this is the story of Culver, the bad rich man, a typically American tale. The resolution—Culver dies; Mature and Leigh get each other—is democratic and classless. It is perhaps significant that Culver as actor is English, Mature and Leigh, American.

The Mau Mau plot line is resolved by an attack on the safari by the Mau Mau, who are armed with spears and knives and one rifle. Mature has a Bren, with which he seems to kill hundreds; it is the kind of magic gun, never needing loading, that used to show up in cowboy movies. The soldiers arrive and they, too, kill lots of Mau Mau. The soldiers are black, and the image of blacks killing blacks fills the screen, a colonial fantasy.

Otherwise, *Safari* is true to its clichés. There is savage dancing, so good that it appears that the safari has run into the Kenyan National Dance Company; Mature says to the dance leader, "Jambo, Chief," as if chiefs always danced their way across the landscape. Leigh's character is threatened by a black man, his eyes glinting in the darkness. All wild animals—lion, hyena, python, crocodile—are constant threats. "Africa" is beautiful (this is often a most handsome film) but inherently dangerous and deceitful: servants murder children, rivers carry beautiful women away, crazy rich men turn homicidal. There is no sense that, as in *Simba*, "Africa is my home." To the contrary: Leigh is presented as a wanderer, going where her patron takes her; Culver is a temporary visitor; and Mature, who had a house and a child, is deracinated, the house destroyed and the child dead. His vengeance on the Mau Mau is "merely personal," as Gatsby has it—a significantly American response; he does not take part in the British attempt to own Kenya and to live in it. Like Tarzan, he is not a colonist.

ROBERT RUARK WAS a newspaper columnist who became the author of several books, long tomes that sought to make their points by the pound rather than by the word. He fell in love with African hunting just before the Mau Mau uprising in East Africa and was thus positioned to churn out a big book about the subject. The result was *Something of Value.*

The film made from the novel (1957) was very earnest but suffered from several bad choices, the first of which was a style of drip-dry realism that gave it the gloss of a tourist brochure. The second was the casting, which put Rock Hudson in the role of a young white farmer and left him there to twist in the wind.

Hudson was one of a group of young men who had been groomed to replace the now aging stars of the 1930s, the megawatt studio kings like Gable, Power, Flynn, et al. Unlike them, Hudson projected both blandness and niceness, qualities perhaps inevitable as the ruthless studio systems declined; he was "good-looking" and "clean-cut," but essentially safe, as the very successful comedies with Doris Day would show. He was not almost femininely beautiful, as some of the older stars had been when young (Cooper, Power, Grant, Taylor); he lacked the sexual danger of Power and Flynn—and, for that matter, Weissmuller—whose appeal had often been associated with exotic but graceful physical activities like fencing and swinging on vines or ships' lines; he did not seem ready at any moment to whisk a woman away to Sherwood Forest or a bower in the treetops. His masculinity was, instead, an urban and modern one, more of the office than the pirate ship. He was, in fact, the idealized corporation man of the 1950s (and, in retrospect, his death therefore takes on added poignancy). Wind him up and set him going and he would walk into the nearest corporate headquarters.

In *Something of Value*, Hudson was required to do the impossible: first, to convince us he was rural rather than urban and colonial British rather than American; and, second, to be more interesting than the charismatic Sidney Poitier. Poitier, however, was even then a far better actor, and he was not safe as Hudson was: in any role, he has passion in every movement of his eyes, every twitch of his mouth, and he is always dangerous. Casting Poitier as a black man who moves from Good African to Dangerous African tilted the movie's balance toward him, while the script tilted it the other way, with the result that a fundamental ambivalence was created.

Something of Value is the story of two boys, Hudson and Poitier, who grow to manhood together between 1945 and 1952 in colonial Kenya. Their fathers are comparable patriarchs, the white a farmer who "understands" the black Kikuyu, the black a tribal reactionary who believes things would be fine "if only they did not teach young men evil in the cities." The two boys play soccer together, hunt together; but the black is humiliated by the white's older brother when the two (Poitier and Hudson) argue as equals, instead of the African's behaving like a servant. The African eventually "goes bad" and joins a gang who are stealing guns from whites. (There is no explanation of why Africans do not already have guns.) In an upstairs room in Nairobi, Poitier and others are harangued by a Kenyatta-like figure: "The whole colored world burns with the fire of revolt. . . . You will need a symbol, a sign—a name. Here it is—Mau Mau. Mau Mau is the machinery that will carry us to freedom." This does to the creation of Mau Mau what Don Ameche did to the invention of the telephone.

Hudson's thoroughly nice young man has meanwhile been falling in love with Dana Wynter, who is inexplicably as upper class as the Queen Mother and as arch as Clifton Webb. The two lovers are shown against beautiful skies, often looking troubled but clean and pressed. Poitier gets messier and messier, living rough with his gang and being cared for by a wife who never speaks a line and with whom the film never allows him the luxury of a relationship. When the Mau Mau attack, it is of course Hudson's family whom they kill and maim. He goes off to fight Mau Mau, seeing some of the seamy side of white soldiering (a concentration camp, torture of a black prisoner). Hudson finally confronts and kills his former friend, Poitier, and Hudson takes Poitier's child and his sister's child and says, "Maybe for them it will be better." Music up, The End.

The party line on this movie is that it presented a balanced picture of the two sides in Kenya; the novel had made the same claim. It won't wash, however: the camera itself has a white sensibility, and Richard Brooks's script and direction keep looking at the whites in normal and nice situations—falling in love, being a family, planning a wedding—and at the blacks in abnormal and horrific ones—plotting revolution, staging a Mau Mau ceremony, attacking a farm. The whites have a society and a stable way of life, the film tells us; the blacks do not. The whites are the center; the blacks are the periphery. The whites are the norm; the blacks are the aberration. Given these emphases, no mere equality of footage could make the film seem balanced. Juxtaposition of scenes makes the discrepancies even stronger: a Mau Mau ceremony, including the taking of blood and the drinking of a potion, is juxtaposed with a white happy-family scene of wedding planning, with the whites making jokes whose basis is how the Kikuyu supposedly behave in marriage—wife-beating, wife-buying with goats, female work. When the whites plan strategy, they are rational; when the blacks plan, they are hysterical. It is an utterly typical example of falsification through "naturalizing"—the unstated assumption that one side is correct by nature. This essential imbalance extended even to the credits: the white stars were shown on the screen as their names and roles were given; the black performers were not. The film's balance was in fact a pose—"pseudo-objectivité," as Guy Hennebelle has called it.

Something of Value was not helped by its unconvincing style. Hudson's and Wynter's clothes were always fresh and neat, their hair perfect. Hudson's big-game rifle had no recoil. The Kikuyu never spoke Kikuyu but always English, with a bewildering mixture of accents. The Kikuyu women were shown as having shaven heads. The whites called the Kikuyu "Kukes" but never "niggers," the favored word. Mt. Kenya, so often hidden by cloud in reality, was always cloudless. And so on—repeated cheats on authenticity, in a film that asked to be taken as authentic—that, in fact, loses all reason for being if it is not authentic.

At the center of this inauthenticity stands Hudson, with his niceness and his urbanness and his Americanness. At its periphery stands Poitier, eyes flashing fire. The camera keeps telling us that it is Hudson, the nice American corporation-man, whom we should believe. Our eyes keep swiveling to Poitier. A new archetype has been born, and we recognize its power: the Dangerous African. The movie shatters like cheap glass.

VOICE OF THE HURRICANE was released in 1963, after its moment had passed. Yet, despite this untimeliness and despite flaws that made it a very unlikely commercial release, it often came closer to the essential conflict of the time than any of the three commercial Mau Mau films. It was a didactic motion picture produced by Moral Rearmament, and its didacticism finally swamped its insight, but it showed up a trivialization like *Something of Value* for what it was. Even the *New York Times* acknowledged that "it appears so confident and guileless that it leaves you submissive and mute."

This film does not name Mau Mau, but it seizes on Mau Mau's history for its environment. In a significant reversal, however, it makes the secret head of the terrorists a woman, Mary/Mbali, a cook in a white household. She has an impassioned speech that is reminiscent of Shylock's "Do we not bleed?", a diatribe against white oppression—white hunting, white sexual exploitation, white homosexual acts with Africans—that ends with, "A storm is coming—and it's a hurricane!" But the film's resolution has this Dangerous African praying to the Christian God for help "to take on the tasks of the future together," and this pious ending is no more convincing than such changes of heart ever are. The difficulty in this serious film is the difficulty of all intellectual drama: its messages can be believable only if they are embedded in action and therefore in character, but, instead, the artists keep embedding them in dialogue. For all its earnestness, then, the resulting work is unconvincing just where it most seeks to convince.

Even more than *Something of Value*, *Voice of the Hurricane* suffers from weak production values: the lack of location filming, actors who are seldom better than acceptable, lackluster direction. What it does have is a willingness to call a spade a spade; it gives a better idea to a white audience of the causes of African discontent than any of the other Mau Mau films. Its seriousness of content, however, is never carried into a seriousness of plot, which remains merely melodramatic (a squabble between father and son, an injured child rushed to the hospital, a threat of Mau Mau attack on the farm). Underlying its own seriousness, as well, is a profound ambivalence about an Africa that it sees as female but subject to a male god.

THE IMPORTANT INNOVATION in these films was the new African archetype. However, it is worth glancing in passing at the whites, too. The women are about what we might expect, sexist images concocted by a patriarchal production system. (Mary in *Voice of the Hurricane* is a partial exception.) They exist as functions: Leigh has the rubber-inflatable quality of the Drag Queen, Wynter an android lack of expression. And why not? They are not characters, as the men are. McKenna is somewhat more textured, physically more a woman—because, paradoxically, she is less a Barbie Doll. These are not films about women, however; they use women as victims and offer them as prizes, little more.

And the white men? They have active roles, but they do not project a new archetype for a changing future. Mature's White Hunter is an archetype getting long in the tooth, one whose relationship to Mau Mau—that is, to the new African archetype, the new and future reality—is accidental, really peripheral for much of the film. Bogarde is a far more interesting piece of casting, but his unsure neurotic is an expression of the confusion that will lead in a few years to the shucking of the African colonies. He is not a new white archetype, any more than Mature is; he is a reaction, a threat of withdrawal.

Nor is Rock Hudson's strong-jawed American the new white African. Hudson is an American actor in a work conceived by an American, filmed by Americans. What he represents, therefore, is not a deep response to Africa but a response to something in America. In pairing him with Poitier—even in making this film for the mass American audience—it is likely that the creators of *Something of Value* were looking at some American crisis and its resolution, not at an African one. Given the historical moment—*Brown v. Board of Education* had just been decided—it is not far-fetched to suggest that what Hudson's casting speaks to is the beginning of the American civil rights movement. There is Poitier, dangerous and black; here is Hudson, reassuring and white: we're okay.

Thus, the only archetype to come from these films is a black one, the Dangerous African. Poitier and Cameron are vibrant with the African future; the white men, unlike their forebears in the imperial films, lack conviction.

But a new white presence does appear in these pictures. Where, we may ask, have all these white families come from all of a sudden? And all these farmers? White men in Africa have been loners, imperial eunuchs; now here are this bunch with sisters and sweethearts and mothers and children. And they are not romantic explorers or hunters or servants of empire; they are *farmers*! What goes?

The answer, of course, is that the ground has shifted from imperial exploitation to colonial ownership; now, instead of running the army or the local civil service, the hero tills the ground—and thus makes it his own. Yet only half the reality is shown: where are the black farmers of Kenya in these films? Where are the black farmers—many of them women—whose only holdings were *shambas*, really extended gardens of a couple of acres, when white farmers had spreads of a thousand acres or more, acquired at pennies per acre? Where are the black farmers who had to spend part of each year working on white farms to pay the "hut tax" that the British government imposed to create cheap labor?

The answers are very simple. Like the thousands of blacks killed by Mau Mau, black farmers do not exist in these films. These are films about white ownership. Black Africans cannot exist as farmers here; they can exist only in the functions that whites understood—as servants or as threats.

Nonetheless, *Simba, Safari*, and *Something of Value* marked an important change in the way Africa was filmed. Made while Mau Mau was still active or very fresh in the memory, they acknowledged the collapse of the British and American idea of a subservient, loving Africa. Britain had been poking at the outline of a new African, at least since *Men of Two Worlds*, without success. Those attempts—ahistorical because self-serving—were brought to an abrupt halt when history showed that Britain was no longer welcome in much of the globe; that Lord Sandy was in fact despised; that white claims to superior civilization, to superior religion, to superior birthright were rejected. The new African, as he and she stepped forward in these films, was a potentially violent and untrustworthy one. Not accidentally, the figure most often selected by these films to commit violence against whites was the servant, the traditional role of the Good African: white-made movies were not going to give up their comfortable archetypes without a struggle.

Black men in these films were muscular, no longer soft and plump, as Hollywood savages so often had been. They wore European clothes and they used guns, if they could get them. They were *people*. Old stereotypes were relied on when Mau Mau were shown attacking in force: there was a reversion to the savage horde, and the Mau Mau ceremony was shown as a reversion to witchcraft. But a new African was being shown, and, embodied by Poitier, he was a star.

With the Mau Mau films, the Dangerous African became a familiar figure, enacted by Poitier, Earl Cameron, Orlando Martins, and less often by actors like Raymond St. Jacques. By the 1960s, film Africans were split between the Dangerous and the Good—between rebels and killers, on the one hand, and nice guys and sidekicks on the other. Only rarely did a black actor get to a play a more complex African, as Cameron did in *Guns at Batasi* and Martins in a small role in *Sammy Going South*. The Good African saw a new variation, the black sidekick, a popular use for former athletes (Rafer Johnson, Jim Brown), but best exploited by Johnny Sekka in the underrated *The Southern Star*. Black women were hardly thought of, the Black Wife of the Robeson films and the Black Eve of the White Man's Grave both vanishing.

The Dangerous African also found a perhaps surprising new venue in the 1960s: films out of South Africa. They marked the rise to stardom of a new black actor who was himself African, Ken Gampu. Gampu was a big man with an expressive face that could seem ferocious, and he was easily typecast in Dangerous African roles. However, he was also a fine actor, and even his brief appearance as a Zulu messenger in the later *Zulu Dawn* was startling: a personality leaps from the screen in that otherwise confused film. However, it was in *Dingaka* (1965) that Gampu's talent got sufficient scope, and the picture, marred as it was by its controlling white sensibility, is still worth watching for his performance.

Dingaka was directed by the white Jamie Uys (now best known for *The Gods Must be Crazy* pictures). It is a film about one of the Dispossessed, about the doomed travel from Zululand to the city and back. Perhaps because an all-black film would have had little chance in South Africa, *Dingaka* also starred Stanley Baker and Juliet Prowse, Baker as a lawyer who helps Gampu's Dispossessed and Prowse as Baker's wife. The effect of this casting, however, was to make it a film about whites helping blacks, or perhaps about blacks needing the help of whites, an unfortunate effect because the Gampu action would have stood by itself and been the better for doing so.

Dingaka is the story of a rural Zulu who finds himself pushed to the city and to murder by the machinations of a "witch-doctor." Gampu, in furs and skins, is the father of twin children, one of whom is murdered by a man who has been told by the "witch-doctor" that he will regain his prowess at stickfighting if he eats the heart of a twin. When the Gampu character takes his suffering to the "witch-doctor," he is told who killed the child and why: the impression we are given is of a formerly idyllic life destroyed by unreason, as if the "witch-doctor" (who virtually rules the village from a cave high above it) were engaging in a particularly perverse kind of fun. Gampu goes to the city to find the killer. The city at first stuns him—he is tricked out of his bit of money, he is overwhelmed by the mines and factories, he suffers the humiliation of putting on Western clothes that diminish and mock him (these events recall similar scenes in *Cry, the Beloved Country*)—but he tracks the killer down and kills him. He is then arrested for murder, and it is at this point, halfway through the film, that Baker first appears, as his court-appointed lawyer. Several otherwise irrelevant scenes take place between Baker and Prowse (she wants to adopt a child; he doesn't; he wants to talk about Gampu; she wants a child, and so on). Gampu mysteriously is able to speak English, although Baker says such things as, "He grew up in the jungle," and "He is ignorant of the ways of the white man." Baker tries to convince the credulous Gampu that the "witch-doctor" is "only a man," and that Gampu must fight the charge of murder. Baker's character seizes the film: he goes to the "witch-doctor" and challenges him, and the "witch-doctor" threatens Prowse. Gampu escapes from prison and confronts the "witch-doctor" and kills him, proving that Baker's white-European rationalism was correct: the "witch-doctor" is only a man, and he has no magical power over Gampu. And Gampu goes off with Baker, presumably back to prison and a double charge of murder.

This series of actions is accompanied by some glorious music, most of it South African choral singing, which gives the picture a feeling of greater depth and importance than in fact it deserves. The music also both glorifies the rural simplicity of Zululand and lyricizes black life around South Africa's mines. The same vigorous group dancing that was shown in *Song of Africa* appears here; in this context, however, it "naturalizes" the impossible situation of black men isolated from their homes, making the dance seem happy, even celebratory. Much of the "Jim-Comes-to-Jo'burg" section of the film, in fact, is a kind of travelogue of black South Africa for whites, seen through the naive eyes of Gampu's sweet revenger. A scene in which Gampu hunts for the killer of his child on a hill where stickfighters are fighting in pairs is chilling, the more so because it recalls that 16mm film shown in 1950, with its blacks turned against each other for "recreation" while white policemen with whips stand by; yet here, the scene, even though it is a vision of hell, normalizes: it seems to say, as travelogues do, not "How terrible!" but "How fascinating!" Finally, the assumptions about black people and superstition are very much those of *Men of Two Worlds* and are patronizing for the same reasons. Worse than patronizing is the implication that it is a black cause (here, witchcraft and revenge) that dispossesses black men and sends them on their tragic journey to the city. (It must be said, however, that Uys did not invent witchcraft as a South African concern: it was a common subject in earlier black South African writing, although there the focus was not white-black but Christian-animist. Nor was it without foundation in fact: the Johannesburg newspapers still contain ads for *sangomas* with 900 lines—dial-a-magicians.)

Thus, *Dingaka* is not only a film split between its black and its white stars, but one split between its black myth and its white exploitation of it. Its gravest fault, considering its South African origin, is its implication that apartheid's horrors are normal, and that the chasm between blacks and whites can be bridged by one white man's extending his manicured hand. You ache for the honest anguish of those whites in *Cry, the Beloved Country* who knew that good intentions were so much dust on the wind.

It is Ken Gampu who gives the picture such power as it has; next to him, Baker seems insignificant. Prowse, of course, is an excrescence and should never have been in the picture to begin with (although the futility of her role nicely embodies the South African notion of women). Perhaps regrettably, Gampu's enormous honesty lights up every scene in which he appears, so that the romanticized village and the whitewashed city both draw authenticity from his presence; yet, on the positive side, that authenticity serves the myth of the Dispossessed. *Dingaka* is thus half of a very good film about the tragedy of black corruption by South African society. The other part is half of a very bad film about how necessary whites are.

Gampu was also prominent in *The Naked Prey* (1966), a picture made in Rhodesia and South Africa. The film, however, was dominated by Cornel Wilde, who both starred and directed. It has a simple story line: in a vaguely nineteenth-century past, four white men are captured by Africans (the location not stated) because all but Wilde refuse to pay tribute. Three of the four whites are then killed with a vividness seldom seen in films of the period. One is tethered within striking distance of a cobra; one is decorated like a grotesque chicken, legs tied, and is chased by women who hack him to death with sharpened sticks; and one is packed in clay, except for a breathing tube, and slowly roasted over a fire. Up to this point, the film rubs its audience's face in racial horror—the black horde, savagery, cannibalism.

Then, however, Wilde's torture begins: naked, he is turned loose, to be run down by several Africans. The rest of the film is this run for life, in the course of which Wilde's character is shown becoming as savage as that of the Africans. Wilde, then fifty or so, was wonderfully fit, and he did a great deal of very real running during the film's making. The African pursuers were fit, too—Ken Gampu in particular—and, with everybody nearly naked, a curious shift took place. The action swung from torture to athletics; the iconography swung from black savagery to human savagery to individual competition between Gampu and Wilde.

At the end, Wilde reaches a British fort and is safe. Naked, he turns, sees Gampu, now too far behind to hurt him. They stare at each other. It is a strange moment—is it the African past looking at the African future? Or two enemies who have learned respect? I find it too ambiguous to read, although I would hazard that the impropriety of white presence in Africa is an allowable meaning. If so, it is a peculiar one for a motion picture made with Rhodesian and South African participation, and perhaps its ambiguity was Wilde's solution to the influence of that participation. Certainly, it suggested where movies were at that moment: the aging white star facing the upcoming black one. It was a portent of things to come in both movies and life.

9 THE HELPER, THE SIMP, AND THE OAF

The emergence of the Dangerous African and the expanded roles it allowed for black actors slightly anticipated the end of colonial rule. It was a preparation for independence. So was the change that is the subject of this chapter: an attempt to shift the justification for white presence from Livingstone's "three C's" (commerce, Christianity, civilization) to altruism. Its roots can be found in early films about Africa, although its full realization came as the wave of decolonization began in the 1950s.

"Animal pictures" figure largely in the body of African films. However, if we subtract nonfiction films about animals as objects (of travel, scientific study, and so on) and fiction films about animals as menaces and monsters, their number is greatly reduced. If hunting films are further subtracted, the remaining number of animal films is small indeed, and it comprises those motion pictures in which African animals are viewed more or less benignly and in which the human heroes help rather than harm them. Perhaps significantly, these are mostly a recent phenomenon. But, perhaps even more significantly, they outnumber by a large proportion the films in which the hero or heroine helps African humans.

Selig had produced a number of silent animal pictures before World War I that show nonlethal meetings between humans and African animals. Selig had a considerable menagerie, first in Chicago and then in Los Angeles; its African pictures were all shot in the United States. A number of these, all starring Kathlyn Williams (an interesting figure who also did some directing) at least have titles or descriptions that suggest the animal-helping theme: *Captain Kate* (1911); *Capturing Circus Animals in the African Wilds* (1911); *Lost in the Jungle* (1911); *The Leopard's Foundling* (1914); and *In Tune with the Wild* (1914). The first two were actually about animal trapping, however (in *Captain Kate*, Kate is trapped in a cabin with two of her dead trapper-father's leopards, and the second may have been a sequel). If the last two were "helping" pictures, as their titles suggest, they were isolated examples and seem to have been variations of the Selig wild-animal picture. They have some significance, however, because they went against the received ideas of Dark Continent and animal menace, and the corollary human domination through killing.

These Selig animal pictures were also different, however, because Williams's Kate was a very early example of a competent white woman in an African setting—wearing practical bush clothes, dealing with animals, *not* simpering or preening. Her posture was like Elmo Lincoln's—chest out, head up—not like Enid Markey's round-shouldered defensiveness. The films' emphasis seems to have been on her ability to deal with the animals, not on her ability to kill them. Kathlyn Williams thus embodied an early archetype, the Strong Woman, in a "jungle" setting where she was neither helpless nor magically omnipotent nor dependent on a man for salvation. She did not last, however: like a very differently empowered female, the vamp, Williams's Strong Woman was a creature of early silents.

The other fictional films in which humans help African animals are far more recent. *Where No Vultures Fly*, the first important one, was a decidedly pro-helping movie released in 1951. It appears to have been the pioneer and prototype of modern animal-helping story films, perhaps because it was the "top British moneymaker of 1952." It introduced, in the person of Anthony Steel, a new archetype, the Helper: the white who is in Africa to help rather than to exploit.

It was the earliest of eleven such animal-helping pictures made between 1951 and 1972: *Where No Vultures Fly* (1951); its sequel, *West of Zanzibar* (1954); *Odongo* (1956); *The Roots of Heaven* (1958); *The Last Rhino* (1961); *The Lion* (1962); *East of Kilimanjaro* (1962); *Rhino!* (1964); *Clarence, the Cross-Eyed Lion* (1965); *Born Free* (1966); *An Elephant Called Slowly* (1969); and *Living Free* (1972, a sequel to *Born Free*). In addition, two human-helping story films were also made, *White Witch-Doctor* (1953) and *Mister Moses* (1965).

A third of the animal-helping films were British, a tribute, perhaps, to the British love of animals; two other very successful films, *Born Free* and its sequel, had British stars and British directors. (The United States was producing at least four times as many films as Great Britain during this period.) The British product, too, was disproportionately successful, the reasons impossible to pin down. Hollywood was in turmoil for part of the period, producing as color features films that would formerly have been B movies (*Odongo*, for example), fighting television, flailing about to find marketable product. A number of the American pictures were simply terrible by any standard (*Odongo*, *The Lion*, *Rhino!*).

Where No Vultures Fly was reportedly the idea of its director, Harry Watt, to make a motion picture about Mervyn Cowie's efforts to create East Africa's first game park (now Nairobi National Park.) In the event, this story film had nothing to do with Cowie or Nairobi, but it did devote itself to a game warden and his attempt to create and then guard an East African park. It was antihunting and antipoaching. Being against poaching was nothing new—every white who ever hunted in Africa was opposed to anybody else's killing the game—but being against hunting was.

Anthony Steel was Bob, the idealistic warden, and Dinah Sheridan was Mary, his apprehensive wife. Bob and Mary go to live in his new game park so as to protect it, taking with them their preadolescent son. Thus, this film puts a nuclear family where previous British films had put a solitary male, and in Steel it has a new imperial type—duller, less elitist, physically stronger, stereotypically heterosexual. A number of the film's conflicts become both professional and familial: Mary doesn't want to live in the bush, but they have to live in the bush; the child loves animals but is attacked by a lion; Bob has to fight the poachers, and the poachers threaten him and the family, and so on. Central to this inclusion of the family in Bob's crises is his insistence that they be with him: Mary is not left in London like *Four Feathers*' Esmee, nor is she an intruder to whom Bob snarls that women don't belong in the bush, as the White Hunter was wont to do.

Where No Vultures Fly relies on some stereotypes: Bob wears a leopard-skin hatband; a snake apears the very first day they go into the bush; a rhino attacks their car; the "Kuwamba" people are shown in skins and feathers, dancing like dervishes. The film can't help itself when it comes to colonialisms: the Africans are referred to as "boys"; the game department staff are white; the Masai are "just as they were a thousand years ago." But the film also includes genuine collisions with contemporary Africa: although the poachers are black, their boss is white, a cynical racist who tells Bob, "Africa's finished; there's nothing in it for a white man; one day that black scum is going to take it over." The chief of the "Kuwamba" wears a suit. And it is significant that the enemy of white civilizaton is not a "witch-doctor" but another white, who exploits black poverty to steal the living wealth of animals, to which the hero's response is to hire other black Africans to fight the poachers—an adumbration of one modern poaching-control tactic.

Where No Vultures Fly is uncertain about the animals, both loving them and fearing them (personalized as Bob's and Mary's views). Far too many animals attack humans; the real Africa has never been like that. Bob's need to keep the Masai out of his park because their cattle bring rinderpest obscures the far greater threat—overgrazing—that cattle pose to animals all over Africa. Nonetheless, this is a fairly honest movie with a fairly honest treatment of a complicated issue.

In 1954, Watt and Steel returned to the character in *West of Zanzibar* (not to be confused with the Tod Browning-Lon Chaney film of 1928), with a new wife (Sheila Sim) and a too-cute child. Lacking this time the strong storyline of the creation of the first-ever game park, the movie actually retrogressed, relying more heavily than its predecessor on clichés and reducing the general even more to the personal. Having found star quality in Steel, too, it relied more on him as action hero. The result was a film with unresolved inner contradictions and a sense of uneasiness with itself.

Nevertheless, this *West of Zanzibar* is one of the very few films to try to show the dilemma of Indians in Africa. The villain is an Indian lawyer, a stand-in for the villainous white of *Vultures*, called by the game warden's wife "the most hateful man I've ever met." He puts the strawman argument that "the black man is doomed to be a savage," so we know that Steel—and we—must believe otherwise. Yet it is also he who says of himself and the British colonial system, "I am a wog! And you ask me to sympathize in perpetuating that?"

The plot has Steel tracking ivory poachers along the coast of East Africa. The central conflict pivots on the Galanas, who are first presented as untouched by civilization (impossible, the more so as they are shown wearing manufactured cloth) and then as corrupted by it—wanting consumer goods and willing to poach to get them. The Galana headman (Orlando Martins) makes a plea for the thousands of Africans being drawn to the cities: "They are thrown into the gutter. They starve in the slums. They need your help—they need your help more than the animals!" The film's answer, as he puts it, is to "destroy the tempter"—that is, the coastal Arabs and Indians who pay for stolen ivory.

This is a quantum leap from *Sanders of the River*. It has the unfortunate effect, however, of replacing one racism (antiblack) with another (anti-Arab and anti-Indian); but for those who are interested only in white racism against blacks it may seem an improvement. It did not seem so to the colonial censor in Kenya Colony, who banned the film, an action upheld by the governor. J. Koyinde Vaughan also saw a dark side of this new Britisher: "There is nothing . . . to suggest that [he] in spite of his platitudes [about loving Africa] would regard Africans as equal partners in his land of hope."

West of Zanzibar has some gorgeous cinematography of the East African coast, of dhows sailing before the wind on that beautiful water, of Mombasa and the coastal landscape. More even than in *Where No Vultures Fly*, this photography objectified the hero's proclaimed love of Africa.

THE REDEFINITION OF the imperial protagonist and the use of a family, or at least a close, married couple, was continued in three more films. In all of them, British actors under British direction played British subjects: the first of them, *Born Free*, struck gold. Based on Joy Adamson's best-selling book about Elsa, the lioness, it starred Virginia McKenna and husband Bill Travers as Joy Adamson and husband George. The actors might as well have been playing Elizabeth and Phillip for all the resemblance to the Adamsons, who were in real life a prickly pair and not the saccharine constructions they were represented to be, but no matter. Nor was there—nor could there have been—any sense of the darkness of the real Adamsons' ends, both murdered in Africa.

Born Free is a movie about the joys and heartache of Being a Mum. It happens that the baby is in this case a lion, but no matter: Mum suffers and smiles, laughs and weeps, and knows the inevitable, sweet heartache of seeing Baby grow up and leave the nest. The gender roles of *Where No Vultures Fly* and its sequel are reversed here: the woman is the protagonist, the man a beloved obstacle (he thinks Elsa ought to go to a zoo). McKenna, as Joy Adamson, narrates much of the movie in voice-over, with treacly results: "That evening [when Elsa is first allowed away from camp] we suffered all the agony of parents whose teenage daughter is out on her first date." Anthropomorphism is the bedrock on which the thing is based, with Joy having insight into Elsa's mind: "Elsa thought I was her mother." "Elsa stopped me from walking into a great big cobra. And knew what she was doing." "I don't want to send her to a zoo! I want to set her free! Elsa would be miserable in a zoo!" (As if other animals aren't.)

As a result of this mindreading, Elsa comes across as a nice, white, middle-class sort of lion. She gets her name because "she reminds me of a little girl at school." Elsa is naughty but never bad or, worse, amoral. When, grown up and returned to the camp with her own babies—Mumhood Forever!—she responds to the distant roar of a male, we are told, "Her master's voice." One expects that Elsa will buy her nappies at Harrod's, prepare her babies for their O levels, and teach them to vote Conservative.

Born Free, with its glacial pace and its gush, was probably intended for children and their attendant parents. It made only an occasional gesture toward the real Africa, as when Elsa causes trouble by stampeding elephants through Africans' fields. It did show black Africans, but only as servants and guards. The only cinematography of any distinction was the animal footage; that of the lions was obtained by using more than twenty lions in locales as far apart as Ethiopia and Uganda. Afterward, a goodly number of these lions were sent to zoos, and there was a flap over whether they could have been returned to the wild, McKenna and Travers writing to the *Times* in favor of the wild. Some were; by 1969, one had been found in critical condition and was returned to captivity.

McKenna and Travers clearly loved Africa. Perhaps they were looking for a way to get a paid vacation there in 1969, for, with James Hill, who had directed *Born Free*, they produced *An Elephant Called Slowly*, a form of home movie with the stars playing the same roles, only as themselves. She is indulgent, capable, and motherly; he is bumbling and ever so dear. Everything they do is accompanied by happy music. They do silly things, like mistaking a cow for a buffalo. She stands in an ant nest, and we know this is supposed to be amusing. It is, again, a kind of children's film, although it has some excellent animal footage and some rarely honest shots of an African town. A sequence with the real George Adamson and his lions now has historical value. The result is a very small film of some charm, marred by a misleading idea of the relationship between humans and animals—Africa as a petting zoo.

It was to be their compensation, however, for not getting to play the Adamsons in *Born Free*'s sequel, *Living Free*. Joy was this time played by Susan Hampshire, a less cloying interpretation, but the script was even more sentimental and less believable, so that, despite Hampshire, Joy Adamson came across as an obsessive neurotic (which, by accident, may have been closer to the truth). The voice-over is again anthropomorphic: "Elsa gave us the gift of her love." "She remained our friend." "[Elsa and her cubs] were a happy family." The stultifying influence of Walt Disney's films can be seen in staged encounters among lion cubs and an eland, lion cubs and a rhino; there is a sense of no plot and much filler. Black Africans are real and contemporary—a Masai on a bicycle, black game scouts—but they have no part in the central action. Whites are not all blameless—the bad poachers are whites—but the sensibility is again upper-middle-class, somewhere about Reading.

The rest of the animal-helping films were American in both origin and feel. With the exception of the comic *Clarence, the Cross-Eyed Lion* and the decidedly odd *The Roots of Heaven*, they were mere exploitations of African settings, with the animal helping an excuse for being there. *Odongo* is bad-tempered and chaotic, its Helper a female veterinarian (Rhonda Fleming) who is afraid of every animal she sees and who wears tight, cute clothes that emphasize her nose-cone breasts; Macdonald Carey is unattractive and boorish and you wonder what either sees in the other. The picture does have a tidy litle performance by Eleanor Summerfield as a Crowing Hen whom we are supposed to laugh at because she doesn't want a wild baboon in the car with her; instead, she seems far more sensible than the two supposed animal experts. *Rhino!* tried to be a funny buddy movie about a bad-tempered veterinarian (Robert Culp) and an animal catcher (Harry Guardino), with Shirley Eaton as a token sex object who stands by a tree and is frightened by a python and who takes a bath in a river and is frightened by a crocodile and who stands by a Land Rover and is frightened by a rhino. Most of the Africans wear enough feathers to join the Folies-Bergères; the *KSM* stampede gets used again.

Clarence, the Cross-Eyed Lion was a comedy that showed its television roots. It starred Marshall Thompson, an actor who oozed good nature, as a veterinarian in charge of a "center for the study of animal behavior." He is (of course) a widower and he has (of course) a teenaged daughter, and she makes friends (of course) with a wild lion who happens to be cross-eyed. This creates gags, of course: she feeds the lion cake. The movie's comedy is not always so benign: when two black game rangers can't use the telephone, they use a drum. The doctor and his daughter are (of course) white, his assistants black; even the most important of the assistants calls the daughter "Miss Paula." A convenient white widow (of course) appears on the scene; the Africans call her "memsa'b." The presence of a comic (white) teacher suggests that this is a movie for school-age kids. The indifference to consequences suggests that no resemblance to real life is intended: Dad gets into a pit with a leopard, wrestles with it, and comes out with hardly a scratch. The film's Africa is the old generic one: the language is bastard Swahili, but the vet has West African kitsch on his walls. A product of the Ivan Tors factory, it was a nonlocation film directed, for a wonder, by Andrew Marton, who had once been able to create the likes of the 1950 *KSM*. A severing of any connection between events and bad consequences is what gives the film its television, and hence its modern, feel. In its favor, it has a secure social center (father, daughter, prospective wife-mother) and a warm male figure in Thompson—the only such male in the American films under consideration. (He was also in the otherwise negligible *East of Kilimanjaro*.)

The Roots of Heaven is inescapably a Darryl F. Zanuck film of the 1950s, immediately recognizable by its pretentiousness and the presence of Juliette Greco. It has an oversized, all-star, virtually all-male cast—Errol Flynn, Greco, Trevor Howard, Eddie Albert, Orson Welles, Edric Connor, Bachir Toure, Paul Lukas, Herbert Lom—and is based, like Zanuck's other gasbags, *The Sun Also Rises* and *The Snows of Kilimanjaro*, on a "great" work, this one by Hollywood's resident French intellectual, Romain Gary. The only thing that saved it from Zanuck's touch of death was the presence of John Huston as director. The result was a merely bad film, not a dreadful one—but one that has arresting moments and some flittingly superb acting; nobody can string a whole film's worth of performance out of it, but the cast is so good that *The Roots of Heaven* is still worth seeing for a moment here, a moment there.

Howard plays the Helper—a half-mad idealist who wants to save the elephants of some unspecified French colony. (French Equatorial Africa? Chad? Cameroon? This is one of the film's problems—it has no specificity.) Like a Biblical prophet, he withdraws to the desert, where he attracts an odd lot of the halt, the lame, and the blind, including Greco as a prostitute (what else?) and Flynn as a broken and alcoholic ex-officer (what else?). (Out of all proportion to the real situation, it is an Africa where the human detritus of World War II—Flynn, Greco, Howard—have washed up, a kind of white Last Resort.) Orson Welles, delicious ham on wry as a media personality, promotes Howard's cause; the government gets involved; allies become enemies; and most of Howard's supporters are murdered when they try to stop the slaughter of a huge elephant herd. Howard and four others escape, totter across the desert, and are welcomed by a huge and approving crowd of Africans, in a scene that was meant to be powerful but that is absolutely flat because the viewer hasn't a clue what's going on.

Tied far too closely to its source, *The Roots of Heaven* almost requires that you know the novel, but that's a trial in itself; as a Huston biographer said, "The film has the same leaden pedantry as its source." At its heart is an error of conception, expressed as the most elementary kind of visual oversight: the death of elephants is never given either reality or poignancy. This lack would seem to have been Huston's fault, or perhaps Zanuck's, but it radiates outward into a general lack of visual power; considering the visual potential of Africa, it is a parched film, full of talk where it should be full of pictures. It keeps going indoors when it should stay outside in Africa. Yet, in wildly different ways (and this is another trouble, that they are never stylistically brought to the same standard), Welles and Howard and even Greco are worth watching. For a different reason, you also watch Errol Flynn, who, in this film as in the ridiculous *The Sun Also Rises*, plays his own wreck and salvages from it an awful gallantry. The actors seem often to be working against the director, however; Huston again and again equates characterization with idiosyncracy, a technique he got away with in *The African Queen* but not here.

The Roots of Heaven does deal with a real Africa of dust and of towns. Blacks and whites argue as equals, although the presentation of an anticolonial "Black Napoleon" is overdrawn. The central figure's desire to help Africa is important, but it is seen to be an outsider's, a non-African's, concern—not for Africa or its people, but for the elephant as mystical beast. "Mankind are the roots of Heaven," the idealist says, but he does not truly seem to mean black humankind; and the macho Huston and his almost exclusively male cast do not seem to mean womankind, either.

Three other Hollywood movies verged on the helping type but do not really belong to it. *Hatari* (1962) and *Africa, Texas Style* (1967) were both about animal catching for zoos and were thus really hunting pictures, but of a nonlethal sort that brought them close to the Helpers. *Hatari* was a John Wayne film with a solitary female (Elsa Martinelli) who jumps into Wayne's bed, apparently to counter any tendency to see homoeroticism in the otherwise exclusively male cast. Wayne, pot-bellied and gravel-voiced, looks as if he could hardly go to bed with anything more interesting than a hot-water bottle. The movie is about male bonding, with Africa as the mere setting and animal catching from trucks as the requisite dangerous activity. *Africa, Texas Style* presented as new a feat that had first been done in 1909, roping African animals from horseback, the subject of Cherry Kearton's *Lassoing African Animals*, which would be far more worth seeing. Hugh O'Brian has Adrienne Corri as his sex object, Tom Nardini as his sidekick (an American Indian), John Mills as the necessary Kenyan rancher, Nigel Green as the now acceptably white (but not British) villain. *The Lion* (1962) was not really an animal-helping film at all, although it does deal with a young girl's attachment to a lion, but this attachment gets all tangled up in a love triangle among very unpleasant people so old they ought to know better. *The Lion* may have been an excuse for the aging William Holden to get to Kenya, which he loved; little else would explain it. Trevor Howard looks ancient; Capucine can't act; Jack Cardiff directs as if it's a staged play. There is actually a scene in which a man can be seen wrestling with a rug that we are supposed to believe is a lion. At the end, Howard gives up Capucine and drives off in one direction as she and Holden drive off in the other, and the question of who gets the house and the furniture—by far the best things in the film—goes unanswered.

None of these films is worth mentioning except that they show several common directions: a continuing Americanization of the white presence in Africa; a perpetuation in American films of an interest in almost ritualistic sexual courtship, rather than in established relationships; and a stubborn focus on whites who pursue profitable activities in Africa that are not available to Africans.

White Witch Doctor (1953) was a human-helping movie in which Susan Hayward played a widowed nurse in "the Congo" in 1907. Thus, responsibility to modern Africa was checked at the door. Greeting her on the dock of the "last port of call" was an irritable and inexplicably rude Robert Mitchum, who at once saves her from a man in a gorilla suit.

Mitchum is eager to leave Africa after months of animal catching, but oily and evil Walter Slezak persuades him to take Nurse Hayward upriver. (Slezak has a scheme to use them as cover while he seeks gold "among the tribes.") Mitchum sets out the producer's and director's theme with forthright honesty: "I can't believe a beautiful woman buries herself in the jungle out of love for mankind." The implications of this seem to be that he could believe that a homely woman would bury herself in the jungle, or that a beautiful woman would bury herself somewhere else (a drawing room? a bedroom?), or that a woman would bury herself in the jungle out of love for something else (a man? money?). Hayward then finds herself in Hollywood's jungle—a python frightens her; a "Leopard Man" puts a big spider on her as she sleeps; a "witch-doctor" contests with her. Mitchum's quest for gold overshadows her nursing, however, and the plot turns toward finding the source of "the Bakuba's gold," which involves Hayward's using an IV drip and novocaine (in 1907) to save an African "chief's son." Anyway, as she confesses, she's not in Africa out of idealism, but out of guilt because she thinks she caused the death of her doctor husband. The latter part of the movie is devoted to getting rid of Slezak, getting the gold, kissing, and getting the hell out, proving that Mitchum's initial question was the right one: What's a nice girl like you doing in a place like this? Answer: Looking for a husband, what else?

A more relaxed and likable Mitchum was himself a Helper in *Mister Moses* (1965), in which Alexander Knox was a human-helping medical missionary and Carroll Baker was his human-helping daughter and amateur nurse. Essentially a comedy, although a slow one, *Mister Moses* has a racialist premise (only a white can guide an entire black village to a new location) but considerable charm. Mitchum plays a charlatan who runs a medicine show—always an appealing type in comedy, although questionable when we contrast his quack medicine with the missionary's real medicine, and his fake religiosity—"Mister Moses"—with the missionary's zeal. He finds himself in charge of moving an African village because only he speaks the Hindustani that a crucial elephant understands. The feel is very colonial, possibly nineteenth century, so it is a shock when a district officer flies in by helicopter. Mostly, however, the film is an ahistorical trek through wide East African landscapes, photographed for their own beauty by director Ronald Neame. Conflict erupts between Mitchum and a black activist played by Raymond St. Jacques, who is "trying to get [Africa] back from the Reverend's shop." The district officer is captured, his chopper destroyed, and a big idol built, giving rise to savage dancing of a sort not seen since the jungle films of the 1930s (actually a perfectly decorous Masai dance of a familiar type). Mitchum saves everybody with his fists and destroys the idol, and St. Jacques gets into Mitchum's mountebank's flame-throwing gear and incinerates himself (suggesting that independence-minded black Africans can't handle Western technology). Carroll Baker of course goes off with Mitchum and his elephant. No questions are asked about the appropriateness of the missionary's work; no mention is made of the independence of East Africa that same year. The movie is handsome and cheerful and often enjoyable, but it could not stand up to a charge of racialism for a whole second. Its "help" is not separated from interference (evangelism, colonial rule, charlatanism) and is mostly temporary (Mitchum, Baker). Self-help, as represented by St. Jacques, is "savage," backward-looking, destructive. This is all wrapped in a singularly beautiful package, from the batik-like titles to the Afro-pop music, leaving the intelligent viewer feeling guilty for having enjoyed it.

TAKEN TOGETHER, THESE films do not make a very strong case for the Helper archetype. The concentration on helping animals suggests an avoidance of human problems, probably of political complications of the sort that the 1954 *West of Zanzibar* got into in Kenya. By and large, the British films seem to have been more successful than the American at finding an effective character for the

Helper, particularly as embodied by Anthony Steel; the British films, too, found at least functional roles for women.

Concern for animals is a complex issue. The films do not address it in the same way. *The Lion* is really not sympathetic to animals at all: the girl's love for the lion is an obstacle; the game warden played by Trevor Howard bedevils animals with his truck. At the opposite extreme is *The Roots of Heaven*, which shows a sympathy for animals bordering on psychosis. The *Born Free* movies are not much saner, the affection lavished on the lions seeming much like that given by childless couples to dogs. A number of the films use African animals merely as devices, the way other films often use children and domestic pets.

The Helper films did raise one of the thorny questions of neocolonialism, however: can non-African whites do anything to interfere in the status of African animals without being colonial and even racist? One of the worst of the films, *Rhino*, tried to answer the question with an assertion: "These animals don't belong just to Africa!" The statement was unconvincing. Otherwise, the Helper films pretty much showed whites doing well by doing good: help, especially help to animals, was a white occupation on a black continent.

Another matter, not having to do with animals, is worth noting in the American films: how charmless the men are—boorish, complaining, selfish: Carey, Culp, Mitchum, Wayne, Holden. They are, in fact, so remarkable that they comprise another archetype, the American Oaf. Although not limited to the Helper films, the archetype is found here in significant numbers. It also occurs in American melodramas of the same years (e.g., *Duel in the Jungle, Beyond Mombasa*). Victor Mature in *Safari* is really one, as well; so is Rod Taylor in the 1973 *Trader Horn*.

Some of the women are correspondingly arch, curved into the men's rudeness like spoons; they preen and present their breasts and look up at the men like cats in an ad for cat food. They have inexplicably large wardrobes and are inevitably made up like fashion models. They, too, represent a new archetype: the Female Simp. Normally paired with the Oaf (Fleming, Crain, Leigh, Capucine, Eaton), they are obsessive and unhappy teases, always flaunting sexuality and always cutting it off.

Africa is a punishment for American women in these films. The plots have brought them there for punishment: the punishment in *White Witch-Doctor*, for example, is quite specific and self-inflicted, for the death of a husband. Africa was an initiation for British men in the 1930s, to prove their manhood; now it is an initiation for American women, to prove to them that they are too inept to deal with the world without men. But it is a punishment, too, for having failed men, usually at some unspecified time, in some unspecified way.

Both the Oaf's and the Simp's sexual behaviors are empty, no longer related to male-female heat (as the smart bickering of 1930s films like *The Road to*

Zanzibar had been), no longer related to real life, no longer related to anything; it is all going through now ritualized movie-sex routines, like Spanish courtiers in a locked palace. Style, which got so many Americans through cinematic trouble in the 1930s, has failed, as if it belonged to youth, and youth has fled. Now the men are older and disenchanted and lower-class, and they bitch and whine; the women are younger but baffled.

You also have to notice how old and used-up the male stars seem—Wayne, Carey, Holden, of course Flynn. The stories and direction, too, are full of used-up situations; it as if Hollywood has no new ideas about Africa and can't give life to the old ones. The men seem mostly loners and losers, middle-aged has-beens on the run from something not very interesting. Why are they in Africa? Because, you suspect, there is nothing for them in America.

It is distinctly odd, then, that we are now told that the 1950s were the era of "family values" in America. Where are family values in these films? They are in *Clarence, the Cross-Eyed Lion.* They are absent from the others. What's going on here?

The answer probably lies in identifying Africa as the only place these men can go. If we look at these oafish American male protagonists, we see that all are unmarried, all are rootless, all are outside society. These are films about oddballs: a charlatan, a wandering cowboy, an animal catcher, uprooted veterinarians. They are outsiders. These are active men pursuing odd and often dangerous professions, which are presented to us as admirable and enviable, but which somehow seem pointless and which are imposed on their location, Africa.

In these American films, then, Africa is no longer the place where Mr. and Mrs. Tarzan live. It is the place where alienated American men go, a last frontier on a shrunken planet. Metaphorically, "Africa" is the name of a drawer where the corporation man, secretly bored with family values, puts his secret (antifamily) fantasies.

Unless he is Bob Hope. Hope made the unremarkable *Call Me Bwana* in 1962, smack in the middle of the Oaf-Simp era. Its premise—that Hope as a fake Africanist is called upon to find a space capsule that has fallen in central Africa—rejected even the Oafs' reasons for going there. Africa, this film said, is a place an American would go only if something he wanted happened to fall out of the sky and land there.

10 GOOD LOSERS, BAD WINNERS

The Helper films were one response to the threat of African decolonization. Another very different one was made in the same years, expressing itself in a group of films that depended on violence for their very nature. If the Helper films seemed ready to attempt to cope with new conditions, these others seemed to turn against those conditions with a ferocious vengeance.

Most African colonies were shucked off between 1950 and 1964: nearly forty new states emerged in Africa alone from the empires of Great Britain, France, and Belgium. (Britain gave up what are now Ghana, Kenya, Lesotho, Malawi, Nigeria, Sierra Leone, Somalia, Tanzania, and Uganda in those years; Botswana and Swaziland, a few years later.) Many of the colonies were not given up easily: besides Mau Mau, there were such bitter wars as that the French fought in Algeria and the bloody aftermaths of Belgium's withdrawal from the Congo and Britain's from Nigeria (Biafra).

The violent cinematic response was expressed in two groups of films, both military: those about disastrous colonial defeats or merely Pyrrhic victories; and those about anti-African battles, fought by a new white archetype, the Mercenary. The first kind are nostalgic and autumnal, full of the color of old uniforms and the glory of old parades, and they celebrate colonial martyrdoms that are to be viewed as, in Thomas Pakenham's words, "glorious defeat in the best British tradition." The second kind are mean-spirited and nasty, full of violence and noise and the dying of black men: they are the revenge for the loss of Africa. For the first time since the 1920s, the influence of South Africa also begins to appear in internationally released films—and it is in many of these military and Mercenary films that it shows.

Guns at Batasi (1964) is a film specifically about the loss of an African colony (apparently Kenya). That loss is reduced to the experience of one post on one day, but it is made to epitomize the loss of the whole empire. It is a small film, made in black and white a decade after most movie-makers had turned to color and so restricted in its settings (mostly interiors) that you expect it to have been based on a play (it was not, however, but came from a novel). Within these restrictions, it is a fine picture with some excellent acting, Richard Attenborough particularly carrying a heavy load as a sergeant-major who is made to stand for the entire imperial mentality. The task rather forces him toward "overacting," a word meaningless outside the context of the performance but one useful here because it suggests his necessary solution to the problem of carrying so much. The text conceives of him as a cliché, gives him cliché speeches and attitudes; his workable solution is to go toward the big gesture, the big emotion and thus into a somewhat different style from the other actors (especially a very young Mia Farrow, whose wispy voice and timid face seem less the product of acting than of coming to).

A fairly intelligent motion picture, it nonetheless perpetuates British film's association of offensive ideas with women: here the Crowing Hen is Flora Robson, who plays an M.P. whose sympathies with a black rebel are meant to be found ridiculous, or worse. Mia Farrow, on the other hand, is a female nebbish with no active role at all.

Guns at Batasi turns on the handing over of a white, British army command to a black interim command at independence. It takes place almost entirely in the noncom mess and bar, opening only occasionally to show huge black crowds in a nearby city or essential events elsewhere on the army post. The new black commander, Captain Abraham (Earl Cameron), is a cautious Good African; he is ready to carry out the phased transfer that has been planned with the outgoing white commander (Jack Hawkins). However, Abraham is supplanted by the more militant Dangerous African, Lieutenant Boniface (Errol John), who wants faster, more violent change, and who seizes control of the base as soon as Hawkins has left it. Abraham, wounded in the mutiny, takes refuge in the white noncoms' mess, where the sergeant-major (Attenborough) defends him.

The sergeant-major then gets some guns, and there is a stand-off, which the lieutenant ends by pointing two field pieces at pointblank range at the mess and threatening to blow it to Kingdom Come: "For the first time in the history of my country, it is we who are putting the shell in the breach, and we who give the order to fire." In an absurd climax, the sergeant-major and a private (John Leyton) creep out and disable the guns, and Jack Hawkins then returns and takes charge. The sergeant-major's triumph is really a defeat, however: the rebel Boniface is made a colonel by the new black government and appointed military governor of the province, and the sergeant-major is ordered out of the new nation. Broken, he throws a whiskey glass at the wall, only to smash the portrait of the Queen that hangs there. Not profound as symbolism goes but adequate to this film, and welcome because its power is visual in a picture that is so word-heavy otherwise.

As a military film, *Guns at Batasi* is an honorable retreat from empire. It is significant that its focus is on other ranks, not officers—that it is the sergeant-major who embodies the old virtues and vices. There is none of the boyish fantasy of *Four*

Feathers, either; the lack of color photography underscores its antiromanticism, gives it a perhaps unearned "realism." It also looks history in the face, unlike the earlier colonial films: it sees the African officers as people and as individuals, although Boniface's "badness" (for which he is rewarded at the end) is overdrawn and is colored by the Crowing Hen's enthusiasm for him. The sergeant-major must be right in his heart, we are meant to feel, or else what would this cow of a female parliamentarian be spouting off about? But if he is right, then rewarding Boniface is wrong, and what is left unsaid at the end is the widespread British belief about the end of empire: those black bastards won't be able to govern themselves, just you wait!

Zulu, also from 1964, is a tribute to a long-ago kind of British courage and to the brilliant uniforms that represented it. The film is still a favorite of military history buffs for its "authenticity," although revisionist African historians may disagree with its version of events. The incident being celebrated is what is now known as the Battle of Rorke's Drift, a strategically meaningless encounter in which a couple of handfuls of British regulars held off thousands of Cetewayo's warriors during the Zulu War in South Africa. The event would hardly warrant a footnote in the books had it not produced a record number of Victoria Crosses, in part because it followed by a day the single greatest British defeat of that war, also at the hands of Cetewayo's impis, the Battle of Isandhlwana.

Magnificently photographed, and directed by Cy Endfield to capture both the splendor of South African landscape and the breath-stopping impact of thousands of Zulus, the film is a spectacular but mostly mindless story of a siege. Characterization is rather minimal, although not merely stereotypical; the emphasis is on spectacle and suspense. While utterly European in its bias (the only question we are allowed to ask is "Can the British hold out?" never "Can the Zulus break in?"), it captures the respect that British soldiers developed for the Zulus, and it justifies that respect: the Zulus, despite their furs and feathers, are not movie savages but disciplined troops. That they exist in such numbers throws the film back to the cliché of the savage horde, however.

Zulu begins at Isandhlwana: dead British soldiers in red coats, littering the ground. A voice-over explains that disastrous defeat. The camera switches abruptly to a Zulu town and to Cetewayo himself. He is entertaining a white missionary (Jack Hawkins), who exclaims, "They are a great people!" (Students of history will be interested to see that Cetewayo is played by a modern Zulu chief Buthelezi.) Lines of half-naked young women form and dance: the sequence presents images of power and barely leashed energy.

Then, in a rugged and beautiful landscape reminiscent of the American West, we see Michael Caine as a young British officer, a dandy, riding back from hunting as if he has been shooting stag in Scotland. With one other officer

(Stanley Baker), he is in charge of the tiny British force at the river crossing called Rorke's Drift. The landscape is huge; the post is infinitesimal; everything is still. The members of the small garrison are quickly sketched in: a malingerer, a Welshman, a malaria victim, a tough sergeant. Then the Zulus come.

The British soldiers either send away those who encumber them (Hawkins's now drunken and half-mad missionary and his family) or are deserted by those they need (a troop of Boer mounted militia). Then they face the Zulu impis, who ring the hills around them, first silent and then hideous with unintelligible, massed cries. These sequences are striking in their impact, communicating as they do the power of non-European armies that fight a different kind of war. (America's war in Korea had ended in 1955; its war in Viet Nam was just warming up; Mau Mau was vivid in British memory.)

The rest of the picture is the siege itself. The British slowly give up ground; one building after another in the small post is abandoned, the most terrifying loss that of the hospital, with wounded men being dragged through a hole in the wall while the Zulus hammer at the doors and windows. The attacks come in waves; between waves, the Zulus pick at the British with rifle fire, "testing our guns," as one of the British says, so that our understanding of the Zulus is one of discipline and military craft. Finally, the remaining British withdraw into a kind of redoubt made of filled sacks, and there Caine has them form three concentric lines, each line firing and then kneeling so that the line behind can shoot while the others load. (Correctly, they are firing single-shot Martinis.) The resulting fusillade is continuous; the Zulus attack but are thrown back by the terrible barrage; and then the impis, instead of attacking again, ring the hills as they did in the beginning and sound their spears on their shield in tribute to their enemy. The British respond with "Men of Harlech," and a voice-over recounts the remarkable number of Victoria Crosses and medals awarded for this tiny engagement.

It is, then, a film about courage in the face of annihilation—about going on, about doing well what you are disciplined to do, even though the effort cannot produce a worthwhile effect. There is no victory, except the Pyrrhic one of the Zulu withdrawal; there is only the courageous performance itself. Yet, the film seems to tell us, that performance is itself the point, not conquest; it is as if we have looked back at Caine and Baker and the others and said, "Yes, once we were this kind of people; once we were worthy." In good part, that worth is defined by the worth of the enemy, a superb if alien opponent.

THE HISTORICAL BATTLE of Rorke's Drift offered no great man at its center, and *Zulu* wisely chose not to create one. Caine's Lieutenant Bromhead is a useful and sufficiently interesting figure for us to see the historical personalized, but he does not expand into archetype—nor should he. The British soldiers comprise a group protagonist (we happy few), and it is around their experience that suspense crystallizes.

The third film of military disaster in three years, however, went for one of the colossal self-made myths of nineteenth-century history as its center. *Khartoum* (1966) was a picture about the long siege and final fall of that city in Sudan, with Charlton Heston as its self-appointed (and self-annointed) hero, General Charles Gordon. The movie is not unaware of Gordon's perhaps vaunting ego: "Vanity was always mixed up with vision," a voice tells us early on. Another character calls him "the vainest man alive." Ralph Richardson, doing a delicious number as Gladstone, hints at Gordon's self-righteousness: "I trust no man who consults God before he consults me." Given this historical sophistication, then, you have to ask why Gordon was thereafter treated unquestioningly in the movie as a tragic hero, and why an actor noted for his rather wooden portrayals of supergreats (e.g., Moses) was cast to play him. The movie gives no answer—or, rather, the movie is its own answer: it is not interested in questioning heroism: after serving these bits for us to chew on, it forgets them and settles into preparing for the inevitable and bloody end. It gives us the bits instead of really examining Gordon, so that the Gordon we see (always more convincing than any Gordon we merely hear about) is the same towering construct of heroic marble that Victorian boys were given: a great man who sacrificed himself for the cause of empire by isolating himself in Khartoum. ("But you'll be all alone!" someone says when this Gordon sends all the Europeans away. All alone with thirty-five thousand dark-skinned people, he means but does not say.)

Khartoum cannot proceed without some ludicrous excesses. Worst of them is Laurence Olivier as Gordon's nemesis, the Mahdi. Olivier was never an actor to be discounted, because he was always experimenting; sometimes, however, the experiments blew up and ruined the laboratory. This was one such disaster: even when supposedly speaking his own language to his own people, Olivier's Mahdi sounds like Peter Sellers playing an Indian waiter, and he looks as silly as any other white man would have in a blackface role in 1966. (This was more or less his Othello period.) Yet Olivier's name above the title, even more than Heston's, brought "class"; this was, after all, a *serious* production—Richardson, Alexander Knox, Richard Johnson, Johnny Sekka. (No women, of course.) Different casting might have been the means to giving the Mahdi moral, as well as dramatic, equality with Gordon; after all, a goodly part of the world's population believed that the Mahdi was an even holier man than Gordon—although Britons might not have wanted to recognize that fact so soon after their balls-up at Suez.

The color photography was sometimes superb. A wide-screen process (Panavision) opened the scenes of the Nile and the desert in a new way (although calling Sudan "the vast, hot African nowhere" threw the point of view back at least a hundred years). The final battle scenes were sometimes beautiful. Gordon's death on the stair, sword in hand—already the subject of any number of paintings and illustrations—was handsomely done. But the script was too talky, with the action scenes hemmed in by words; finally, the words did little to deepen the movie, and Gordon remained the exemplar of juvenile hero worship he had always been.

There is nothing wrong in making a film about hero worship aimed at a child's mentality. However, *Khartoum*, with its megastar cast, its wide-screen process, and its "seriousness" seemed to be something else. It seemed to be history: an examination of an earlier loss in Africa, in the light of more recent losses. Instead, it was nostalgia, even rather vengeful nostalgia, for a time when one magnificent Englishman could hold off an army of those black blighters for a year, and then go down in wonderful, heroic defeat. No red-blooded boy would forget, either, that Gordon's death set up the punitive expedition that revenged him at the Battle of Omdurman—the climax of *Four Feathers*.

WHAT THE BATTLE of Little Bighorn is to American popular history, Isandhlwana is to British: both represent the astonishing destruction of an industrialized force by a preindustrial one. The American catastrophe, however, has a focal figure in Custer, who has served equally well as a tragic hero and as "one of the great dumb-assed men of history" (as Arthur Kopit's *Indians* has it). Isandhlwana lacks such an exemplary center, and that lack is one of the things that is wrong with *Zulu Dawn* (1979), the often incomprehensible film about the event. You should be able to view *Zulu Dawn* and *Zulu* in sequence and respond to both the defeat and the Pyrrhic triumph; the events happened only hours and a few miles apart. But, where *Zulu* is tight and suspenseful, *Zulu Dawn* is fragmented and unsure, and it comes off in the last analysis as a picture about nothing.

It opens magnificently—and, indeed, its cinematography is its greatest strength throughout. An opening sequence in Cetewayo's "royal kraal" suggests that we are in for a shared experience of the battle, both Zulu and British, with equal time given to the two sides. Both male and female impis dance and display: the camera looks down a seemingly endless line of black bodies.

But then the film gets serious and starts looking at the white folks. What could have been a work about the two sides and how both got to the field and how one suffered crushing defeat and the other triumph becomes, instead, a work about certain white individuals and, to some extent, how the white army got to Isandhlwana, and what happened to some of the white individuals there. But if you come to this film to learn anything about the reasons for defeat or the follies of war or how the British leader, too, may have been one of the great dumb-assed men of history, you are disappointed. *Zulu Dawn* sets out to be comprehensive and ends by being diffuse.

Stars are scattered like birdseed: Ken Gampu plays a Zulu messenger; Burt Lancaster is a one-armed, supposedly Irish colonel of some sort of mounted infantry; Peter O'Toole is Lord Chelmsford, leader of the expedition; John Mills is Sir Henry Bartle Frere, Commissioner of Natal; Simon Ward is somebody or other. By and large, they are names and little else; the characterization is on the level of those outdoor dramas that you can see on hot summer evenings in the United States. Men on horses gallop onscreen and off; the odd female— identifiable by her dress—says a few words; the camera devours landscape and pans across an army on the march. Some interesting history bits flicker by: a troop of black cavalry; a white officer lamenting the drowning of black transport workers; hundreds of black laborers pulling a raft loaded with white soldiers across a river; three blacks being tortured by the soldiers for information. Then everybody gets to Isandhlwana and things settle down to battle scenes and spectacle. The British Little Bighorn turns out to be meaningless, given importance only because of who lost.

You wonder why it was made—until you notice that it, like *Zulu*, was made with South African cooperation, and you ask yourself, Is there a pattern here? Are the South Africans trying to tell us something? A South African film released internationally, *Shangani Patrol* (1970), helps to answer these questions. Like *Zulu* and *Zulu Dawn*, it celebrates another lot of white martyrs to the black horde, this time during the trumped-up Matabele War, with which Rhodes grabbed western Rhodesia. You then recall that one of the great films of the first years of the South African industry was *Symbol of Sacrifice* (1918), a remarkably sophisticated work for its time that celebrated the same military agony as *Zulu* and *Zulu Dawn*. What we are in fact seeing here is the internationalizing of South Africa's national myth, by way of films that allowed Great Britain and the United States to bemoan the end of the old Africa. Keyan Tomaselli, who has written most penetratingly of this development, has suggested that the use of South African facilities by international producers (South African locations, South African technical facilities, and above all the South African Defence Force for battle scenes) opened such productions to implicit censorship, including SADF approval "at the script stage." It shows.

SOUTH AFRICAN INFLUENCE, however, has not been limited to great moments in military history; it has also been applied (again, largely through outside producers' use of the South African Defence Force) to a series of filmed thrillers in which a new archetype, the Mercenary, was glorified.

The thriller is a conservative form, often a reactionary one. A branch of melodrama, it partakes of melodrama's Manichaean view: us/them, good/bad, white/black. In the hands of a master like John LeCarré, it can capture the paranoia of an age like the Cold War, turning the reactionary morality back on itself; in lesser hands, however, the perception that corruption (i.e., spying, subversion) corrupts those who wield it becomes the sophomorically cynical "man is vile," and all morality gushes out through this hole. What is left is a Blimpish assumption that we are nonetheless right and they are nonetheless wrong—a bedrock that is particularly flinty when "we" are white and "they" are black, as in the African thrillers that followed independence.

The African Mercenary thrillers were special-mission plots. ("Your mission, if you accept it, is to. . . .") All took for their model those books and films that have posited a killer elite, perhaps based ultimately on Britain's SAS; all took as gospel the notion, popular among less thoughtful military people, that a handful of trained white soldiers could cut their way with ease through any nonwhite nation or army. All took for their hero the Mercenary, a soldier-emeritus of one of the great European armies: it is he, with a few carefully chosen colleagues, who will perform the mission, obliterate the black horde, and return to tell the tale. He will necessarily be cynical, proficient, sentimental (about children, whores, and comrades), and masculine.

On the face of it, the clichés of the thriller, even as strained through the Mercenary, would not seem to doom out of hand any attempt to make African films of them. In actuality, however, they produced motion pictures of an unrelieved mediocrity—and an unequaled racism.

Dark of the Sun (more frankly titled *The Mercenaries* in Britain) capitalized on the turmoil that wracked the former Belgian Congo between 1960 and 1966. The audience are not expected to know whether they are looking at the mess made by Moise Tshombe, Patrice Lumumba, Joseph Kasavubu, or General Mobutu; indeed, a "no names, please" policy puts the film into a convenient nonhistory that lets it exploit the Congolese situation without bothering to be responsible to it. All we know is that Rod Taylor is a white mercenary with a black sidekick (Jim Brown)—of course, the white is an officer and the black is a noncom—who has come to Congo to carry out a mission. The goal is to bring out a lot of diamonds that were mined "up north," presumably by a European company headed by the fat Belgian who gives Taylor his instructions. However, the mission is complicated by the necessity to get up north by train and then bring the train back loaded with both the diamonds and a lot of whites who are fleeing the country. (This scenario would seem to put the action in 1960-61, with Moise Tshombe as the president in whose palace this plan is hatched. Not a very savory environment.)

In the first reel, Taylor manages to put down a UN peacekeeper and a newspaperman with equal bursts of machismo: we are to understand that peacekeepers are wimps and newspeople are traitors. He then goes about signing on his band of killer elite, which is to include an ex-Nazi (Peter Carstens), an alcoholic doctor (Kenneth Moore), and one of those one-of-each groups already familiar to us from war movies. They board the train and head north, suffering air attacks, panic, and Yvette Mimieux, who climbs aboard with her clothes askew from a run-in with the dreaded "Simba," the Congolese version of Mau Mau. The ex-Nazi of course behaves very badly (he shoots two black children because they might tell the Simba about the mission; naturally, Taylor disapproves, because real soldiers don't shoot children, do they?). Jim Brown gives a little speech about why he doesn't hate whites. Taylor fistfights with the ex-Nazi, who uses a chain saw. They reach their destination, and white civilians mob the white mercenaries in a frenzy of gratitude—with not a black mercenary in the shot.

In order that nothing trite will be left unused, Moore's alcoholic doctor nobly volunteers to stay at a mission hospital, Simba or no Simba. Taylor lets him go, despite a scene only a reel or two back in which he said that a doctor was essential to the mission. The Simbas raid the mission hospital and do in the noble drunk, the nuns, and everybody else in the vicinity.

Taylor and friends take off on the train. The Simbas arrive—paint, feathers, the whole savage-horde stereotype—and, horror of horrors, the car carrying all those relieved white folks uncouples from Taylor's train and rolls right back into Simbaville. This potentially comic development is, of course, meant to inspire fear and loathing. (Rape! Torture! The horrors of Black Africa!) Then Taylor and Brown have to go back into town to get the diamonds (not the white folks; too late for that—scenes of black rapine and excess.)

Brown and Mimieux have a talk about Taylor and what a swell fellow he really is. Taylor and Brown have a talk about being a mercenary. "I'm a paid hand, and I'm doing a dirty job." The ex-Nazi gets fed up and murders Jim Brown with a bayonet (he wants those diamonds). Taylor is overcome and actually sobs; then, full of righteous indignation (*very* full—he has a noticeable paunch) he tears off after the bad Kraut. The ex-Nazi makes a raft and heads for the border; Taylor catches up, and the two fight. They hang on parallel vines over a gorge and bash at each other. They grunt and gasp. They fall in the water and have at each other. Taylor at last kills the bad man with Brown's bayonet, at which point a black mercenary appears and tells Taylor that he has reverted to savagery. Oh, right, Taylor seems to say, and gives himself up for court-martial for murder. Far too late, we have come to the end.

Cinematically, *Dark of the Sun* does its best work early, showing an authentic Africa of urban scenes, a countryside with roads and houses and electric poles, crops growing in fields instead of jungle. Visually, however, it chooses to go nowhere from there, neither to find beauty in this landscape nor to look for a different one. The real visual interest is in scenes of violence—the mass rape, the final fight between Taylor and the ex-Nazi, the Simbas' rampage—but the camera looks at these without originality. Otherwise, the film is often static, with talk scenes stuck in to tell us things we should understand from the action (Taylor's mercenary is a misunderstood hero; it is possible to be African and yet to fight on the white side; and so on).

The film's triteness weighs on it like chains. There is no reason for Mimieux's presence; she is an object and an agent (barely) and so uninterestingly conceived that her irrelevance announces itself. So, too, does the roster of the mercenaries (why not a sober doctor for a change, or a female doctor, or a homosexual doctor, or an elderly doctor?). So, too, does the tokenism of Brown's black sidekick, who we know will die before the film is out because he is a Good African. So, too, does the predictability of Carstens' ex-Nazi (why not a rotten ex-American GI? or an ex-SAS killer? or an ex-*pied noir*?) These transparent devices wrap around the characters and the action and pull them down, until, inert, they are merely the matrix for a meaningless sensationalism. That that sensationalism works at all is the result of its exploitation of white fears of black Africans.

Like other Mercenary movies to come, *Dark of the Sun* is constructed around a central conviction (white superiority) that it then cannot face. All the Mercenary films show some version of it. This one at least tries to resolve it (with the "reversion to savagery" of the protagonist).

THE WILD GEESE (1978) was a violent "mission" movie, but one with better than average actors (Richard Burton, Richard Harris, Stewart Granger) and no token females. Its credits boasted that its "military and technical advisor" was "Colonel Mike Hoare," a name on the label that, if you were an aficionado of the Mercenary, assured you of the genuineness of the contents. Presumably, Hoare kept his mouth shut about the age and physical condition of Burton and Harris, both of whom were too old for their roles and both of whom cause you to look away when they start to do anything as strenuous as trotting a few steps.

The Wild Geese begins with a map of Africa in flames; the flames become crowds, urban turmoil, troops. Need anybody go into further detail about whose notion of Africa we are dealing with here? Then Burton—"the colonel"—gets set up for his mission by a silver-haired, nasty old man named Matheson (Stewart Granger), and then he puts together his killer elite—Harris, Hardy Kruger, Roger

Moore, et al.—and then they all go off to train under a stereotypical sergeant-major. The training scenes are full of he-man, macho nonsense. The group is more varied than that in *Dark of the Sun*, including a homosexual and a South African who likes blacks (Kruger). Diversity can go only so far, however: when they line up to start the mission, forty-nine of the fifty have white faces.

The actual mission takes up the final two-thirds of the film and is mostly about annihilating black Africans in large numbers. The killing begins with four black soldiers, three killed with cyanide darts and one with a knife; it then escalates remarkably as two hundred are killed with cyanide gas as they sleep. Then a Cuban; then six more Africans, with machine pistols; then two more, with silenced pistols; then twenty or so, with a grenade and automatic rifle fire; then one more Cuban, with a pistol. The killing takes a short recess while Kruger and a black politician have a discussion about blacks and whites and Africa—"We have to forgive you for the past, and you have to forgive us for the present; if we have no future together, white man, we have no future"—and then back to it, with another dozen or so done in with machine pistols, and then (revenge for the panga killing of a nice white medic) thirty or so Africans with more grenades and more machine pistols. Most of the white mercenaries run right through opposing fire as if the blacks are shooting jelly beans.

Then there is a final rush for a getaway plane, after some to-ing and fro-ing about having been betrayed, and poor Burton is huffing and puffing to get there and get aboard, with pursuing Africans dropping literally by the score. The plane taxis; Richard Harris tries to get aboard, can't quite make it, and Burton shoots him so that he won't suffer a fate worse than death. Then Burton shows up in London again and does in Matheson (Granger) for the betrayal: the mission was one of those thriller clichés, the switcheroo from which nobody was supposed to come back alive.

At bottom, *The Wild Geese* is a film about racial revenge: show as many black deaths as possible. Another level up, it is, unintentionally, about the built-in contradictions of The Mercenary Way: if you kill for money, you have no business objecting if somebody betrays you for money; or, on the other hand, if you think you are a band of brothers bound by machismo and love of danger, why are you racists? At its surface level, it was so full of contradictions that it wasn't about anything at all.

Richard Burton was once an actor too good for this sort of thing. Still, he had a perfect right to piss his talent away as he chose—and he chose *The Wild Geese*. Little acting was required or delivered; the characters were thin, the actions strong (run for your life), the superobjectives more than a little murky. Take the money and run was probably the strongest (and what's a little white supremacy between friends?).

* * *

THE DOGS OF WAR (1980) at times looks like a remake of *The Wild Geese*—same Mercenary training, same untrustworthy white man who gives the mission, same mindless carnage visited on black men. In Christopher Walken, it has a younger but far less interesting leader; you don't wince when he runs, but you do wonder if spare parts may drop off, Walken's rigid face and manner suggesting something put together in the lab. (This is fitting, as the movie has the same feeling of being put together from this and that—a little Carré, a bit of Peckinpah, a lot of *Wild Geese*.) The country is called Zingara, its dictator Kimba; its officials are presented as universally dreadful, as Walken learns on a recon trip when he is cheated, insulted, arrested, beaten, and humiliated. Worst of all, they are *uppity*, behaving as if Zingara is their country. The final third of the film offers high explosives and low drama, with the only really pleasant moment coming when one of the white mercenaries bursts into a hut and finds a black woman crouching with a child; he turns away, and she raises a pistol and shoots him in the back. You want to cheer. At the end, Walken and the other good whites install a new president—not the one that their mission was supposed to install, but a Good African whom Walken met in prison. Take that, uppity black men—now you see whose country it really is.

Pauline Kael said of *The Dogs of War* that it was "a swift and intelligent demonstration of how the conventions of action movies can be adapted and given new meaning." True, it has its swift passages (although it has some painfully slow ones, too). Intelligence and meaning, however, seem to have been in the eye of the beholder. *The Dogs of War*, like its protagonist, is robotic. Like *The Wild Geese*, it dare not think, in fact, lest it discover what it is.

After this (*The Dogs of War* being, in 1980, already an anachronism), the Mercenary should have faded from movie myth, his stock falling as it did in the real world; a bunch of real-life mercenaries, for example, made the evening news for an adventure in the Seychelles that was more hilarious than heroic, and *Soldier of Fortune* magazine turned The Mercenary Way into a kind of comic-book fantasy. However, South Africa, unable to laugh at a number of things the rest of the world finds risible, continued to exploit the archetype for its own purposes; those films (of the 1980s) will be discussed in the next chapter.

THE HISTORICAL PROBABILITY is that the white mercenaries who went into Congo and other new, black countries, really were white racists; indeed, the aspects of the Mercenary myth that persist in American pop culture suggest that it is still racist there. By the time that *Dark of the Sun* was made, however, unalloyed racism would no longer sell lots of tickets (outside South Africa), and so several of these films have a racial corrective built into them along with their core racism—Jim Brown in *Dark of the Sun*, Kruger's character and the Good African in *The Wild Geese*, the good politician in *The Dogs of War*. These tokens were not enough, however, and the films' makers apparently knew it; consciously or otherwise, the makers often relied on the turnabout trickery of the thriller to undercut both the racist mission and the people carrying it out. The effect in each case was to make not only the Mercenary but also his Africa immoral. *We are all bad*, these films seem to say, thus asking to be forgiven for universal failings. Yet the films' characterizations will not allow all men to be vile: Burton's colonel asks to be seen as a noble sufferer when he "has to" kill his friend; Walken's Mercenary asks to be seen as politically idealistic when he puts the Good African into office. Thus, these films want it both ways—they want an easy cynicism that will let them slip the noose of an obvious racism, but they want in their hearts to celebrate white superiority. If we doubt that they want to celebrate it, we should ask Pauline Kael's question: "A reasonably accurate test of whether an action movie is racist: Do the white heroes slaughter people of color in quantity, either affectlessly or triumphantly?"

Obviously, the answer in the Mercenary movies is Yes. As surely as they place black carnage at their climaxes, they are racist, and they fail as coherent movies precisely because they cannot face this in themselves.

11 FREEDOM *NOW!*

I t could not have been apparent in 1970 that South Africa would become both a dominant subject and a dominant player in international film. Rather, several Africas would have been seen to exist simultaneously, treated in very different ways, with South Africa merely one among a cluster. However, a settling-out was going on at the end of the 1960s, suggesting a partial adjustment to the realities of a mostly decolonized Africa: the Helper films ended (*Living Free*, 1972); the last regressive comedy was made (*Carry On Up the Jungle*, 1970); the last nonfiction film appeared (*The African Elephant*, 1971). A partial vacuum seems to have followed: the 1970s saw the number of films about Africa plummet. Only fifteen fiction films were made (compared to at least thirty in the 1960s). That vaccum was gradually filled with two different approaches to Africa: one that would treat some version of its present, often violently (the subject of this chapter); and another that would treat its colonial past, more often than not with nostalgia, occasionally as camp (the subject of the next chapter). South Africa would figure prominently in both.

Films about the present ran right on from the 1960s, carrying with them, in good part because of their increasing interest in South Africa, violence. They rejected most of the approaches already tried but held tight to the thriller and the Mercenary. Extreme black-white violence also characterized a number of other films of contemporary subject, in good part because they dealt with some form of terrorism. As already discussed, such films were expressions of racial fear and racial hatred, and they were not about to go away while a national government at the tip of the continent condoned racism and violence—and had its oar in film production.

Several films began to take a pro-black stance as early as the 1970s, however, without dealing with South Africa and apartheid. Thus, slavery was rediscovered as a subject—although skeptical blacks would say that little courage was needed in condemning an evil that no longer touched European culture. There was, nonetheless, an inevitable movement toward overt attacks on apartheid, first outside South Africa, and finally inside South African film itself.

RICHARD ROUNDTREE BROUGHT his black exploitation character, Shaft, to Africa in *Shaft in Africa* (1973), thus extending his range but not really doing anything for portrayals of black Africans. Shaft was still American, still violent, still the aggressive cocksman; Africa, the film suggested, was only a convenient background. Shaft is there to break—what else?—the slave trade. Vonetta McGee, as an emir's daughter, is a beautiful sex object who gives up virginity and a clitoridectomy (and thus her culture) to be made love to by Shaft. A bad white woman also has to have him (you know she's bad because she engages in kinky sex, but also because she's white). Bad white men reveal their badness by killing Shaft's dog. And so on. Shaft kills at least twelve men with his hands, a gun, a crowbar thrown like a spear, and who knows what all. He is, as they say, ba-a-a-d. The movie was filmed in Ethiopia and had some splendid location work and authentic language, for once (although where Shaft learned Amharic remained a mystery), but, like most other thrillers, it never rose above its genre (or tried to, for that matter). However, in making a new equation—black equals good, white equals bad—it may have accomplished a necessary purging of outdated values: the irresolution of *Dingaka* and *Something of Value* had turned into a knee-jerk ethos of black goodness. For black men, that is; for black women, nothing really had changed.

Roundtree was in Africa again in *A Game for Vultures* (1978), which had an impressive cast: Richard Harris, Roundtree, Ray Milland, Denholm Elliott, Ken Gampu, Tony Osoba. (And, not so impressive, Joan Collins.) Its setting, the Rhodesian civil war, before Zimbabwe came into being, was a perfectly respectable one for an action thriller that offered predictable but workable niches for Dangerous Africans. However, the plot was so tormented that it became impossible to keep it straight: Dave Swansey (Harris) has a new sister-in-law whose brother (got that?) is a mixed-race terrorist (or rebel, depending on your point of view); Ken Gampu is a (different) terrorist/rebel who shoots a storekeeper because the storekeeper sold his men a booby-trapped radio because they had raped the storekeeper's daughter. (Got that?) Roundtree is a terrorist/rebel who goes to London to queer a deal that Harris has made to buy American helicopters illegally from Ray Milland, who kills himself because his company's sanction-violating is going to be made public, while Harris's sister-in-law's brother escapes from prison and disappears, but reappears to murder his sister, although back in London a U.S. embassy official's black mistress (Alibe Parsons) is giving secrets—and sex—to Roundtree. However, the helicopters are brought by air to Southwest Africa (Namibia), where the South Africans let Harris in to fly them to Rhodesia, but Roundtree and Gampu are there, too. After much carnage (during which Harris kills Gampu), Harris and Roundtree end up in the Rhodesian bush again with each in the other's gunsights.

While this much complexity may have worked in a novel, it certainly doesn't work in a film, the more so when the film's real interest is in raw sensation, really of only two kinds, sex and violence. Harris seems too old for both (he and Collins appear to be making an instructional video, "Sex Fun for the Aging") but he is an actor who always has a tremendous urgency—he is apparently able to invent objectives for himself when patently none exist—and thus he often makes the movie seem more coherent than in fact it is. Roundtree, the film's black parallel to Harris, also has an obligatory sex scene that recalls his stud status as Shaft. This parallel structure (the white and black plot lines develop in alternation) creates a separate-but-equal, black-white movie that was meant to suggest, perhaps, the segregations of Rhodesia itself.

Analysis of other nonwhite characters, however, suggests that the film is more racist than the Harris-Roundtree parallelism suggests. The unsegregated Denny is made to seem monstrous because he is both black *and* white, and his monstrous behavior is symbolic of racial mixing; he recalls the albino black villain of the South African *Whispering Death* (1971). Gampu's Killer African also approaches the monstrous, so that Harris's killing of him seems to be an almost allegorical killing of black violence. This was another movie made with the cooperation of the South African Defence Force, and so its killing of blacks, its fear of racial mixing, and above all its paranoid hatred of black terrorists, are its real meanings.

The only black woman to find an African role of any importance in the 1970s was Beverly Johnson, in the idiotically titled *Ashanti, Land of No Mercy* (1979). Cast as Michael Caine's wife, she seemed about to create a new female African; however, she hardly got a chance to do more than take her clothes off and walk into the ocean before she was kidnapped by—who else?—Arab slavers, and the script thrust her back into the stereotype of the suffering female slave. The rest of the picture was about Caine's pursuit of her captors, with Peter Ustinov trotting out a schtick version of an oily Arab, and Omar Sharif getting away from the bridge table long enough to be a bad Arab prince, or something. The film, which seemed to promise so much, repeatedly withdrew into genre (the pursuit thriller) to solve its problems and so was inconsequential.

QUITE DIFFERENT, BLITHELY escapist, and very successful, were three comedies— two farces set in the Kalahari desert that nevertheless managed to attract charges of racism, and one set in an Africa more fantastic than Haggard's that nevertheless escaped such charges. The first two, by Jamie Uys, looked backward at the Noble Savage; the other, by the American pop-culture star Eddie Murphy, created a postmodern black myth of Africa.

For many audiences, the two small comedies from the same director who had made *Dingaka* seemed to free them from both old-fashioned racism and newly fashionable guilt. *The Gods Must Be Crazy* and *The Gods Must Be Crazy II* followed a Kalahari Bushman through a series of comic encounters with the greater world; audiences have delighted in them, although serious critics have laid down a political line that condemns them as racist. Part of this charge comes because of Uys (his "sly artistry makes a comic mockery of Africa in defence [sic] of apartheid"); part of it comes because the films have South African origins; and part of it comes because of perceived racism in the colonial gaze that Uys turns on his Bushman hero. Some critics have gone to extremes of nit-picking—complaining, for example, that the first of the two films shows blacks and whites working amicably together in an office. The location of that office, however, is apparently in the capital of the major Kalahari nation, Botswana, an avowedly multiracial society; what would these critics have?

Some have complained that the films mock the Bushman; to the contrary, however, the real fools in both films are whites, and in one a particularly foolish Land Rover. And black Africans can hardly win medals for their own treatment of the Bushmen, who have been often treated with contempt and sometimes enslaved, as by the Herero of Namibia, not to mention their treatment by the black cattlemen of Botswana.

If the *Gods* movies are racist, then, they are so in ways that are not today important (for example, reviving the archetype of the Noble Savage, turning the camera on him); what is more significant about them is their air of cheerfulness and immense good humor, and their complete rejection of such filmic stereotypes as jungle, savagery, savage dancing, and witchcraft. For Jamie Uys, at the very least, they represent a quantum leap from the stereotypes of *Dingaka.*

Coming to America was a 1987 vehicle for the American television star Eddie Murphy. Murphy produced it; presumably, therefore, it is the product of a black, not a white sensibility, and its creation of a new African myth is therefore the more remarkable.

Coming to America begins with a long pan over a green "Africa" that is all unpeopled forest. There are no cities, no slums, no townships. In the distance, a fairytale palace appears, something out of the Emerald City by way of Disneyland. This is the home of a black king and his son—Murphy. Here he lives in unending luxury, as defined by display, physical comfort, and indulgence, much of it represented as realizations of adolescent sex fantasies: a pneumatic young black woman surfaces, sponge in hand, in Murphy's pool-sized bathtub and says to him, "The royal penis is clean, your majesty." Much of the rest is represented by high-level consumerism—clothes, decor, glitter.

This postmodern Africa has no savagery. Blacks wear business suits and polo clothes, unless they are women, in which case they wear Las Vegas showgirl costumes. The bare breasts of the old nonfiction films and the *National Geographic* are here uplifted to leitmotif, the bigger the better. The only animals are tame elephants, zebras, and giraffes that wander through the palace gardens.

The dangerous animals seem all to be dead, their skins worn as costume accessories by the royal family, including James Earl Jones as the king.

This civilized and jejunely glamorous (or tacky; take your pick) Africa does not satisfy Murphy's prince, however. Like an American teenager, he is obsessed with "love" and choice: he wants to pick his own bride. Africa's women are too servile. (In fact, they recall the blacks of old movies, being barely visible, "curiously unintelligent menials.") Taking with him a sidekick (Arsenio Hall) and traveling incognito, he flies to New York, commits some comic princely blunders, and finds the girl of his dreams. Thereafter, the movie has to do with that time-honored plot, hiding one's wealth from the object of love. It becomes straight television sitcom, even to its settings and its faces, most of them familiar from the American tube.

Coming to America is finally a movie about the delights of consumer culture. It is all surface. Its world of reference is American television, except when it is male adolescent sex fantasy (which may, in fact, be the same as American television). Because of some obvious similarities, however, it demands to be compared with Robeson's African films. For example, it moves in precisely the opposite direction from Robeson's films, which moved from interiors (the docker's flat, Sandy's office, Jericho's ship) to African exteriors, often with Robeson posed heroically against the sky to sing. *Coming to America* begins with a panoramic "Africa" and focuses down to New York streets and then down to the overdecorated but lifeless interiors of television shows. Robeson's films seemed to say that the black man's problem was to break out of the world where he was defined by whites and to find his Africa; *Coming to America* says that the black man's problem is to find Miss Right and own a lot of things. Robeson's black man went to Africa to find "our people" and position; Murphy's black man leaves Africa to find love and style. Robeson's docker went to Africa to claim kingship; Murphy's prince goes to America to work in a fast food joint.

The comparative triviality of the Murphy text—a television script masquerading as a major movie—underscores these differences. The trivialization of "Africa," a plastic setting, is a setup for the "reality" of the movie's America. The difference marks a shift from Robeson's concern with white hegemony to Murphy's concern with materialist hegemony: Robeson was black in a white world, Murphy is rich in a consumerist world.

Coming to America is disturbing for two reasons. One is its reduction of women to functions—sex object, mother object, love object. The other is the elevation of materialism to the status of dominant culture, even of ethos. *Coming to America* is a supremely selfish film, one in which mere self-indulgence ("freedom of choice") is given status above such formerly important cultural and ethical matters as nationality and history. Its rejection of Africa is dazzling, the more so because Murphy is "African American." If a white producer-star had made a film in which Africa was stripped of its people, its cities, and its contemporary concerns; in which its animals were reduced to stuffed toys and its women to prostitutes; and in which the landscape was exploited as a false comparison to make another place look good, we would say the film was racist. (This last is precisely a charge laid against the *Gods* movies.) Presumably, we cannot say this of Eddie Murphy. Certainly, those scholars who have found Jamie Uys to be racist have not found Murphy so.

We can say, at least, that a new African black archetype has been created, the Selfish Escapist. It is a marked change from all the others, most notably from Robeson's, and not necessarily in a promising direction.

BY CONTRAST, *GORILLAS IN THE MIST* (1988) put a woman at its center and an endangered animal squarely in its viewfinder. This film about Diane Fossey, a real woman who spent years with the mountain gorillas of Zaire-Rwanda and was murdered for her work, is so different from the helping films of the 1950s that it seems to have been made on another planet. Sigourney Weaver, an actress often at her best playing loners, is compelling as an obsessive, angry Fossey. Only the fact that she is white suggests racial causes for her diatribes against the local poachers and their allies. Nothing in her or the film suggests that she is "only a woman" or less than competent; like Kathlyn Williams three-quarters of a century earlier, she radiates competence. Nor does the film make the mistake of *The Roots of Heaven*; its animals are shown with such heart-breaking poignancy—a gorilla hand, cupped in death, about to be severed to be turned into an ashtray—that they take on importance without being anthropomorphised. The creation of a mystical beast is achieved here (as it was not in *The Roots of Heaven*), so that even the sentimentality of the film's end—Fossey's grave joined to that of the gorilla Digit by a line of stones where their hands would grasp each other—is acceptable. Where *Gorillas in the Mist* falters is probably where Fossey herself was cold and unsympathetic, a woman perhaps emotionally crippled, irrational to the point of pathology about her mystical beasts, with the result that Weaver loses sympathy about where Fossey herself did. There is some marvelous footage of gorillas and their habitat, a visual correlative for Fossey's addiction to the beasts and the continent.

AS SOUTH AFRICA increasingly surfaced in the world's news after 1970, it inevitably became a subject of film. Both inside and outside South Africa, however, commercial film was at first timid about attacking apartheid head-on, choosing instead the end run of genre. Nonetheless, for the first time since *Cry, the Beloved Country* and *Come Back, Africa*, films treated official South African policy as wrong, even evil. These films were at first non-South African.

Michael Caine was on view in the first antiapartheid film of the period, *The Wilby Conspiracy* (1974), this time with Sidney Poitier as a South African opposition figure on the run. Both Caine and Poitier looked as if they were on automatic pilot, as well they should have been, the plot being one of those fake-cynical 1970s tangles that had everybody screwing everybody else, with only Nicoll Williamson as a very bad baddie seeming to put his guts into it. His performance would have done for an evil Nazi in one of the 1940s serials and was thus an interesting reversal, as well as a new white archetype, the White Torturer: he was evil *because* he was a white South African security cop. Poitier's character was good because he was black and pro-ANC. Needless to say, this was *not* a South African film or one in which the SADF played a part. Not a bad chase film, it is now worth seeing as an early, non-South African critique of apartheid. Its technique of using a genre to criticize would later prove useful to South African filmmakers.

Richard Attenborough's *Cry Freedom* (1987), an antiapartheid picture about the black activist Steve Biko, was another film about South Africa that was made beyond its borders. It elevated the Dangerous African to the level of African Martyr. More pious than serious, the picture stood on the ethical platform already occupied by most of the world's leadership (it came long after sanctions and long after "Free Nelson Mandela" T-shirts were being worn on white torsos everywhere), and, by concentrating more on white Donald Woods than on Biko (Denzel Washington), rather patted itself on its white back. Nonetheless, *Cry Freedom* is a significant film, an advance from *The Wilby Conspiracy* (although hardly so important as *Cry, the Beloved Country**).

However, *Cry Freedom*'s release did not celebrate the triumph of anti-apartheid films or the disappearance of pro-regime product. The Mercenary archetype was wound up again in the very same year by South African producers, and *Skeleton Coast* (1987) proved to be the worst of the genre—maybe the worst movie ever made about Africa, no more worth discussing than are the video games it imitates. Lacking even the shrewdness to suspect its own motives, it is a "jeep opera"—a mechanical exercise in violence against Africans, without even the contradictions that, in the other Mercenary films, suggest an awareness of where that violence is leading. Its enthusiasm for a Jonas Savimbi lookalike and its Namibian locations show its indebtedness to the SADF. *Mercenary Fighters*

---

* Attenborough also produced the similarly worshipful *Gandhi* in 1982. Although only a small part of the film concerns Africa, *Gandhi* stands alone for its serious (if brief) concern with the Indian community of South Africa.

(1988) and *Red Scorpion* (1989) came from the same impulse, the latter film exporting the remarkable South African view that the people really oppressing African blacks are foreign communists.

Another powerful critique of apartheid came from outside South Africa, however, in 1989. MGM's *A Dry White Season* had impeccable credentials: adapted from a novel by Andre Brink, it starred Donald Sutherland and Marlon Brando and featured such important South African actors as Winston Ntshona and John Kani. Dealing directly with Afrikaner culture, it challenged that culture's complete dependence on a police state for its existence.

The picture is unrelenting. Sutherland plays Du Toit, a white South African history teacher whose black gardener's child is brutalized by the police after a demonstration. At first dismissing the incident and advising the gardener to "let it go," Du Toit is drawn in by his own conscience as, first, the child disappears and is then reported dead, and the father is arrested. Against the strong desires of his family, Du Toit appeals to the police, then goes to court when the black gardener "commits suicide" in prison.

The courtroom sequence is a hinge upon which the film swings: before, Du Toit is tentative and trusts in "justice"; after, he trusts nothing and seeks publication of the truth. He has become an example of a new white archetype, the Awakened White—the white who learns what South Africa is really like. Brando's cameo role as a cynical attorney is pivotal, and his scenes need this great personality's presence: fat, slow, ironic, he impales the justice system's corruption on its own pretensions. Brando then disappears from the movie, his work done: justice and law, as he tells Du Toit, are "not on speaking terms" in South Africa.

The film careens to an inevitable and heartless end: Du Toit's Afrikaner wife leaves him, calling him "an Afrikaner traitor"; his pretty, grown-up daughter betrays him to the security police. (Her defense is that "I just want everything back to normal.") Only his young son and a black activist remain, and with them he gets the truth to a liberal newspaper before himself being murdered by a policeman (another White Torturer, the torture scenes themselves shocking).

This bleak tale is rather flatly photographed but superbly acted and directed in a straightforward realism. The picture does its work by personalizing the unbearable South African dilemma: true to its vision, it destroys its hero, although that destruction probably does not go down well with audiences. It also uses (perhaps unconsciously) what has become the cinematic iconography of apartheid: the walled, green gardens of the white suburbs; the dusty clutter of the townships; the motorized violence of the police; the teaching of Afrikaner history to children, scenes of which recur in these films like the probing of a sore tooth; torture. The film is worth seeing, if only for Sutherland's or Brando's performance; in fact it offers far more. Thanks to Brink's novel, this is not merely safe and fashionable liberalism; it is brutal, brilliant social dissection, a great advance on *Cry Freedom* and light years beyond *The Wilby Conspiracy*.

AS REAL-WORLD HISTORY belatedly caught up with South Africa in the late 1980s, South African film was finally able to create products that were not themselves agents (sometimes unconscious, even unwilling) of apartheid. A real breakthrough came with *Mapantsula* (1988), which used the gangster genre to show the life of Soweto's streets and the police state that surrounds them. Focusing on black characters who spoke a polyglot street slang, it self-selected an audience outside the American-European mainstream; its simple story of a petty thug who learns to sacrifice himself for a cause is reminiscent of De Sica's *Generale Della Rovere*.

As even members of South Africa's National Party began to question apartheid, English-language South African motion pictures also began to do so. The speed with which they picked up the cue suggests that filmmakers had been waiting for the moment—on the evidence of *City of Blood* (1987) and *Sarafina* (1992), none more than director Darrell Roodt and producer Anant Singh. (Their *Place of Weeping* [1986] had already dealt with racial injustice and had had a black woman at its center.)

City of Blood is a bizarre, disturbing film that looks as if it might have been made in Eastern Europe under communism. It has no "real" or "normal" life: *everything* in this film is weird. It is generically a horror film, partly a police procedural, but its strange visuals and selective sound transcend genre to become expressionism: this is a film about a society of horrors.

Henderson (Joe Stewardson) is a depressed forensic pathologist for the city of Johannesburg. He has nightmares that parallel a series of brutal murders of prostitutes. The women flee through grungy night-time streets, down concrete stairs, through urban cellars, to be murdered by half-naked black figures wearing ritual masks and wielding a five-pronged war club. A black power symbol is drawn on a wall with blood. The pathologist, his sanity crumbling, dreams even when awake: his estranged wife appears and disappears, and he talks to her. "Things aren't what they used to be," he says to this phantom. "Murders aren't the same."

The present becomes unbearable for him when the security police ask him to sign a blank death certificate. He demands an explanation, is told only it is "a matter of national security." As the prostitute murders continue, he is drawn into this other labyrinth of crime: the president himself asks that he sign the death certificate, which is to be for "Makena" (a Nelson Mandela figure), who has been beaten to death in prison. (This was before the real Mandela was

The British films of Paul Robeson pioneered a new idea of Africa and black humanity, as in his *Song of Freedom*—Robeson with Elizabeth Welch, 1936. *(Photo from British Film Institute Stills, Posters and Designs.)*

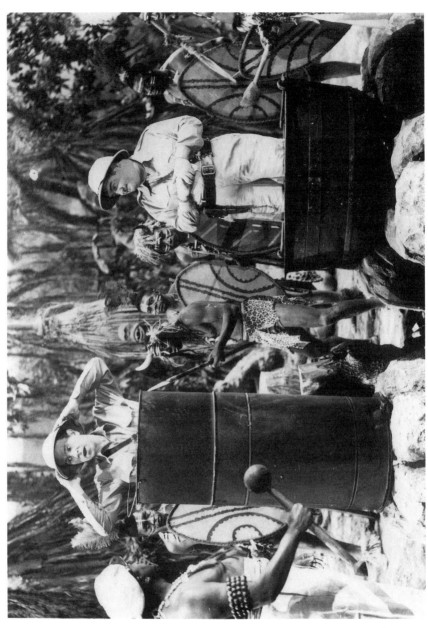

What was funny about Africa in 1949 never got beyond what had been funny in 1880, so even Abbott and Costello replayed the old imagery of cannibalism, animal skins, and jungle. *Africa Screams. (Photo from the Library of Congress.)*

Cry, the Beloved Country brought together several huge talents, including director Zoltan Korda, writer Alan Paton, and (shown here) actors Sidney Poitier and Canada Lee, with the result that it may be the best non-African film ever made about Africa. *(Courtesy Lumiere Pictures Limited; photo from British Film Institute Stills, Posters and Designs.)*

Sidney Poitier's charisma shattered old stereotypes, and, in *Something of Value* (1957), brought star quality to a new and dangerous African. (Right, Rock Hudson) *(© 1957 Turner Entertainment Co. All Rights Reserved.)*

Strong women were rare in African films, but Kathlyn Williams was an outstanding example in Selig silents like *Lost in the Jungle*, 1911. *(Photo courtesy Library of Congress.)*

Anthony Steel was a new colonial man as colonialism was ending, and director Harry Watt tried to confront new realities with him in *Where No Vultures Fly*, but they were too late (1951). *(Courtesy Lumiere Pictures Limited; photo from British Film Institute Stills, Posters and Designs.)*

In movies as in life, one answer to the end of colonialism was mercenary violence—
Yvette Mimeux, Rod Taylor, and Jim Brown in *Dark of the Sun*, 1968. *(© 1967
Turner Entertainment Co. All Rights Reserved.)*

The Tarzan tale
deserved to be told
from Jane's point of
view, and it was—in
Tarzan, the Apeman,
with Miles O'Keefe
and Bo Derek.
*(© 1981 Turner
Entertainment Co. All
Rights Reserved.)*

It may not look it here, but the new black hero was a lot more dangerous than the lion: Richard Roundtree in *Shaft in Africa*, 1973. *(© 1973 Turner Entertainment Co. All Rights Reserved.)*

A surprise from South Africa: the cheerful, cheeky comedy of *The Gods Must Be Crazy* and (here) its sequel, *The Gods Must Be Crazy II*, 1988. *(Courtesy of Elrina Investment Corp. and Mimosa Films.)*

Lush romance, nostalgia as history, and Africa for Baby Boomers: Meryl Streep and Robert Redford in *Out of Africa* (1985). *(Copyright © by Universal City Studios, Inc. Courtesy of MCA Publishing Rights, a Division of MCA Inc.)*

Clint Eastwood as an American not directing a movie about Africa, and Boy Mathias Chuma as the African he admires, in *White Hunter, Black Heart* (1990). *(White Hunter, Black Heart © 1990 Warner Bros. Inc. All rights reserved.)*

released.) If he does not certify that Makena died of heart failure, the nation will be plunged into bloodshed, he is told.

But he knows that it is already plunged into bloodshed. He refers to South African society as "this shithouse." He knows that the police are being misused. "Take some people off these idiot riot squads," he tells a fellow cop; "Stop arresting children and priests." He says to the White Torturers of the security police, "You're what's wrong with this country."

We know, from footage that begins the film, that the prostitute murders replicate others done two thousand years before, with the same clubs by the same kind of masked figures, although then they were black male on black male. The pathologist understands the connection when an ancient skull is found with the telltale mark of the club; he then traces it back to a tribal area and learns the truth from a dying shaman. "The past is creeping into the city."

The two lines of story come together when the pathologist is chased by the masked figures; instead of killing him, they take him to a nondescript urban spot where he finds a shaven-headed Ken Gampu looming over him. Gampu wears a suit and tie and sounds more urbane and civilized than anybody else in the film—yet it is he who directs the horror killings. "But you can't just kill people!" the pathologist screams at him. Then, both he and Gampu seem to understand the irony of what he has said: if the whites can, why can't the blacks? The pathologist at last signs the phony death certificate and then kills himself.

This bleak and perhaps unpromising story yields remarkable results. The horror line is full of holes: the scary stuff is too pat, the solving of the puzzle too easy, the shaman too confiding. What makes the film work is its intelligence—in acting, script, and cinematography. Joe Stewardson's pathologist is masterful: depression, age, and despair are beautifully conveyed. Susan Coetzer's prostitute is eerie, emotionless but compelling, like somebody from an Antonioni film. The dialogue is tight and lean, never condescending to its own genre. The visuals turn Johannesburg into an expressionist nightmare: gone is the sunlit capital of modern consumerism; in its place is a gritty, unyielding, angled place of pimps, hookers, trash. Interiors are sometimes elegant but somehow wrong: the pathologist's house has almost no furniture, the few pieces pure white; a couch in a lobby at police headquarters becomes odd because looked at head-on, symmetrically framed, with a lone figure bang at the center. This may not be the way we dream, but this is the clutch of conventions that we recognize as an equivalent of dreaming.

It is wrong to say that the film is allegory. However, it is meaning-heavy: the pathologist has South Africa for his patient; the pathology he finds is social and spiritual. This city without normality is *all* pathology, the film tells us; only a nightmare will diagnose it. And, when its pathology is understood, the only cure is suicide.

It is too bad that *City of Blood* had to fall back on African witchcraft as an image for black retribution; it calls up the wrong associations, as in *Dingaka*. Nonetheless, this does allow the film to insist on the wrongness of the Afrikaner idea that nobody lived in southern Africa before the whites came. You cannot understand the plot unless you accept the premise that black Africans lived there thousands of years ago, and that the pathology is not theirs (i.e., the film contradicts Afrikaner history).

Parts of the film are hard, perhaps impossible, to decipher. I was unsure about the distinction between nightmare and "reality" toward the end; perhaps the confusion was deliberate. The style may seem mannered. The horror plot is shaky. But the overall film is compelling: flawed, it is nonetheless an important South African motion picture made on the cusp of historic change.

Sarafina, the 1992 film also directed by Darrell Roodt, saw the anti-apartheid South African film come to maturity. Made from Mbongeni Ngema's play, it is a straightforward attack on apartheid that combines the Strong Woman with the Dangerous African, creating an archetype—the Strong Black Woman—already seen in Roodt's *Place of Weeping*. The result was a picture that showed its rebelliousness in its recycling of aspects of apartheid South Africa: the casting of a black, female international star (Whoopi Goldberg) instead of a white male action hero; the casting of Miriam Makeba as a mother, an almost symbolic reference to her role in the 1959 *Come Back, Africa*; the use of subject matter and form derived from the black stage musical originated by Gibson Kente; and the use of indigenous music and dance, including the athletic, calisthenic laborers' dances from films like *Song of Africa*. The result was a strong, deeply painful film of passionate statement.

Sarafina is a Soweto schoolgirl, Goldberg's character her history teacher. The film begins with the fire-bombing of a schoolroom, then is briefly idyllic as the schoolgirl fantasizes (she talks to a picture of Nelson Mandela, still in prison), then begins an escalation toward torture and death. The teacher disappears in the middle of the film, taken by the ever-present white police/White Torturers; toward the picture's end, Sarafina is told she has committed suicide by jumping from the tenth floor of the prison. Sarafina herself has been imprisoned after being caught up in a riot, then again in the burning-alive of a hated black constable. At the picture's end, looking older, wrung out by torture, yet gaining strength, she throws away an AK-47 she has been hiding. Goldberg's voice comes back to her: "I cannot kill. . . . I want to come home to kindness."

This is a film about women—strong women. For all its violence, it is often a film with great gaiety; it is a musical, and its songs and dances have the vigor of southern African group singing and dancing. The first musical number is a fantasy in which Sarafina sees herself as a "star," wittily shown as if it were produced by the kids in her school themselves, so that the full-size convertible in which she rides is made of wire, like African street toys. The number is really too happy, too glitzy; I think it is a sendup of those overproduced white musicals like *Oliver*, thus both an example of Sarafina's fantasizing and a demonstration of the stranglehold of white culture. Later musical numbers are more African, often somber, especially a funeral for children gunned down in a schoolyard riot.

The females of Soweto are at the film's center and give it its style. The men of the film are mostly peripheral, except for the white police. The police raids, often at night, have a sci-fi quality because of the harsh lighting, the armor plating of the vehicles, the weapons; it contrasts with the daytime realism of Sarafina's Soweto. Black men are often seen in long shots or group shots; the white police—especially Sarafina's interrogator and torturer—are in medium or close-up shots. The only white women (and children) are Sarafina's mother's employers, never seen in close-up; they are truly peripheral, coiffed and well-dressed blonds always playing at something in a white suburban garden, protected by gates, walls, police, apartheid—the inescapable iconography of contemporary South Africa.

"The boys, they can fight—what can I do?" This question, Sarafina to the Goldberg character, is the film's heart. It is never answered literally, except by the throwing away of the gun and her embracing of her mother, whom she had earlier rejected because she spent her life as a servant. It is answered symbolically, however, by the example of the Goldberg character, who suffers but cannot kill, who teaches truth, who waits and hopes and works for freedom. And it is answered by the musical finale, another fantasy in which Sarafina *is* Nelson Mandela, released from prison, singing of freedom.

Leleti Khumalo is a beautiful and effective Sarafina. Goldberg, despite leaving the film in the middle, makes a huge contribution, an authoritative woman who is tender, thoughtful, passionate; it is with her that Khumalo's best emotional scenes are played. Miriam Makeba is far less effective, almost wooden; yet her presence alone is important in this referential film.

Sarafina and *City of Blood* and *Mapantsula* brought South African film right smack into the last decade of the twentieth century. They were African in the best sense. British and American audiences will probably not recognize their movie Africa in them, and so may think them inaccurate or melodramatic. I would say that they are both inaccurate and melodramatic, except that recent South African history is itself so much more overdrawn, with its killings and burnings, its government-sponsored murder and its anarchy, that the films actually approach reportage.

12 SIGHING FOR YESTERDAY _____

The nineteen-eighties were politicized decades in all three countries producing English-language films about Africa—Reaganism and Thatcherism in the United States and Britain, the Nationalist-ANC battle in South Africa. Recent films about the African present are, arguably, results of this politicization. That recent films about the African past were also the direct product of such politicization seems simplistic; rather, the films' common attribute seems part of a broader tendency to avoid the risks of experiment by dealing with selective "history"—to be conservative in the wider meaning of the word. Like the triumphalist architecture of the decade (oversized but acceptable, with reference to traditional details like the arch, however out of scale), films also dredged the past for elements that could be recombined—an attribute of postmodernism, despite the conservatism of the styles selected ("the past is fiction"). Too, this was the decade of the creamy Merchant-Ivory films and a nostalgic return to the values of Edwardiana (including greed and snobbery, to be sure), which may have been a reaction against the mind-boggling vulgarity of movies from *Animal House* to *Grumpy Old Men*.

By contrast with the films treating the present, the backward-looking ones had a much lower level of violence—as if, perhaps, one of the things they yearned for was the nonviolence of the old days of colonialism and the Good African. (The violence of colonialism was ignored.) Nor did most of them take racism for their subject. Rather, they assumed a set of values in which racism tried to become invisible, one of the givens. This is not quite true of all the films, for at least two of them (*The Kitchen Toto*, *Mister Johnson*) tried to become critiques of colonialism, and two others (*The Power of One*, *A World Apart*) dealt with aspects of South African apartheid. By and large, however, these films suggested a culture seeking not to learn from the past but to hide in it. It is worth noting that, as a group, they probably commanded a bigger audience and made more money than those films about the African present.

Some of the films recapped old favorites: the period saw a White Queen, two Tarzans, three Haggards, one film about Imperial Men, and a movie about making an African movie in 1950. There were, as well, prestige productions of literature (*Mister Johnson*, *Out of Africa*), and of a snob murder case (*White Mischief*). One, little seen (Athol Fugard's *The Guest*), dealt with a South African artist's drug addiction in the 1920s in a way that may have intended the addiction as a metaphor for apartheid.

Two other historical films came from Australia. Both were concerned with the Boer War and, therefore, with South Africa (*Breaker Morant*, 1979, and *Torn Allegiance*, 1982). They were not, however, concerned with Africa or its archetypes; rather, as with the contemporaneous and non-African *Gallipoli*, they looked critically at Australia's involvement in Britain's colonial adventures. *Breaker Morant* was an excellent film, with a compelling performance by Edward Woodward, and *Torn Allegiance* raised painful questions about the morality of war, but their Africa was really only a tabletop on which to play out the game of condemning the British Empire, as Australians got ready for independence.

Several films re-upped old archetypes. The United States extruded *Sheena*, Columbia's resuscitation of the White Queen, in 1984. It would be hard to guess the target audience: children had the requisite lack of discrimination but not the taste for T & A; adults conditioned even to television were too smart for it. *Sheena* was a carnival of ineptitude that took a couple of seasoned names down with it (John Guillermin, Lorenzo Semple), managing to be awful without being charming and to sick up the past without anybody's feeling better as a result. It had the worst dialogue heard since Ruth Roman's *Jungle Queen*, and a cast beyond badness. Filmed in Kenya, it was still the subject of derisive tales there years later among both blacks and whites.

It mobilized all the stereotypes: an orphaned blond, unexplained magic, B-movie Africans who can't get off their thumbs without help from a white goddess. Orphaned Sheena grows up into a woman with a body that won't quit and jiggles her way across the veldt on a horse painted to look like a zebra; when trouble comes, she saves everybody by summoning the animals. As slow as a doctor's waiting room, this might have worked if the director had had the sense to steal everything possible from Steven Spielberg—who has shown, after all, that flat acting and dialogue can be overcome by great effects and a fast pace—but he decided, sadly, to rely on his own abilities.

The picture is utterly exploitative—of its audience, of Africa, of animals. The use of the animals is particularly painful, for we are to believe that elephants and rhinos can defeat automatic weapons, when it is these very things that have slaughtered them mercilessly.

Two attempts were made to reinvigorate the Tarzan story. Both were of the 1980s, but—perhaps surprisingly, considering the treatment of the White Queen—neither was a sendup. *Greystoke: The Legend of Tarzan* was to be part of the "British film renaissance" of the 1980s, an expensive production that would treat the legend with genuine artistry. The film, however, was often merely earnest where it sought to be serious, pretentious where it sought to be important. Pauline Kael blamed the director, who "doesn't seem to understand that if viewers don't identify with Tarzan . . . the story has no power." She asserted that the original script was "marvelously detailed" but survived only in "bits and pieces" of the director's "scraggly mess." Another critic dismissed it as "Chimps of Fire." As a resurrection of the Tarzan "legend," the picture certainly failed, but the attempt was far more interesting than these remarks suggest. It restored the Greystoke story, with its freight of upper-class—and very dated—values, not to mention its storytelling difficulties. Heavily weighted, as well, toward environmental concern—the Green Party version of Tarzan—it examined the great apes, particularly, in far more detail and with far more sympathy than other Tarzan pictures. The apes were not the articulated haystacks of earlier versions, but seemingly real animals, so that when the stunned, French-speaking Tarzan finds one of them in a cage in an urban zoo, dying, and cries, "Mon père!", the audience feels genuine anguish. Less emotionally effective is his return to Africa to put the world of the drawing room behind him, perhaps because we know that he, unlike Weissmuller's Tarzan, is not and cannot be "happy." Certainly, this film doomed itself by asking questions of the Tarzan story that it simply cannot bear (What are the great apes really like? How does Tarzan really become civilized? How does Tarzan manage to be both Tarzan and Greystoke?). The resulting answers, if pursued with any rigor, tear the story apart and prevent its being put back together in anything like its mythic form. Nor could such an attempt reinvigorate the myth: new wine could not be put into a now broken old bottle.

John Derek's *Tarzan the Ape Man* was a more interesting effort. It is fashionable to pooh-pooh Derek's soft-core films of his wife, Bo, but in this version of Tarzan, Derek tried something that needed to be done and that nobody else had attempted: he made a Tarzan movie about Jane, from Jane's point of view. (From the 1918 *Tarzan of the Apes* through at least the 1936 *Tarzan Escapes*, both story and point of view wavered between Jane and Tarzan.) Regrettably, the camera work and the narrative sensibility were entirely male.

Structurally, the film begins as a remake of the 1932 picture: Jane (Bo Derek) is in "West Africa, 1910" to find "the father she has never known," who turns out to be Richard Harris in a performance that would have included chewing up the carpet, if there had been one. Papa and Jane make the expedition to find the elephants' graveyard, climb the Mutea Escarpment, and hear Tarzan's cry, to which Papa replies, "Oh, shut up, you boring sonofabitch!" The father shows off for the daughter, preening and posing and bellowing, with hints of incestuous flirtation. They find "the great inland sea," and Derek takes a nude bath, into which Tarzan and a pet lion intrude. "This ape sonofabitch wants *you*," Papa concludes. And Jane wants him: for the first time since Maureen O'Sullivan, this is a Jane who is going to become the Wild Mate.

And so Tarzan does want her. Seemingly endless sequences follow—Tarzan fighting a python in slow, *very* slow, motion to save Jane; Jane, a chimp, and two orangs (from Borneo, of course, not Africa) tending Tarzan; Tarzan and Jane swimming together in a scene that tries to copy the 1932 one but merely goes on too long; Tarzan feeling Jane's breasts and her saying, "God, if the girls back home could see me now!" All this leads up to the capture of the party by black Africans of a grotesqueness far beyond that of the 1932 dwarves, led by a monstrous man with a shaved head, who first impales Papa on an elephant tusk and then lumbers toward the supine, nude, white-painted Jane. (It is part of this people's strangeness that they bathe and whiten their victims.) Tarzan intervenes, engages the monster in another slow-motion fight and finally breaks his neck. Papa dies; Jane grieves; and Jane and Tarzan take a bath and then roll on the beach with the orangs and the chimp in a slow festival of polymorphous perversity.

The problem with the film is that director Derek cannot let go of what he considers a good thing (usually, his wife's body), with the result that every important visual goes on far, *far* too long. Derek is really a still photographer, not a cinematographer, and, while he can compose really gorgeous pictures, he cannot see them actively. His camera work is absurdly and sophomorically voyeuristic, and visualized sex is really his subject, not the Tarzan or the Jane myth. The film does do refreshing things with Jane's father, but the father is on the periphery, no matter how much an actor like Harris rants. It also seeks to escape from the racist strait jacket of Burroughs: Papa has an African mistress (whom he calls "Africa"), and black Africans are treated less as part of the furniture. Nonetheless, nothing substantive has been changed: Africans are still the great menace, still grotesque, still "other."

Some day, somebody must make a Tarzan film from Jane's point of view again. The director must be a woman. The camera work must be something other than voyeuristic and male. The result may be a film that really does put new wine into an old bottle.

WHEN THAT OTHER great source of African fantasy, Rider Haggard, was filmed for 1986-87 release, two linked movies were the result: *King Solomon's Mines* and *Allan Quatermain and the Lost City of Gold.**

The principal connections were Quatermain and the two stars, Richard Chamberlain (Quatermain) and Sharon Stone. The second film benefited from the presence of James Earl Jones but proved a stinker, anyway. The first was better, if no match for the 1950 version.

---

* A Canadian company had made a film titled *King Solomon's Treasure* in 1979. It evidently was a version of *Quatermain* but was not widely seen.

Both these films are out of Haggard (rather far out) by way of Indiana Jones and *Romancing the Stone*. Both have, or aspire to have, the same quality of sendup, including such jokes as, of Africa, "It's a jungle out there." The period has been advanced to World War I, so that the Germans are baddies and white supremacy is parodied through them. Nonetheless, the vantage point is ineluctably Euro-American, and black Africans are mostly present to be run over, jumped on, shot, or treated as part of the furniture. Such clichés as cannibalism loom large: Chamberlain and Stone are put into a pot so enormous it has to be reached by a staircase, where they float among the vegetables, to be turned into stew.

Quatermain now appears to be American, but he is still "the Great White African Hunter," as she calls him (although she pronounces his name "Quartermain"). In this *KSM*, Curtis and Good have disappeared altogether, and the quest is rather vague—a father and a map—and takes a distant back seat to such matters as Chamberlain's and Stone's mutual seduction. It does include a peculiar and charming sequence in which they blunder into a culture of people who live upside down, hanging from trees like fruit. Despite the rather Swiftian conceit, the scene is Edenic, as the upside-downers bring food and flowers and seem to want to crown Stone as their queen. "Unhappy with the world as it is, they live upside down, hoping to change it." The scene could better have been saved for *Allan Quatermain and the Lost City of Gold*, where its charm is sorely needed, and where its fantastic quality would have been more at home. A few other details suggest vintage Haggard: the white queens of the (black) Kukuana, frozen in their caves; a treasure with which "you could buy Iowa." All of it is defanged by the air of camp, however—surely the intention—so that the imperial meanings of Haggard's original are rendered insubstantial.

Allan Quatermain and the Lost City of Gold is even wispier. Although it tries to preserve the structure of the quest for what Quatermain calls "a lost city, a great lost white race," it never takes its own goal seriously enough to make the quest vital. Quatermain is now searching for his brother(!); Stone would rather go to America. This is not much of a conflict. They set off for the Lost City, of course, with a comic Indian in place of the comic Frenchman of Haggard's novel; they do the underground river of the novel, pass the pillar of fire, and encounter some giant worms in place of Haggard's nasty crabs. None of it has much urgency, however, probably because neither producers nor director could choose between thrills and sendup, and they couldn't find how it's possible to have both, as in the Indiana Jones films. These sequences would be acceptable, perhaps, if what lay at the end of the quest was itself truly worth a quest, but the Lost City of Gold is nothing more than a steam-cleaned hippie commune from the sixties. Folks wander about in white robes looking spacey, with the lost Quatermain brother as head spaceman, a surfer with Peace Corps idealism. The city has both black and white citizens, but everybody in power is white, including the two queens from Haggard's book. The bad one—the brunette, of course—wears costumes of the sort that used to turn up in Italian films about Hercules. Of course the bad queen loses and all the good folks win, but it is all so awful that it's impossible to care. If this is Utopia, I'd rather be in Philadelphia.

Taken together, the two films represent the emptying of Haggard's imperial mythologizing. Slangy, sexy, unsubtle, they admit through their self-mockery that they are about nothing. What they have kept of the old archetypes is debased: the White Hunter is reduced to a handsome, gun-toting action hero; the True-Blue White Woman is merely a sexy klutz; the white queens and lost white civilization are the stuff of comic books, not myth. What remains more or less intact is "Africa" as a place of danger, but we have the sense that it could be interchangeable with "South America" or "the Near East" or "the center of the earth." The two motion pictures probably mark the end of Haggard's usefulness as a movie source.

However, the two films were made with South African input at a time when all South African filming was subject to racist policy. The films' racism, therefore, cannot be considered a benign oversight: the utopian vision of subservient blacks living peacefully with whites under white rule, the violence done to blacks, the white queens of the Kakuana, are images acceptable to apartheid. So, too, presumably, are the White Hunter and the True-Blue White Woman in these incarnations.

THE BACKWARD LOOK of the 1980s turned to recent history as well as to Burroughs and Haggard and their spinoffs. Two films treated apartheid itself as history, both from a white point of view. *The Power of One* dealt with a boy's growing up, from the early 1930s to 1948; *A World Apart* dealt with a young girl's experience in 1963.

The Power of One is probably best seen as a film for adolescents. It deals with the staples of that audience: parents, school, first love, the currently fashionable teen self-esteem. It also has the self-centeredness of adolescence: no matter how monumental the events of history, the hero is always seen at the center, uncritically. The film follows his rise from seven-year-old orphan to eighteen-year-old boxing champion; along the way, he suffers more than David Copperfield. The only boy of English stock at an Afrikaner school, he becomes the butt of all cruelty. When World War II approaches, the prime tormentor dons Nazi garb, and the hero is his victim. Buffeted anew by fate, he leaves the school and is befriended by an emigre Jew, who is imprisoned when war comes; off goes the lad to prison with him, there to learn boxing from a black man. By war's end, the boy is a stellar boxer. His farewell to the prison is a concert in which he conducts the thousand black inmates in choral singing. He prances about the stage and waves his arms, and the glorious Zulu harmony rolls out, all, the film would have us believe, because this white boy is showing black men how to make Zulu music. (It's as if you decided to make a film about the white kid who taught Fats Waller to boogie.)

The erstwhile Nazi becomes a cop; the first apartheid laws are passed; the boxer falls in love with a girl who just happens to be the daughter of apartheid's prime architect; and township blacks beg the boy to teach them English. Of course the boy finally beats the daylights out of the villain, and of course the girl is killed helping the boy, and of course the boy goes off with his black buddy. To get all this in, *The Power of One* is a very long movie.

The film's heart seems to be determinedly in the right place. However, reflection suggests that it is not so utterly different from the Afrikaner myth it takes as its easy enemy: women in this film are mothers and girl friends and servants, nothing else; blacks, as in the White Goddess movies, cannot act without white help. And the staunchly anti-Afrikaner tone denies (except for one inaccurate title at the beginning) the complicity of Anglo-South Africans in apartheid. Plus, how worthy of a film is the suffering and triumph of a white child in the presence of the South African reality?

A World Apart also deals with a white child, but in a context that does not diminish black suffering. A slow film that works through accumulation of emotional detail, it deserves attention because its writer, Shawn Slovo, bears one of South Africa's most famous names. Apparently in good part autobiographical, it follows the pain of an adolescent girl whose idealistic (i.e., pro-ANC) mother has little time for her.

The mother is an uncompromising foe of apartheid, and, when the Ninety-Day Law is passed in 1963 (allowing detention without charge for ninety days), she is imprisoned for supporting the then banned ANC. (The father—apparently a Joe Slovo surrogate—is "away," presumably underground on ANC business.) The deterioration of the family under the impact of political upheaval is painful to watch: the children are left first with a grandmother, then without even her when the strain is too much. The mother barely makes it through her ninety days, then gets as far as a telephone booth outside the prison before she is rearrested—for another ninety days. With torture imminent, she attempts suicide. In the remainder of the picture, she and the adolescent daughter make tentative moves toward understanding each other, and they reach a kind of resolution at an ANC funeral, a scene that provides an ending for the film, if not for its familial conflicts.

A World Apart is an honest, rather too-low-keyed film. The performances are good, especially Jodhi May as the girl. Barbara Hershey as the mother is so believably undemonstrative and distracted that she is sometimes opaque and therefore uninteresting; the understated script does not help her much. There is a structural problem, too, in the necessary switch from the daughter's to the mother's point of view in the prison scenes, so that the picture seems abruptly to be about the mother, then about the daughter again; this division is not very well resolved. Many of the scenes go on too long, with the daughter's angst too long dwelt upon, and, because the worth of the mother's pro-ANC work must be taken for granted, and because we never really see her doing that work, her distraction from her daughter has no life. It is not accidental that lots of time is spent watching the daughter be unhappy—mooning about, looking at other people, waiting— because the problem of how to dramatize this unhappiness was not really solved.

Nonetheless, *A World Apart* deserves our attention. Its uncompromising honesty and lack of pyrotechnics are admirable. As a daughter's homage to the mother she did not understand, it is touching and historically revealing.

THE REMAINING BACKWARD-looking films of recent release were all to some degree "fiction" and thus showed an uneasy relationship with history. Biography and novels were the principal sources; in none was a distinction between fiction and history entirely clear, a confusion that could be blamed on fashionable postmodern theory—if anybody involved could be suspected of postmodernism.

Even when these films were about "historical people," they had problems. *The Mountains of the Moon*, for example, was about the "real" Burton and Speke and the discovery of the source of the Nile, a great subject since at least Alan Moorehead's *The White Nile*. It had a luminous performance by Fiona Shaw as Burton's wife, but its introduction of homosexual love into the Burton-Speke relationship was a dubious invention, as was an African befriended by Burton and then tortured by a sadistic black ruler. Both these intrusions smacked of fashion, not fact. *Mountains of the Moon* had some superb African scenes, however, and believable detail—the scenes of the failed initial expedition in Somaliland were superb. The film's paradox is that it would have been better if it had tossed out the rather clumsy fictions altogether and stayed with what we know of these two eccentric men and their expeditions—not to mention their role in turning Africa into what it has become. In short, history would have been better than half-baked fiction.

What we want from history—questions, ideas, detailed data—we do not want from popular fiction. The two are sometimes allowed to come together, however, in autobiography, where a certain amount of self-justifying fiction is to be tolerated. "Isak Dinesen"—Karen Blixen—wrote *Out of Africa* as a form of autobiography, an almost poetic version of her eighteen years in Africa. Real names were used, real places described. Yet, it is in good part an inner landscape that dominates the work, and those who people it are poetic creations: not the historian's attempts at truth, but the poet's—and the egotist's.

Any film of *Out of Africa*, therefore, faces a problem: whether to show that the work is fantastic in the best sense of the word, or to stress its history, its re-creation of place and time. It is the second thing that commercial film does well, and so the makers of the 1985 *Out of Africa* seemed wise in going for historical re-creation. To that end (and perhaps for legal reasons) they credited both Dinesen-Blixen and other recent research. In doing so, however, they created a problem they seem not to have identified: in adding to her poetic memoir, they took on a responsibility to history that *Out of Africa* itself would not bear. This is largely a responsibility to a changed view of colonialism, a burden that hardly existed when *Out of Africa* was published in 1937 but one that has grown heavier and heavier and is now enormous. The resulting movie was nonetheless successful, and for good reason: it is a beautiful film, grandly romantic, centered by a superb performance by Meryl Streep.

Streep was the True-Blue White Woman, Karen Blixen; Klaus Maria Brandauer was her husband, Bror (and wonderful in the role). Robert Redford was less successful as her supposed lover, the sometime White Hunter Denys Finch Hatton. Vincent Canby's unkind "a total cipher, and a charmless one at that" seems excessive, but he pinpointed the real problem: "There's no role for [Redford] to act." This lack was another consequence of staying inside Karen Blixen's personal fantasy: the "Denys" of her poetic memory has no substance, as a reading of the work will show. Presumably, some of the credit given to other works was for material that resulted in Brandauer's picture of Bror; why was not the same done for Redford's Finch Hatton?

The film covered the years from the Blixens' engagement of convenience (c. 1913) to her departure from Africa in 1931 after Finch Hatton was killed in a plane crash. Like a few other African films, its visual beauty communicated its characters' love of the land. Its story—romantic rather than sentimental, sad rather than tragic—was accessible. Its presentation of an upper class in the first third of the century flattered the tastes of the mid-1980s.

However, contradictions between Blixen-Dinesen's vision of herself and history are inevitably revealed by the film's quiet insistence that it is historically accurate (settings, costumes, names, events). Dinesen the author—the Baroness Blixen by her marriage to Bror—gained much of her early reputation from English readers who approved what was then her political correctness: acceptance of the rightness of both colonialism and class. Blixen-Dinesen's social sense, as demonstrated in *Out of Africa*, was virtually feudal. If the film had been careful to show that this was a poetic vision—that, for example, the hard-working, Karen-loving Kikuyu were her personal myth and not fact—then I would have no qualms about it. When, however, it does not give the signs of fantasy (not necessarily billowing dry ice, but camera angles, focus, music, and so on), and its photographic realism says that it is history, I have very real qualms. A feudalism that was acceptable to elitists in 1937 simply will not pass as an unexamined idea in 1985, but such it seems if the film is seen as history.

The trouble is, it is inaccurate and self-serving history. Michael Gough, for example, seemed far too old (at sixty-eight) and harmless to play the developer Lord Delamere, who was a tough forty-three in 1913; Gough brought a warm fuzziness to that rather ruthless entrepreneur. Robert Redford, denied a British accent, was right only in Hollywood terms—bankable, handsome—but physically wrong for the tall, bald Finch Hatton of reality. Finch Hatton was widely liked in Kenya. Redford is likable, but not by the folks who liked Denys—what they liked was Denys's combination of charm, courage, and snobbish wit (and hypocrisy— his comments on an American client's vulgarity, for example, did not prevent him from taking the man's money). The real Denys could write to Kermit Roosevelt, of a pipe of port put down in his English cellars, that the bottles lay "like black virgins, waiting to shed their blood for me, row on row." Redford's American Denys is far too swell a guy ever to dream of causing black virgins to bleed—like Gough, in fact, far too nice a person ever to be in Africa to exploit it.

What is smudged in the film (because smudged in Dinesen's autobiographical romance) is the real reason why there was money to be made in "British East": land and labor were deliberately undervalued. Official efforts to force Africans to work for virtually nothing (beginning with a tax system that made it necessary for them to earn money, something they had never needed until the British arrived) were both contorted and successful, although they would end in Mau Mau and *uhuru*. Karen's sweet behavior toward "her" Kikuyu in the film, which is meant to show us her goodness and modernity and which is right out of Dinesen, is, if seen as history, the Lady-Bountiful behavior of the aristocrat who gives the serfs a sweet at Christmas. It was apparently unthinkable to the real Karen Blixen that these wretched people made her crystal and her aristocratic adultery possible; it was unreported by her, too, that she lived high for eighteen years on other people's (mostly her family's) money, trying to get Africa and its cheap labor to pay off. Both these ignorances would be perfectly acceptable as character traits in a closed system—i.e., a personal fantasy; they are howlers when opened up to history.

So is Karen's supposed syphilis, which, in the real world, is much questioned and which may have been an imagined stick with which she belatedly beat Bror. So is real time: Karen was forty-six by the time Finch Hatton died, but Streep doesn't look it. So are the reasons why Bror left her. So is the question of what it would really have been like living with a woman whose idea of fun was telling you stories, hour after hour, night after night.

Out of Africa, then, is a film that wants contentually to be fantasy but pretends visually to be history, and thus is neither. Yet it was a successful American motion picture, keyed to the status-hungry Baby Boomer audience of the 1980s, which also confused autobiography and history, and which also saw political correctness as something only other people practice.

Out of Africa remains an important film for two reasons, its source and its star. In giving Meryl Streep a good role, it justified itself; in enabling a visualization of Blixen-Dinesen's almost obsessive love of Africa, it approached excellence.

White Mischief also looked at Kenya's past, this time the "Happy Valley" crew of Kenya and the real-life murder in 1940 of somebody called Lord Erroll. The source was a nonfiction book, but the film presented as fact some obvious fictions, notably its solution to the puzzle of who shot Joss Erroll.

Happy Valley is always spoken of as a sink of delicious depravity; its people, we are assured, were very different from the other whites in Kenya Colony. " *We* work; *they* play," seems to be the refrain. This difference is all but invisible to Africans, however; Happy Valley had the same exploitation, the same entrepreneurial brutality, the same need for money, as Nairobi and the Ngong Hills. As a result, the decadence of these people—expressed as drug-taking, wife-swapping, and interracial sex—seems merely an intensification of the colonialism of *Out of Africa*. The people themselves, however, are less interesting: except for their corruptions, they are nonentities. And they had no Isak Dinesen to fantasize them.

Charles Dance was Lord Erroll, very handsome and charming, a man who is murdered while out in his motorcar. One look at the brutal face of the real Lord Erroll would suggest why somebody shot *him*; Dance, however, suggests that murdering him would be an act of bad taste. This casting, and that of Greta Scaachi as the heroine, transforms a problem of morality into one of looks (a movie speciality); and by giving Scaachi an unattractive husband, the film makes a very sordid matter seem romantic, or at least worth our attention, like the doings of the famous in the tabloids.

In fact, if Lord Erroll had been Bill Erroll of Leeds, and an angry husband had whacked him with a spanner as he rode his bike behind the gasworks, nobody would care. No amount of wife-swapping or drug-taking would have earned him the starring role in a movie. Yet Lord Erroll and his friends are no brighter, no pleasanter, no greater, than Bill. If we ask (but we are meant not to), "Why am I watching these people?" the only answer is, "Because they are *these* people."

Oh.

Within this narrow limitation, it is possible to enjoy *White Mischief* as a handsomely made period film and a murder mystery. Sarah Miles is particularly diverting as one of the depraved. And the film shows, in a fantastic scene of a party of ghosts after Errol's murder, how *Out of Africa* could have protected its poetry against the rigors of history, had it wanted to.

Victim's tales have low dramatic potential, and *The Kitchen Toto* (1987) was no exception. Again a film about colonial East Africa, it tried to deal with the Mau Mau horror from an African child's point of view. *The Kitchen Toto*, however, was simply not very good as dramatic narrative, and so, for all its good intentions, it fell flat. Had it been produced in 1955, it would have seemed shocking and wonderful, and its lack of dramatic through-line would have been hidden by its audacity.

A *toto* is a child (Swahili), and a kitchen toto is a cook's helper. The toto of the film's title is the child of a black minister murdered by the embryonic Mau Mau. To help his family, he goes to work in the household of a white police official. There, he meets the casual racism of British colonials (the child of the family uses him as a target for his air rifle, as a human ladder, and so on) as well as the virulence of Kikuyu rebellion, as Mau Mau recruiters force him and the adult servants to take a vow to kill whites on command. The boy is thus put into a classic victim's position, and the film does nothing to extricate him. Both sides oppress him. Although it can be argued that his situation accurately reflects that of typical Kikuyu during the Mau Mau years, it must also be said that repeated oppressions do not make very good dramatic action: what we sense most viscerally is the repetition (not the oppression); what we want from dramatic narrative is progression. Like nineteenth-century melodrama, the film seeks to solve this structural problem by pumping progression into the degree of oppression: little hurts become big ones, misunderstandings grow to torments, and the boy is finally given the water torture by his presumably well-intentioned white employer, then killed by a black policeman as he is trying to return the white officer's child.

The Kitchen Toto suffers, as well, from a refusal to go inside its characters. We are meant to read them from gestures, looks, words, but in fact many of those signs remain opaque. So, too, do many of the film's incidents, which seem irrelevant because not given significance: the white officer boffing the D.C.'s niece in a car; the white child taking up valuable film footage to dissect a dead snake. The kitchen toto himself remains most opaque of all, a wide-eyed sufferer who moves through the film's horrific events without giving us enough clues to his inner state. Again, progression is frustrated; what is communicated is stasis, mute forbearance—and dull filmmaking.

Mister Johnson (1990) accreted authority from its source, a novel by Joyce Cary (who once was a bankable name in English fiction, and who had been a colonial officer and contributed to *Men of Two Worlds*). That it was a pretty dull motion picture seems to be the fault of neither Cary nor the actors; the performances, especially by Maynard Eziashi and Edward Woodward, were fine. Pierce Brosnan seemed to lack variety in a pivotal role, but the script gave him none, turning Cary's comic Imperial Man into a serious bore.

Mister Johnson is the story of the downfall of a young Nigerian (Eziashi) gifted with intelligence and cursed with ego—a potentially tragic combination, and one not uncommon in African governments. Johnson is a minor clerk in a far outpost of Britain, where his enterprise is divided between serving his boss, a district officer (Brosnan), and serving his own dreams of status (which Cary himself saw as a love of "romance," calling Johnson a "poet"). He embezzles; he cheats; he sells British secrets; yet he is a charming and fascinating figure. A flaunter of success, he has taken on the attributes of an Englishman: umbrella, pith helmet, white suit. (Comparison with Robeson's identical costume in *Song of Freedom* is inevitable.) He speaks of the British as "we." England, where he has never been, is "home," although we are supposed to laugh at him for thinking that Hertfordshire is a village. It is the more disturbing, therefore, that British justice executes him after he kills a trader (Woodward) during a theft.

In the novel, Johnson's tragicomedy was distanced by Cary's directing our interest toward the effect of Johnson on his stilted English boss: the story was as much about the young white bureaucrat's confusion as it was about Johnson's fall. In the film, however, the point of view becomes diffuse. Too much attention is given to the white man's marriage, even to an adumbrated and irrelevant sex scene, which in the novel was farce and here becomes seriousness. Johnson's very real abilities (shown in his building of a road) are undercut by his being shown in exactly the same ways as in other scenes in which he is either comic or dishonest, so that his positive abilities are smudged. The result is that a character who should be seen as a mixture of tragic hero and poetic buffoon becomes a comic Uncle Tom with jarring lapses into seriousness. The Brosnan character's role in Johnson's execution (he shoots Johnson to save him from hanging) is merely "sensitive," not comic and horrifying, as Cary made it.

Paradoxically, *Mister Johnson* was a more penetrating critique of colonialism in its early (novelistic) form than in its cinematic one. It is odd, for example, that notions of correctness never indulged by Cary have been imposed in 1989: the lower-class trader played by Woodward uses "nigger" and "nig," as in the novel, but Brosnan's district officer and his wife never call Johnson "Mister Wog," as the novel's couple do. In sum, one wonders why such a film was made just now. Perhaps it seemed a likely black-white vehicle; if so, it is to be regretted that it was made so as to be so lacking in edge.

The filmic obsession with a lost past was taken to a new level—and a new intelligence—by *White Hunter, Black Heart*, a Clint Eastwood film of 1990. Written in part by Peter Viertel from his own novel, it was about a movie director named John and a young writer named Pete who are making a movie in Africa in 1950. It helps the film greatly if you know that in 1950 a real director named John Huston and a real writer named Peter Viertel made a movie called *The African Queen*.

In fact, the connection with *The African Queen* is both the film's strength and its weakness. Strength, because for those who know Huston and his film, *White Hunter, Black Heart* gains complexity and depth by an extended artistic allusion: but weakness, because if you do not know *The African Queen*, simple matters of plot and character remain mysterious. It is as if Viertel (and perhaps Eastwood) knew both Huston and his film so well that they forgot to dot the *i*'s and cross the *t*'s of the most fundamental kinds of information.

The story is simple, and not very far removed from the facts surrounding *African Queen*. An independent and almost obsessively macho director decides he wants to kill an elephant while he is in Africa directing a film. However, the elephant hunting and filmmaking are mutually destructive activities, although not enough is made of this conflict early in *White Hunter, Black Heart*. Indeed, one of the uncrossed *t*'s is the amount of money and talent that ride on the director's ability to move shooting forward quickly. The director becomes fascinated, then obsessed, with killing a tusker (although, again, we have to guess at this transition); he becomes enchanted with the kind of manhood embodied by an illiterate African tracker (although we have pretty much to guess at this development, too). His film, delayed by weather and then by his going off hunting, is imperiled (but we never adequately understand how serious this is). Then, by insisting on going after an elephant when his professional hunter tells him to back off or the other elephants will cause trouble, the director causes the death of the African tracker. Only then—weeping—does he get down to film-making and the picture's final word, "Action."

Along the way, the macho ethic gets a pretty good going-over. The director is shown as a charming bully, as a defender of Jews against anti-Semitism and of blacks against brutality, as a practical joker whose jokes are challenges, as a compulsive cocksman, and as a competitive man's man who falls back on charges of cowardice whenever another man (including his friend the young writer) will not go along with his posturings. The character's sexism becomes the film's: it has no female character of any importance at all.

At the same time, elephant hunting becomes a complex metaphor for ethical action: the writer refuses to hunt because he says killing an elephant would be a crime; no, the director corrects him, it would be a sin. The writer soliloquizes on the elephant as divine beast, extrahuman, better than humans. There is insightful critique of British colonialism, and a brilliant little scene in a London nightclub when a dance act unwittingly parodies African film clichés: a man in a gorilla suit captures and strips a jungle princess while a tom-tom plays. Thus, the film acknowledges both the real Africa and its cinematic stereotypes and concedes at least some of the reality of its people (although it remains a picture about white visitors).

This is much more thoughtful than most movies ever try to be. It doesn't entirely work, alas. Textually, the problem is that too much of the idea is left in the dialogue—this is an extraordinarily wordy film—and not embedded in action and character. For example, we do not see enough of the greatness of elephants, despite Simon Trevor's excellent footage, of which the final cut gives us too little. This elementary error has been made so often (*The Roots of Heaven*, et al.) that it seems that directors assume that people understand the value of wild animals, and clearly we do not: we have to be shown anew, each time. The stereotype of "wild Africa" may hide this trap.

Dramatically, the film's problem is Clint Eastwood. Always an interesting actor, he here seems to have shackled himself with too much homage to Huston. The result is that he seems always to be acting in quotation marks, and a real person never shows. Eastwood is not Huston. He lacks Huston's hamminess, his stage-actor's voice, but he provides no substitute, and therefore he seems either uncertain or uncommitted. Yet this is a film about passion—passion for films, passion for the elephant, passion for an ethical idea—and it needs commitment. We never *see* how important the elephant is to him; we never *see* how important the African tracker is to him. We hear him say these things, but words are never enough. On the other hand, Jeff Fahey as the writer is compelling, always believably impassioned; Eastwood seems casual beside him.

This is not to say that *White Hunter, Black Heart* is a bad picture. It is quite a good one—but you want it to be a fine one, and it isn't. Nonetheless, it is surely one of the better ones made by an American about Africa—for me, certainly better than Huston's too-cute tour de force. And the two pictures together make a great double bill.

THERE IS NO indication that many movies about Africa will stop looking backward. As South Africa comes to terms with its new reality, a spate of retrospective films is to be expected, some probably revising the widely hated Afrikaner myth. Revisionist movies about the Day of the Vow and the Great Trek should be expected, as well as harrowing repetitions of the horrors of the apartheid years, which will take a lot of exposure to exorcise. East Africa, the other focus of filmmakers just now, still has potential, too. Its white glamor will probably continue to appeal, and certainly it still has more stories of white courage or depravity or wealth to offer. Whether black Africans will be included in the films to come is a question. Loving servants, of course, are to be expected, as are, perhaps, comic wogs. The fiction, however, that East Africa was white, and that the whites there were charming, is probably too useful to both filmmakers and audiences to be turned over to the realities of history.

Expect more of the same, then.

PART 4

Beyond Black and White

13 CONCLUSIONS

That many films about Africa were and perhaps still are racist was an admission with which this book began. What it did not admit was to what extent films were racist, and in what ways, and why—and which films, if any, escaped racism. For example, I have used "savage," "savage dancing," "fur and feathers," "dangerous animals," "witch-doctor," and similar terms to identify racist aspects of many of the films. However, these terms clearly have not applied to all the films discussed in this book, nor have all the terms applied equally.

Any idea of a monolithic racism—which I questioned at the beginning—is disproved by the many changes in films over their century of life. Tarzan movies, for example, moved from an original eugenics hero to Mr. and Mrs. Tarzan to world-wandering righter-of-wrongs; the Haggard films moved from *She* to *KSM* to camp reworking. As well, new kinds of films appeared at several points that reflected contemporary history (Mau Mau, Mercenary, Helper).

A racist monolith, therefore, is a fiction; so is an unchanging iconography of racism. That said, where are we? It remains to try to determine the kinds and severities of racism, and their chronology and changes, as well as any counters to racism that the films have shown. Too, issues in addition to racism (especially sex and class) need to be addressed.

It is well to recall the gross symptoms of racism in film: the savage and jungle imagery already noted, the most prevalent form; dehumanization of Africans of all kinds, and specifically the playing of black Africans by white actors in blackface; scenes or signs of abuse of Africans, and above all their mass murder; denial of inner life and worth to Africans, and the assigning of negative qualities to them (e.g., Black Eve); the denial to Africans of the cinematic respect accorded whites—size and numbers of fictional roles, centrality, value; and creation of an "Africa" that renders Africans invisible.

However, counters to racism also exist in film: the denial or overt avoidance of stereotypes (as in *Cry, the Beloved Country*), or the use of scenes that overtly stigmatize racism (for example, the scene in the 1940 *Safari* in which the seating of a black guide at the white hunter's table is a deliberate means of distinguishing the hero, who insists that the black man sit with him, from the villain, who objects). Probably the most important counterracism, however, was the creation of African roles that allowed inner life, that gave African characters families and desires, and that then placed those characters and those qualities at the center of a film where they did not serve a white cause. *(The Zulu's Heart*, 1908, gave an African a family and emotions and made him central, but it also used a white actor in blackface and made his action the saving of a white child and her mother.) Such counterracism was emphasized by the casting of black actors. This creation of larger, more central roles began in the 1930s, ultimately realizing star status for black male actors (e.g., Robeson, Poitier, Roundtree, Washington, Murphy).

This is not to say that racism disappeared from films in proportion to the appearance of black actors; the astonishing increase in "jungle" films in the 1940s and 1950s shows that that the hoariest of racial imagery was being perpetuated even as black actors began to achieve stardom (see Appendix, Table 2). With the death of the cheap jungle films, however, that imagery became less common, although not until two decades after the first important crack had appeared in the black archetype.

That crack, of course, was Paul Robeson. Until Robeson's third film, the only black male (African) archetype was the Good African, who was faithful, obedient, even loving to whites, often unto death. The Good African in his early forms embodied the reassuring white conviction that whites were loved. The Good African continued long after other black archetypes appeared; indeed, it is, overall, the most common one. However, the Good African changed as films themselves changed; he has been embodied as a token equal (Jim Brown in *Dark of the Sun*, 1968) and a smartass sidekick (Johnny Sekka in *The Southern Star*, 1969) on the way to becoming the empowered, individualized Umslopogas played by James Earl Jones in the 1987 *Allan Quatermain*.

Robeson himself played a Good African in both *Sanders* and the 1937 *KSM*. Nonetheless, in *Song of Freedom* and *Jericho* he created an entirely new archetype that shucked off racist imagery or turned it on its ear. Robeson also created space around himself for black actresses to play real women, and these two small films are significant for these innovations.

Still in the 1930s, the Educated African was a long-overdue filmic admission that "savagery" was outmoded. Real-life educated Africans were getting doctorates by this time, but the issue of education was still one about which many whites were ambivalent and to which some were unequivocally opposed. The Educated African was, of course, a white construct—an attempt to deal with the reality of Westernized, sophisticated Africans, but on white terms and in the context of white domination of the continent. In his first embodiment (*Old Bones of the River*, 1939), the Educated African was made villainous and was poised against a Good African. In *Men of Two Worlds* (1946), on the other hand, the Educated African was positive, if powerless. When he reappeared as the doctor in *Simba* (1955), he was suspected of being a leader of Mau Mau; here a taint of savagery was feared to have dominated Western education, while the education itself was feared to have given him leadership and intelligence. This Educated African was the more remarkable because the contemporaneous and real-life Jomo Kenyatta, holder of a doctorate, was widely believed to be the founder of Mau Mau. In making the doctor in *Simba* innocent, therefore, the filmmakers deliberately turned their backs on easy racism. They could not resist killing him off, however: a good Educated African had to be a Good African, apparently.

With the creation of the Dangerous African in the 1950s, however, films empowered male African characters, thus taking another step away from the old racisms. The initial examples were melodramatic projections of white fear—Mau Mau killers—but the archetype later embraced many kinds of African urgings toward self-realization. The Dangerous African was "dangerous" because he wanted identity and power; he could be the Killer African, but he could also be an African revolutionary or an African politician. His danger was like the Good African's goodness: in the eye of the white beholder. The archetype thus included Sidney Poitier's Mau Mau killer in *Something of Value* (1957), his South African rebel in *The Wilby Conspiracy* (1975), and Denzel Washington's Steve Biko in *Cry Freedom* (1987). (Until the late 1980s, it also included only one woman—Muriel Smith, in *Voice of the Hurricane*). This shift from Mau Mau to martyrdom paralleled a shift in Western attitudes, from colonial fear of Mau Mau to worldwide disgust with South African apartheid—but it has to be emphasized that opposing kinds of Dangerous African were often simultaneous, the result of opposing racial agendas. Out of the anti-apartheid black male came the significant emergence in the 1990s of powerful black women (*Sarafina*); their success at the boxoffice must be seen as a rejection of the old filmic racism by at least a significant part of both audience and industry. It is the more significant because the only other central black woman had been Black Eve (although last seen many years earlier, in 1942).

Eddie Murphy's *Coming to America* (1987) represents a quite different rejection of racist iconography and archetypes. It did not utterly reverse the old order: it did not go so far as to create a black colonialism or a black enslavement—unless it is the new colonialism of pop consumerism, and the enslavement of black women. Whatever hash Murphy made of "Africa," however, he destroyed traditional racist imagery, and that is the issue here.

MOST FILMS ABOUT Africa were made by whites for whites, and so it is not surprising that they concentrated on whites. Nor is it surprising that they abounded in white archetypes. What I have called the White Hunter, the Jungle Lord, the Imperial Man, and the White Queen were most common. These four (and others) are not all racial to the same degree or in the same way, however.

In the real Africa, "white hunter" was so racially charged that after African independence it was replaced by "professional hunter," and Nairobi's White

Hunter Bar was asked to change its name. However, as he appeared in films, the White Hunter was primarily a social and sexual ideal, less so a racial one. That is, "white hunter" usually had accreted associations of competence, class, and sexy masculinity, not overt racism. He could even become the center from which *counter*-racist meanings radiated, as in *The Macomber Affair* (1947) and the 1940 *Safari*; in both those films it is the White Hunter's authority that makes a counterracist scene important. Contrarily, the White Hunter in the 1956 *Safari* slaughtered Africans, so he can be seen as a racial hero. In two of his final embodiments in the 1980s, on the other hand—Chamberlain's Quatermain— the White Hunter was again merely white. That he remained white is, of course, inescapable—and is, for some, proof of racism.

Other white archetypes had strong racial underpinnings. The White Queen was racist almost by definition, her whiteness the key to her magic and her dominance of Africans. Tarzan, the first Jungle Lord, was conceived as a genetic hero of "Nordic" racism. However, the Thalberg-Van Dyke decision to throw out the Greystoke background freed him from eugenics and made him in effect American, certainly no longer a hero of a racial myth, except insofar as he continued to battle—and murder—black Africans. In his post-Sol Lesser avatars, however, he shucked this off, too. The Imperial Man was colonial by definition; his racism was less a matter of overt act than of posture, of assumption. The imperial movies, however, often ended in mass black death, so I conclude that the Imperial Man was based on a racial superiority and a commitment to racial warfare. In some imperial films (*Zulu, Khartoum, Zulu Dawn*), the whites lost this warfare; the triumphant Africans then remained "other," but they were hardly the "unintelligent menials" or "picturesque crowds with spears" of one critic's idea of racism. Thus, the racial message in the imperial films was mixed. It was sufficiently strong, nonetheless, to get South African approval of several of them.

However, it was with the Mercenary, first seen in 1964, that films got a new embodiment of white racism. The Mercenary films do not work very hard at disguising their racism: they are carnivals of black death. They also employ the standard racist imagery, especially savagery in dress and superiority in numbers (the black horde). It is justifiable to say that the Mercenary films are the expression of not merely racism, but of racial hate, and the virulence of that hate is not mitigated by casting a token Good African, as in *Dark of the Sun*. Again, it should be noted that the Mercenary films (except *The Dogs of War*) were made with the cooperation of the South African military and were thus subject to its approval. When Mercenary films were made entirely by South Africans, they turned Africans into monsters (*Whispering Death*, 1971) and generally turned up the racial heat.

By contrast, the Helper—for a while a contemporary of the Mercenary (1960s)—rejected overt racism but inherited racist imagery; black Africans, however, were not equal partners in the Helpers' schemes to help. The Helper was a filmic step away from the Imperial Man, but he and she were still colonial at heart. To a degree, they represented a real-world future that nobody then quite guessed at: the continuation of colonialism in the form of benevolence into the 1990s.

The films' racism, then, as expressed in what I have called archetypes, was widespread but not monolithic, and it fluctuated across the decades, both in degree and in kind. Judged on the basis of the most common white archetypes and the relative lack of positive black ones, it seems to have remained more or less constant through the early decades of the century, then to have increased. It gathered strength (or at least filmic examples) in the 1930s and peaked in the 1940s and 1950s, then fell rather abruptly through the 1960s, to surge again in the 1970s and 1980s in the Mercenary films. Judged by nonfiction films, which relied heavily on both the savage and the jungle imagery, however, racism peaked in the early 1930s and then fell off rapidly and never recovered—but this pattern is probably the result of the collapse of nonfiction as a genre.

Clearly, however, another attitude was also taken toward race in fiction films. This counterracist one was minor for most of film's history, sometimes showing in ways that do not appear in the archetypes. For example, in *The Macomber Affair* (1947) it was Macomber's beating of an African that characterized him as weak and unsympathetic. After the 1960s, of course, the counterracist line became more marked and eventually crossed the racist one. A deliberately counterracist direction can be seen in films about South Africa starting with *The Wilby Conspiracy* (1974); such films had a new, anti-apartheid white archetype, the Awakened White, seen most clearly in *A Dry White Season.* These films and others also needed a new white to represent the evils of apartheid, and the White Torturer occurs in films from *Wilby* to *Sarafina,* most often as a policeman or security officer.

What is the cause of these fluctuations in kind and degree of racism, and of the appearance of counterracist films? It is easy to say that they are responses to historical change, but *which* historical change? To begin to get at an answer, it will be helpful to discover which kinds of films were made by which national industry.

Both of the Robeson African Returner films were British. So were the Educated African films. So was one of the two Dispossessed African pictures, made the more significant by its being *Cry, the Beloved Country.* In addition, the first Helper films were British. Finally, it should not be forgotten that two nonfiction British films of 1929-1930 were, if not antiracist, certainly revisionist: Kearton's *Tembi* and the Treats' *Stampede,* both with "native" casts and African protagonists.

On the other hand, *all* of the Jungle Lord and White Queen movies before 1980 were American, and the Jungle Jim films that caused the anomalous rise in White Hunter films in 1950–1959 were, as well. All but one of the Black Eves were American. Three of the four non-South African movies in which mercenaries kill black Africans in great numbers were American, as was the 1956 *Safari*, with its scenes of black carnage.

It appears, then, that racism, at least as it is represented in "jungle" films, in negative images of black women, and in the race hatred of the Mercenary films, is an American specialty. Counters to such racism, on the other hand, are almost always British. Although these tendencies are far from justifying any such claim as "American films are racist but British films aren't," they do suggest rather different racial preoccupations in the two industries.

Some of this difference may be accounted for by the work of individuals. That is, the Robeson films were what they were because of Paul Robeson, not because of the British film industry; *Cry, the Beloved Country* was what it was because of Zoltan Korda and Alan Paton (just as *The Macomber Affair*, although American, may have got its counterracist tendency because Korda directed it.) *Where No Vultures Fly* and the 1954 *West of Zanzibar* had in common a new attitude toward Africa—and Harry Watt. The importance of individuals to nonracist or antiracist filming is probably reinforced by the relative scarcity of such films; that is, only the rare individual could swim against that tide. Individualism also explains some of the racial fluctuations: counterracism is notable by its eccentricity, its appeal to special audiences (the old "art houses," film festivals), rarely for its appearance in a mainstream movie until the way has been prepared by a smaller, individual's film (as Robeson's films prepared the way for *Men of Two Worlds*).

What the British film industry did *not* do must also be considered: it did not produce jungle pictures, and it did not, except for the internationalized *The Wild Geese*, drench the screen with African blood. What it did do was employ black actors (Martins, Adams, Cameron, McKinney, Welch, Robeson, Poitier) and permit the expression of non- or antiracist ideas (Harry Watt's pictures).

At first glance, the apparently greater American racism is surprising. After all, by 1950 Hollywood was probing around the edges of American racism with films like *Home of the Brave* and *Pinky*. Hollywood was thus, it seems, capable of examining racism, *but not in African settings*.

Two significant differences between the two nations that may have influenced their films must be noted: Britain had a stake in Africa, and the United States did not; and the United States had a large number of black citizens, and Great Britain did not. One result in Britain was an apparently greater tolerance for the individual black person in the 1930s—a tolerance that had drawn Paul Robeson away from his native America before he ever thought of making *Sanders*. This individual tolerance may be analogous to the industry's tolerance of the individually counterracist film.

The American situation was different. Money was to be made from racist iconography (the jungle movies). After 1940, the audience for such films was mostly juvenile. Thus, movies could be made about American racism (*Pinky*) for an adult audience, including blacks and racially liberal whites, that would not destroy another lucrative, juvenile genre that depended on African racism. The reason for the very large disproportion in American jungle archetypes and iconography probably lies, then, not in a conscious conspiracy to perpetuate racism, but in the consumer-driven American movie industry.* Suffice it to say here that nobody in power gave a damn about their content so long as the cheapies turned a profit.

Among adult American films about Africa, then, little counterracism was evident before the 1960s. American fiction films continued mostly to recycle the savage-jungle footage from *KSM* or to make Africans invisible, as in the American Oaf movies. Some minor tendencies showed: *Duel in the Jungle* used the beating of a Good African to characterize its villain; *The Lion* had a minor incident about Africans, but it was couched in the grammar of savagery and was included really to set up the denouement; *Odongo* had a nonwhite child, but it is an old truism of racism that children don't count. A few quality films took another direction: *The Macomber Affair* has already been cited. As well, *Something of Value* was an American film about African race relations that won praise at the Venice Film Festival. *Something of Value* was unquestionably an improvement on most of what had gone before; the very fact that it starred Poitier was significant. But it was a film of many equivocations, one that more often gave the appearance of racial balance than the reality. By comparison with the counterracist British films of the same years, it was a tepid gesture.

And what of Great Britain? Was its smaller proportion of racist films real or apparent? The answer seems to be that the proportion was real. British film seemed less racist than American because it relied less on the timeworn imagery of the jungle, perhaps because it so often focused on imperial men who were not adventurers in an Africa of fantasy but who were, rather, workers at the task of governing. The jungle-savage imagery was offensive (and probably ridiculous) to the colonies themselves, and Britian had to be cautious of offending colonial populations; better to show the positive side of British rule. And, of course, to

---

* Possession of "jungle" and "savage" footage, which was recycled for decades, was probably a factor in perpetuating these films—and their racism. So was juvenile naiveté, which helped inexpensive film-making through reduced shooting schedules, reuse of settings and properties, lower salaries for second-rate people, and so on. As well, children's ignorance encouraged the use of outdated information. As Jan Nedereen Pieterse has pointed out, "In the Western world the culture of the nursery, of children's stories and songs, toys and games, is still in many respects that of colonialism and not that of the 'Third World.'" The very hoariness of the jungle image, which was hardly more sophisticated than the pictures in *Little Black Sambo*, made it accessible to children.

inhibit cinematic criticism of the army, the clergy, or white women. Thus, the *films* may seem less racist; the structure and intent behind them were not necessarily so.

Britain thus had a stake in showing itself as not racist, and it had a structure of censorship to enforce that desire, particularly in its muting of violence. British racism after the end of censorship, on the other hand, could be both real and evident and has erupted into race hatred, as in the carnage of *The Wild Geese*. Overall, racism in British films has come more to resemble that in American films since the 1960s—the same period during which Great Britain increased its domestic black population.

JUST AS THESE films were made mostly by whites and thus show a white bias, so were they made mostly by men and show a male bias. The female roles were significantly fewer and less interesting than the male roles: there were few female protagonists between the mid-1920s and the 1980s; and the females in most films were agents rather than characters. The scarcity of female characters is even more vivid among black females than among white, and only five black female archetypes have been identified (one in a single example from *Voice of the Hurricane*). One black archetype (Black Eve) was negative. The only positive black women in major roles before 1980 appeared in two of the Robeson films and in nonmainstream productions (two of them from the black film industry): *A Daughter of the Congo, Son of Ingagi*, and *Voice of the Hurricane*.

This scarcity of female roles, both black and white, was particularly marked in British films. The British imperial films were virtually womanless. When they had female characters, those characters were either inactive or negative (the Crowing Hen). Other films were womanless or included token women who were marginal (Mia Farrow in *Guns At Batasi*), or they included women who were active and central but negative, like Black Eve. In fact, active women who were also sympathetic were rare in British films about Africa before the 1950s—the 1937 *King Solomon's Mines* was a rare example. Slightly later women were wives, usually wives of Helpers, then wives *and* Helpers. In these Helper roles, however, they functioned mostly as mums. Mum or wife, the British female of later African films remained powerless and found her being in others, at least until the 1980s.

The only significant exception in British silent films was Ayesha. In the 1925 *She*, she was an ambivalent figure, both sex object and monster—in fact, a film vamp. She was more than this, but she was at least this. Her sexuality empowered her, both as a fictional character (erotic obsession as action) and as a woman (men could not resist her). However, Ayesha suffered the vamp's separation from society. She was literally part of an underworld; the men who survived her returned to the "real" world. She was not a woman who could be taken to that real world; the real world—presumably, the world of other British films—had no place for empowered women.

The Black Wife of the British films with Paul Robeson was quite different. She was not a vamp; to the contrary, especially as embodied by Elizabeth Welch in *Song of Freedom*, she was a warm, comforting, supporting woman of great personal courage. Empowerment came through her husband; expression of self was also made through his desires, especially the return to Africa. Yet she stands out in British African films of this period because she was a woman who was a central character; so was Bosambo's wife in *Sanders* (Nina Mae McKinney). And they stand out because the Robeson characters *did* have wives.

In contrast, Sanders didn't have a wife. The district commissioner in *Men of Two Worlds* didn't have a wife. Rhodes didn't have a wife. The soldiers of *Four Feathers* didn't have wives.

One could say that imperial plots didn't have time or space for wives, but this is circular. Imperial men didn't have wives because women were trivial; only men were important. Only when women and children were needed to express the ownership of colonial real estate did they come into British films: *We own this because we have put down roots here. This must be our land because we have put our women and our children on it.* That is, women were important only insofar as they represented male ownership.

Such women still had no power, but they had value. This was a kind of step forward—like putting your hand into boiling water instead of the fire.

The Robeson characters, however, had wives twenty years before other men in British films. In Bosambo's case, a wife and child became a critique of the eunuch of empire—the putative hero of the film—because Bosambo now seems more human. Zoltan Korda may have thus undercut the film's imperial content, perhaps unconsciously. By giving Bosambo a wife and child, the film—in later British terms—seemed to be saying that the land was theirs, certainly the opposite of the film's stated intention. In the case of the other Robeson heroes, love also enabled a more fully fleshed man. In *Song of Freedom*, he took his wife with him to Africa; in *Jericho*, he married when he found a place for himself there. The women were secondary characters, but they had individual identities, and they were much more than the surveyor's pegs of a property line.

But other than these Black Wives, London found very little room for women in Africa until the Mau Mau crisis.

America never had any national interest in Africa—no colonies, especially— and no real knowledge of it. It had no reason to stake a claim by showing wives and families. (The family in *Clarence, the Cross-Eyed Lion* is a rarity.) What

America did have (from Stanley and Roosevelt—both Americans, although Stanley was only a temporary one) was a complex male imagery of adventure, action, search, and self-aggrandizement. The early nonfiction films showed a male landscape: there were virtually no white women in Cherry Kearton's pictures of East Africa during Roosevelt's safari, for example, and none at all in Paul Rainey's films. Even in the 1920s and 1930s some of the appeal of Osa Johnson in her husband's African footage was her supposed rarity, perhaps her vulnerability. The realities of contemporary Africa—wives, children, schools, sweethearts, old women—were irrelevant.

One female archetype has dominated American fiction films, the White Queen. All but three of the White Queens were American; those three exceptions were early British Ayeshas. What made the figure so attractive to Americans?

Not, clearly, aggressive female sexuality, Ayesha's dominant quality. The last entirely American *She* (with an African locale) was made in 1917, and the 1925 version was rejected by American reviewers despite its American star.* Ayesha's overt eroticism and power were not to American taste, apparently. Neither was Haggard's ambivalence toward female sexuality. At least after 1925, then, American taste wanted a virginal White Queen—in the form of the female fantasy queens of the serials and Bs—but not the vampish, rather literary and explicitly erotic Ayesha.

By comparison with Ayesha, the American White Queen spinoffs—jungle princesses, jungle goddesses, white priestesses, et al.—were mostly rosy-cheeked and scrubbed. Some were jungle girls; some were magicians; a few were bad; but most were good and sweet and as American as Chase Manhattan. And, sexily though they were dressed, they were chaste, waiting for Mister Right.

The salient quality of the White Queen, American style, was that she was in black Africa at all. She was *white*—inescapably, inevitably—and so she didn't really belong there: she was there only to be rescued from her surroundings. By the time we see her in a movie (when she is an adult, or at least a shapely adolescent), she has established her separateness from black Africans—as well, often, as her dominance of them. She is outside the tribe that raised her—unmarried, virginal, "other" to their otherness.

This, then, was one characteristic of the archetype: she was waiting for a white male. That such waiting utterly defied what common sense and anthropology would tell us is beside the point: within the probabilities of the White Goddess fantasy, she was untouchable by blacks. When the white hero appeared, he was inevitably "the first white man she has ever seen." So the White Goddess was an

---

* Other vamps did occur in American silent films about Africa, however, notably Louise Glaum in *Leopard Woman* (1920).

archetype of a racial myth, one in which she both escaped the fear of black sexuality that underlay *Birth of a Nation* and opened instantly to the white male.

She was also the virgin who has to be "awakened", a Sleeping Beauty surrounded by a jungle of African thorns. She was a valuable object to be searched for (and this was one of the fictional fringe benefits of the archetype, that she set up a quest story). Once found, her very existence elevated the man, making him even more of a real man (because she "falls in love with him") as compared to false men (the Africans who never touched her and who represented no threat to her virginity, neither from them nor from her own desire). Once the American white man had appeared, she became a woman—*only* a woman—and had to be defended, often saved, from the very Africans she had been ruling. Thus, not only did the man expand his own identity and reduce that of black men, but he also destroyed the White Queen's power and demonstrated his own superior strength.

Unlike Ayesha, who could not be taken above ground, most of the White Queens could be taken home to mother—and father. By then, however, she was no longer a White Queen; she was just an American girl in a leopard skin, glad to be swept off her bare feet and turned into a wife.

The White Queen movies, then, were myths of white (American) patriarchy. They were not set in Africa because of any intrinsic interest in Africa; they were set there because Africa was a suitable locus of American white male fantasy.

Tarzan was usually an idealized patriarchal hero, powerful, ruthless, xenophobic; his taking of the virginal Jane was the other side of the White Goddess-white man coin. The remarkable intensification of the rate at which Tarzan, White Goddess, and similar movies were released in the 1940s and 1950s (sixty-seven jungle fantasies in twenty years) indicates an audience saturated with myths of white patriarchy—kids sitting in the darkness on Saturday afternoons, learning how to be American dads and moms from Tarzan and the White Goddess.

These decades also managed to insert sexism into even the casting of the films, suggesting, in the replicability of the actresses who played with Weissmuller and Johnny Sheffield (the Tarzan, Jungle Jim, and Bomba movies) a throwaway idea of women. After Maureen O'Sullivan, the Janes began to come and go every few pictures; after Weissmuller turned to playing Jungle Jim, he had a different female for every film, and so did Sheffield, and so did the post-Weissmuller Tarzans.

The only constants were the men who starred and the men who produced and directed. This vision of Africa was really the work of a small circle (which is not to say that it was atypical). Ford Beebe directed all the Bombas at Monogram; Spencer Bennet and William Berke directed ten Jungle Jims between them at Columbia, most produced by Sam Katzman. But it was Sol Lesser at Columbia who produced that seemingly endless chain of Tarzans, with their throwaway Janes and knee-jerk exotics—Amazon, she-devil, slave girl, leopard woman, huntress, mermaid, jungle goddess, even an old woman renewed by a magic fountain. Some of these women were evil, and so when Tarzan wasn't saving women because they were weak, he was beating them because they were strong.

This was also the period (the 1940s and early 1950s) when American women were being driven back into the house after their brief fling in the bomber factories. Perhaps, too, it was a period when boys needed to be prepped for a competitive world that had jobs again (for men). Only a few years earlier, Maureen O'Sullivan had brought real femaleness and individuality to the role of Jane: in 1932–1936, her first three films saw her as the Wild Mate, the suitable consort with her own inner life. It is no accident that she was the contemporary of two of the three Witty Women in American films about Africa and of the women of 1930s Hollywood comedy. In the late 1930s, however, she withdrew into the Mrs. Tarzan of the later Depression, and the other Janes and jungle girls followed.

Other white female archetypes gave somewhat mixed messages. The Strong Woman, who was effectively manless and endangered, but competent, occurred in widely separated decades. She was imitated in nonfiction in the 1920s and 1930s by Osa Johnson (dressed, like Kathlyn Williams' Captain Kate, in mannish clothes, sometimes shown with a gun). The Strong Woman's reappearance in the 1980s was hardly surprising—why so late? is one's response—but her early appearance is more difficult to understand. Before 1915, the Strong Woman was the film contemporary of the vamp and of such vulnerable virgins as the first Jane. Like the vamp, the Strong Woman had her own setting (the jungle), which was markedly abnormal by most female standards. Unlike the vamp, she was no threat to other women or to marriage. She even needed saving sometimes, but saving her did not automatically confer love on the savior. Nor did she present herself as endangered (and therefore virginal): unlike Enid Markey's Jane, for example, Kathlyn Williams carried her head up and her chest out, and her body was almost beefy. She was also rare among white characters, male or female, in seeming to belong in "Africa". The vamps and the Strong Woman would suggest that early silents expressed some of the protofeminist consciousness of the first part of the century, but that both were essentially outsiders. The endangered virgins and similar females in silents (e.g., the two women of *Son of Tarzan*), on the other hand, were admitted to the (male) world; so were the heroines of a number of melodramatic "women's pictures" set in Africa (*Poppy*, 1915).

The True-Blue White Woman had her biggest decade in 1950-1959, when her ability to endure without complaint suited an America bent on security and family. The archetype is too generalized to do justice to Deborah Kerr's luminous performance in *KSM*, but it at least explains that character's grit and its ability to stand up to Stewart Granger's snarl. The archetype was well suited to Susan Hayward in *The Snows of Kilimanjaro*, too: her principal task there was to nurse Gregory Peck while he nearly bored himself to death with the rest of the movie, which was made up mostly of ludicrous flashbacks. Hayward, in fact, was the ideal woman-in-Africa of this decade (*The Snows of Kilimanjaro, White Witch-Doctor, Untamed*); no other actress suffered so stoically or breathed so heavily.

The Female Simp was a creature of the same years. Molly Haskell has anatomized the American women of the 1950s films; her analysis explains the Simp's contradictory nature—the relentless eroticism and the relentless withdrawal from contact, the utter inappropriateness of her huge wardrobe, and her childish lack of skills. Such women were "robbed of their identity and intelligence on film" and became mere carriers of huge breasts; "the mammary fixation is the most infantile—and most American—of the sex fetishes, and indeed the fifties, in which bosom power was supreme, was the least adult decade in movie, and national, history." This "dehumanization" of women is recognizable in the Simps—the wide-eyed idiot look of Rhonda Fleming and Jeanne Crain, their lack of reason for being. No wonder that their counterparts, the American Oafs, were surly: they had come to Africa to find what earlier male heroes had found (White Goddesses, wealth, adventure), and here they were with these overdressed and lobotomized pompom girls. No wonder that 1950s movie males were, in Joan Mellen's words, "alienated from the world." Indeed, a case can be made that it was that alienation that drove them to Africa in the first place, where now there was no place for them. Nor was it accidental that most of the Oaf actors were getting on in years: the Oaf films, and the Oaf roles, were American responses to a changed world, one in which the old American male personae were ill at ease.

As the number of African films decreased after 1970, so did the number of female roles, although they fell so low proportionally that it is fair to say that both British and American films about Africa were shying away from women in that decade. What roles existed, were, if anything, retrogressive.

In the 1980s, on the other hand, the number of films increased, and both British and American films found room for women again: Sigourney Weaver's Strong Woman/Helper in *Gorillas in the Mist*; Fiona Shaw's wonderfully realized proto-feminist in *The Mountains of the Moon*; the Barbara Hershey role in *A World Apart*. However, the decade's rush toward nostalgia and camp generally positioned white women in secondary roles or took control of events away from them, as in *Out of Africa* and *White Mischief*. Bo Derek's Jane sometimes seemed to be a Strong Woman, but the camera treated her as a soft-core sex object. By the early 1990s, however, real strength and identity came to black women in films like *Sarafina* (which included an American star [Whoopi Goldberg] but was not an American film).

Until at least 1970, then, American women's roles seem rather different from British. American males created a fantasy of White Queens and black enmity; British males created a fantasy of bad African women and no white women at all. American films included women but defined them in the narrowest terms; British films simply excluded them.

Thus, one looks almost in vain for a film from either country before 1980 in which a woman drove the action, made the definitive moral choice, or existed and acted independently of a man or romance. One looks almost in vain for a film from either country in which a woman was *not* the object of male quest, or was not taken along on a male quest, or was not the reward for male action. The exceptions are Kathlyn Williams' roles before 1915, the woman in *Voice of the Hurricane*, and the female doctor in *Son of Ingagi*. Black women were even more invisible than black men, less seen and certainly less individualized than white women.

Indeed, it is safe to say that for both British and American mainstream motion pictures, Africa has been that continent where women have been kept in their place. South African film, which would introduce the Strong Black Woman in the 1990s, was even more male-centered than British or American. The South African idea of white women was similar to that in the Simp movies, but with far greater emphasis on motherhood (*Dingaka*). Women are notable in most South African films by their absence, making *Sarafina* the more remarkable.

MATTERS OF CLASS are less visible in these films than race or gender, perhaps because the films so often fail to show people at work—that is, there is often an implication of white upper-class indolence, but little insistence on it. The result until after World War II was a distorted picture of colonial and postcolonial Africa, whose workers here seemed to consist principally of professional hunters, imperial civil or military officials, and black menials. The lack of working-class and middle-class people in these films contradicted the African reality of Indian shopkeepers, Goan and female clerks, black schoolteachers and civil servants, white and black farmers, and all the others who in fact made and make Africa go. In their place were a hugely disproportionate number of treasure seekers, explorers, and recreational hunters, most of them apparently millionaires. They, however, were visitors, so that the distortions of class were further bent by the distortions of nonresidence. Africa, in so many of the films, was a place where wealthy or would-be wealthy whites visited, helped by a few resident and apparently upper-class white officials.

Before sound, class emblems were mostly sartorial, with substantial help from aristocratic or military titles. Putting the actors into formal clothes represented money or status—evening dress, tail coats, the elegant shipboard gowns and suits of a film like *The Missing Link*.

Sound brought a new emblem to the representation of class: accent. British accents were usually not, in fact, upper-class, but "stage British"; this neutralized Oxbridge sufficed for a range of social levels, from prime ministers and peers through generals and second sons; in America, this sort of British accent always "had class." The implication seems to have been that these men could go directly from their posts to a London drawing room, as they seemed to have come directly from a top-level public school to Africa. By the 1960s and Michael Caine's officer in *Zulu*, however, this stereotype would seem to have lost its force.

Class was also important in stigmatizing the man (never a woman) who had "gone native" and was thus declassé. The emblems of that fall were class-based: unshaven face, improper clothes, sometimes heavy drinking (Bogart in *The African Queen*). Class was also a factor in the wrongness of certain characters who were "un-British"—i.e., foreign, like the hotel manager in *The High Command*, a film whose other characters were British officers and therefore genteel. In general, class distinctions suggested by casting, especially accent, were more typical of British than of American films. British casting can be seen as an important exploitation of class stereotypes in British film, with the conventionalized "stage-upper-class" actor—e.g., Leslie Banks as Sanders—used to elevate imperial male figures.

Other than the Imperial Man and the man who has "gone native," however, major male archetypes did not have close class associations. The White Hunter was perhaps surprising in this regard, but, except for the British accent of Douglas Fairbanks, Jr., and Stewart Granger, actors playing White Hunters have rarely suggested class. Many film White Hunters have been played by Americans without class implications (Harry Carey, Gregory Peck, Victor Mature). The casting of Robert Redford in *Out of Africa* was true to this pattern, even though untrue to his character's real-life model. Sometimes the Americanized White Hunter was contrasted with a client who was wealthy or upper-class; in that case, the White Hunter's classlessness was a virtue associated with masculinity (the 1956 *Safari, Mogambo*). This democratized American maleness also typified the American Oaf.

A similar anti-elitism Americanized Tarzan. With the excision of his aristocratic background in 1932, Tarzan's *enemies* were frequently played by British actors—film aristos who wanted to capture him or find the elephant's graveyard. The thoroughly Americanized Tarzan generally took a democratic, anti-upper-class position.

Generally, then, American films before the 1970s tended to elide "British upper class" with weakness (in men), unless the men were middle-aged or older (Cedric Hardwicke, C. Aubrey Smith); thus, Donald Sinden in *Mogambo* was no match for the American Gable. Even when the British upper-class man was not weak in American films, he was often villainous, like Tarzan's enemies or David

Farrar in *Duel in the Jungle* or Roland Culver in the 1956 *Safari*. To be sure, there were exceptions: Stewart Granger in *KSM* and *The Last Safari*, for example (although he was a villain in *The Wild Geese*).

Martin and Osa Johnson did for nonfiction films what Weissmuller and Thalberg did for fiction. They erased the Explorer's class; determinedly Midwestern, plain "Mr. and Mrs.," they did without British-accented voice-overs or associations of aristocracy. Only in *Across the World With Mr. and Mrs. Martin Johnson* do their evening clothes suggest the class that used to dress for dinner.

Women were also subject to stereotypes of class. The Witty Women in American films were presented as lower-class or working-class: Ann Sothern in *Congo Maisie* was a "chorus girl," as was Ava Gardner in *Mogambo*; Una Merkel in *The Road to Zanzibar* had a vague theatrical connection. The "chorus girl" association was probably allied to an actress-whore stereotype; such women were outside normal society and thus had both special privileges, such as their wisecracks and cleverness, and special limitations, such as being less attractive to the hero than a "classier" woman. The very upper-class Grace Kelly, for example, was neither a wisecracker nor a working woman in *Mogambo*, and for most of the film Gable was crazy about her; Gardner's sexually easy, clever chorus girl couldn't compete. Like Gardner in *Mogambo* and Janet Leigh in *Safari* (1956), Madeleine Carroll (*Safari*, 1940) "traveled with" a wealthy man whose only attraction seemed to be money; Dorothy Lamour was planning the same sort of liaison in *The Road to Zanzibar*. These Depression-era "kept women" conflate class and gender and are implicitly exploited in both.

The three Crowing Hens, all from British films, were working women (journalist, author, member of Parliament) but were cast and played as upper-middle-class types, at least to judge from accents and clothes. Because the Crowing Hen was meant negatively, the fact that the women had careers probably said more about gender roles than about class: they were, like the American chorus girls, "unnatural." None of them had any inner life, nor was any of them allowed any sexual self: unlike the American chorus girls, they had been desexed.

The vamps generally, including Ayesha and Glaum's Leopard Woman, were *déclassées*. So was the Black Eve, although she was below, rather than beyond class; when she attracted a man, he fell out of his class.

Class stereotypes became less clear after the mid-1960s, then veered back again toward class consciousness after 1980. By the 1960s, a British film like *Guns at Batasi* could concentrate on other ranks as well as officers. By the 1970s, the British effeminate-aristocrat stereotype was pretty well gone, perhaps a victim of British military prowess in World War II, and perhaps of "classy" British superheroes like Bond. Such changes were not permanent, however. The British aristocrat returned with force in the 1980s. Tarzan's noble heritage was restored in *Greystoke*; *Out of Africa* and *White Mischief* revered high class. *White Mischief* presented that class as corrupt, to be sure, but the film would not exist if its central figure were not a British peer. *Out of Africa's* social world was an elevated one, the historical Lord Delamere included; the opening sequence in Denmark was as beautifully Edwardian and aristocratic as anything in *Greystoke*. Older stereotypes of accent and manners, however, were rather shaky, most of all with the casting of Robert Redford as Denys Finch Hatton. *Coming to America* may also deserve inclusion among recent films of class awareness, although its awareness was based entirely on consumption. Royalty was expressed as wealth, often as a vulgar display of wealth. Only James Earl Jones's king had the older associations of class through his accent and his manner.

South African films after the early sixties were idiosyncratic. The white-black chasm was social as well as racial, but within white society a generalized look of middle-class privilege has prevailed (*Dingaka*, even *A Dry White Season*). The Promised Land of the *voortrekkers* is now, in filmic myth if not in fact, a place of malls, washing machines, and universal (white) consumerism. Class distinction would violate both the myth of the chosen people and the solidarity of race. *City of Blood*, however, foregrounded an urban underclass of white pimps and prostitutes—one of the reasons why it was an innovative film. *Sarafina* did not seem to consider class at all, but focused instead on race and power.

IT IS TOO much to expect that a nation's films should reflect the specifics of its experience in every detail. Francoise Pfaff opined that "Africa is seen by the West as a reflection of America rather than Africa," but this can hardly be true— British movies, as we have seen, are not at all "reflections" of America, nor are South African. Nonetheless, it seems true that film sometimes does show a connection with national or cultural history; in the case of at least one country, South Africa, the history of motion pictures and the history of sociopolitics seems quite close.

South African films (and those international films with South African participation) rather specifically mirror South African history, probably because the machinery of government, which drove both policy and censorship, has been so pervasive and so powerful. Certainly since World War II, South African film has been a branch of propaganda, and even in its genres (e.g., subsidized black films in tribal languages) it has expressed policy rather than merely following policy. It is too strong to say that South African propaganda was overt in all international films in which South Africa participated in the 1960s, but it would be foolish to deny that it was often influential. Even a run-of-the-mill production like *Sands of the Kalahari* (1965) seemed to have been affected by apartheid when the only black character in its source novel—an American intellectual—was cut from the film version.*

Great Britain and the United States are, by comparison with South Africa, far more complex in the relationships between their cultures and their films. They do not demonstrate national "agendas" so much as the limited diversity possible within the currently fashionable idea of hegemony: harmless alternatives to established power, within a context of large demonstrations of that power (i.e., mainstream movies). Each country had a partly official machinery for censorship, but neither was as rigorous or as political as South Africa's, and censorship in both countries disappeared decades ago. The result was a mild diversification of ideas, with sometimes opposing views appearing in different films, the result of both individual expression (*Cry, the Beloved Country, Song of Freedom*) and the rise of multiple audiences, probably as a result of the breakdown of the studio system and the monopoly theater chains.

Two salient points about British film before African independence have been noted: that it used less obviously racist imagery than American film and allowed more dissident racial views; and that it was male-centered and even misogynistic in its exclusion of women. To these could be added a less clear third point: that it tended to conflate upper-class characteristics and male centrality, at least in the imperial films. Taken together, these tendencies suggest that British film until the 1960s was conceived from a position of privileged, male, white confidence rather than from one of insecurity—that is, the very lack of insistent racism, sexism, or classism suggests that conditions of race, gender, and class in British Africa suited Britain just fine. They were evidently found so "natural," and they so suited British power, that they did not need to

---

* Early British and American films *about* South Africa suggest how a filmic stereotype satisfies a cultural hegemony and then abruptly fails when real events intervene. Pre-1924 films, both South African and foreign, associated South Africa with wealth—specifically diamonds—and British culture. These "diamond" films ended with the Nationalist (Afrikaner) victory of 1924. The pre-1924 stereotype was revived just after World War II (*Diamond City, The Great Adventure*) but seemed archaic; subsequent films adopted the Afrikaner rather than the British myth (e.g., *Untamed, The Fiercest Heart*), or an apparently neutral tone not offensive to South African censorship (*Rhino, Sands of the Kalahari*), or a violent one (*The Wild Geese*). Certainly, one reason was that such films could be distributed in South Africa; and another was that they could use South Africa's cheap technical facilities and rent-a-grunt army. However, when films have been made about contemporary South Africa but without South African participation, the Afrikaner myth has been rejected.

be forced in film. The 1935 *Sanders*, it should be remembered, was conceived as a celebration of British competence, not as a defense of it. The later Robeson films were allowable alternatives because, probably, they were no real threat.

This upper-white-male cluster in British film was not adaptable to fundamental change in Africa. At best, it appears to have been always behind the curve. Attempts to adapt to independence movements were too late and too little (*Where No Vultures Fly* and *West of Zanzibar*). Put at its crudest, it appears that British films could imagine Africa on British terms or not at all. When Africa was no longer British, an orgy of hand-wringing ensued in the form of white male reversions to the past, often produced in South Africa or with South African cooperation (*Zulu*), or bleak white male looks at the black African future (*Guns at Batasi*). A non-British Africa literally had no white male British film imagery, and such Africa as appeared in the 1970s did so either as more of the doleful white male past (*Zulu Dawn*) or as a violent white male present (*The Wild Geese*). Later, in the early 1980s, only by looking back toward an all-white, all-British, male-privileged past could British pictures create African images that were not also anti-African—and that were not made with South African help (*Greystoke*, *White Mischief*). This nostalgia, however, was won at the expense of a rein-vigorated classism. Very recent British films suggest a new ability to look at black Africa itself (*The Kitchen Toto*) and to include women in the imperial picture (*The Mountains of the Moon, Mister Johnson*).

The British nonfiction films reflected the same shift and the same rather abrupt loss of confidence. They exploited the "colonial gaze," and those, particularly, that used the airplane's ability to cover vast distances (*With Cobham to the Cape, Wings Over Africa*) projected the imperial embrace over large chunks of the continent. British nonfiction films were generally optimistic motion pictures that showed Britons getting where they set out to go, shooting the animals they claimed as theirs, leapfrogging over dangerous terrain in frail aircraft. That all this ended abruptly in 1940 indicates that, as with the fiction films, no alternative Africa was filmically imaginable. "Africa" was actually "Our Africa," and when it ceased to be Britain's in fact, the camera looked elsewhere: there was no iconography for an Africa without British power.

The American experience has been somewhat different. America and Britain have cultures of common origins but very different histories. One most significant difference is worth noting: slavery. The United States was a slave nation; Britain was not. Britain became an antislavery culture after an early history of profiting from the trade; its vigorous private and official moves against the slave trade in the nineteenth century represented, perhaps, penance for earlier acts. America did not do such penance; instead, it fought a ghastly civil war in which slavery was one of the major issues. The end of slavery after that war did not, however, remove slavery from the white American consciousness, and it is likely that it still remains there, taking two forms, guilt and fear: guilt for what was done, fear of reprisals—above all sexual reprisals. Guilt produced such mythic types (not restricted to films of Africa) as the Tragic Mullato and the Weeping Slave, even while slavery flourished; fear produced—and produces—images of black violence. *Birth of a Nation* set out that fear in cinematic terms.

Many of the films considered in this book suggest that Africa cannot be separated from that American guilt and fear. The guilt is perhaps partly assuaged by reinforcing the dehumanization of Africans, picturing them as unfeeling, subhuman, without inner lives or family structures. The fear can perhaps be assuaged by giving it a cinematic name—a film image—and destroying it on film. The fear-inducing savage runs through the underbrush of scores of American movies; his painted face peers from the leaves; he is glimpsed, weapon in hand. He sometimes takes dream forms: the pygmies of *Tarzan the Ape Man*, like evil black children (a visual play on the derogatory "boy"), or the gross giant of John Derek's *Tarzan*, a nightmare rapist. American fear demanded that this figure be crushed before the dream ended. Scores of American movies end with the destruction of African villages, from the 1914 *Won in the Clouds* ("closing with the burning of the whole savage village with lyddite bombs dropped from the airship!") to the 1932 *Tarzan the Ape Man* to the 1980 *Dogs of War*.

We might ask why the major carrier of this iconography (the serials and Bs) were let die in the 1950s. One answer appears to be that a more modern fear-guilt object appeared in Mau Mau, producing *Something of Value* and the 1956 *Safari*; another is that the American civil rights movement was grasping white attention. American society was at last confronting its own apartheid, Southern style, with the movement that restored civil rights and destroyed the Jim Crow laws.

The American psyche had to change. American films about Africa did not, however, lead this change; they followed it, and not too closely. American films about Africa did not relax racially until the end of the 1960s, and then only slightly; the real-life racial violence of the 1960s fed the first of the Mercenary films. Paradoxically, however, that real violence may have substituted for cinematic violence, the more so because images of it were so available on television. Their effect may have been to neutralize much of the old fear, which, being realized, was confronted. The very worst of it then moved into the Mercenary films, where it took forms theretofore unseen—multiples of violence, death, rape, racial vengeance. It is significant that the first of the Mercenary movies, *Dark of the Sun*, showed the rape and murder of a whole trainload of whites and could not avenge it: this was the upper end of racial fear, that which could not be assuaged by television and reality. Yet, this is not the whole story: at the very same time, other parts of the industry were making the Helper films and the Oaf films. Again, it was a divided industry and audience, with competing images representing competing ideas.

It should not, then, be surprising to find that some American movies began a rapprochement with South Africa at the same time. White South African culture apes American culture in many respects, above all in its materialism and its pose of classlessness; the two societies resemble each other in their enculturated violence, as well. Seen in this context, the films the two societies had in common through the eighties and nineties were to be expected, from *Dark of the Sun* to *Sarafina*. The American South, on which America used to be able to project its idea of race (*Birth of a Nation, Gone With the Wind, Pinky*), changed; the African South took its place—or, rather, its places, for American audiences have had both *Dark of the Sun* and *Cry Freedom*. However, it must be said that of the anti-apartheid films that have appeared since 1970, few were American.

It would appear, then, that the likely bedrock of American films about Africa is white male guilt and fear. Predictably, this psychological foundation has been indifferent to the real Africa. (It did not, in fact, conceive of it as real.) Changes in the real place, therefore, have had little effect on this foundation. What has affected it has been change in America.

The real Africa has little or no reality for America. Postcolonial Africa appears to have no reality, or at least no accessible filmic imagery, for Great Britain, as well. In the 1980s and what we have seen of the 1990s, both cultures appear to have lost all interest in the contemporary Africa that stretches from the Sahara to the Limpopo; instead, both have shown nostalgia for old archetypes, old events, and old class distinctions (*Greystoke, Out of Africa*).

It remains to be seen whether a new cinematic Africa can be created in Britain and America. It would not be for lack of subject matter: even granting that both cultures will want to make films about whites, there is enough white involvement throughout modern Africa to justify hundreds of movies that need not be racist or colonial. Novelists like Maria Thomas and Doris Lessing (not to mention Olive Schreiner), real-life figures like the Leakey family, the experiences of Peace Corps workers and Fulbright scholars and aid workers—these and hundreds more could supply materials. The new white Africans of Kenya and Zimbabwe have yet to be looked at. America has also a large African–American population with its own African films to make, both of the diaspora and of its reverse. Modern Africa abounds in novelists, both black and white, whose work would translate into film.

Whether such films will ever be made is another question. The real puzzler is whether the psychological need exists for the creation of a new Africa. At the moment, it appears not. In the midnineties, at the end of the first century of filmmaking about Africa, the two major producers seem able only to look backward, longing for the psyche that was, or southward to the third producer, signing on to the psyche that is.

APPENDIX _____

Table 1 British and American films, by decades*

TYPE	PERIODS								
	1900–1909	1910–1919	1920–1929	1930–1939	1940–1949	1950–1959	1960–1969	1970–1979	1980–1989
Fiction									
US	3	32	27	24	36	57	26	5	10
GB	0	6	10	12	2	7	11	3	4
Other	0	10	4	0	1	2	2	4	4
Nonfiction									
US	9	9	13	9	3	7	4	2	0
GB	1	7	14	17	0	1	0	0	0
Other	1	3	1	2	0	3	3	1	0

* Figures from films in the filmography only.

Despite a skewing in the first decade (when most American films were short Boer War actualities), it is clear that nonfiction film-making was primarily a pre-1940 activity and that Britain, which outproduced the United States in the two biggest decades (31 to 22), had a far higher proportion of nonfiction production. In fact, the proportion of US to British nonfiction films was 7 to 5; if the first decade is dropped, the proportion drops to barely 6 to 5—very different from the 3-to-1 American dominance of film production overall.

Among fiction films, the totals (220 to 55) show a virtual 4-to-1 ratio.

Table 2 American jungle fantasy films, by decades

TYPE	PERIODS								
	1900–1909	1910–1919	1920–1929	1930–1939	1940–1949	1950–1959	1960–1969	1970–1979	1980–1989
Tarzan		2	7	7	8	11	4		1
Jungle Jim				1	2	10			
Bomba					2	10			
Other*		1	3	9	16	8	3		1

_____

* "Other" includes all American serials and B movies in the genre; such classification is hard to apply before 1920 and after c. 1960. Such films are fantastic (including the white queen and jungle princess movies, the lost tribes and lost civilizations) and, generally, are films made cheaply for a very unsophisticated, usually juvenile, audience.

These films account for 39 of the 57 American films in 1950–1959, 28 of the 36 in 1940–1949; altogether, they account for 106 of the 220 American fiction films—just about half.

Examination of the filmography will show how availability of videos is skewed toward these same films.

ENDNOTES

Introduction

Page
11 . . . with Africans often presented as heroic and beautiful. Relich, 1990, 10, 18.

11 ". . . provided a pseudo-scientific . . . imperialism." Gerard, *African*, 181.

12 . . . the same as Britain's and were in fact derived from Britain's. Cameron, *Into Africa*.

12–13 . . . what Pierre Sorlin has called its "capital. . . ." Sorlin, *History*, 20.

13 It has become a truism. . . . racist. Vaughan, 1960; Wiley, 1981; Pfaff, 1982; Stam and Spence, 1983; Ukadike, 1990.

13 "'. . . master race' narcissism" and "the voyeuristic gaze. . . ." Ukadike, "Images," 38; Stam, quoted in Ukadike, ibid.

13 ". . . colonialist," forever "entrenched in the dehumanizing spirit of slavery?" Ukadike, "Images", 31.

14 . . . South African . . . separate study. Tomaselli 1986A, 1986B.

14 . . . beyond discoveries of racism. Much current criticism has identified a racism in commercial film that is seen as so monolithic that it is usable as a weapon with which to berate commercialism itself, and, through it, capitalism. (*e.g.*, Spence and Stam, 1983). It would be convenient and neat if, in fact, the villains of racism identified themselves so easily. Regrettably, they do not, and locating the ultimate cause of racism in film is often difficult if not impossible. Nonetheless, for these authors, racism and capitalism are the same thing, the test of racism being a reductive *cui bono*? I take this to be a fashionable marxism-with-a-small-m (Marxism, like apartheid, having both a petty and a grand form), and so it seems often to have as its actual subject capitalism and not the ostensible one—in this case, racism. Now, marxism-with-a-small-m has been very helpful in enabling new critical attitudes and destroying a great deal of nonsense; on the other hand, it is full of nonsense itself, as recent history has shown. It is ultimately reductive, too, and it is used polemically by people who otherwise wrap themselves in the mantle of scholarship. If one must take a marxist stance, far better to take a Gramscian one, and acknowledge that hegemony has much room for exceptions. Otherwise, one starts out to look at racism in film and winds up saying that capitalism is a bad thing, but we already know that—just as we know that, like democracy, it is probably the best thing we can hope for.

Chapter 1 The White Queen and the Hunter

17 ". . . with [my own hands] hoisted the British flag over the Transvaal. . . ." *London Times*, 6 April 1920 (8c).

19 Will Arda. *London Times*, 23 June 1917, 4a.

19 "Never had an idea . . . drawing quality of the film." *Variety*, 27 April 1917: 25.

19 Within a year, Lucoque had bought film rights. . . . Higgins, 224.

19 "possibly . . . the best . . . during the war." Low, *1914–1918*, 178.

19 "a most modern and intelligent vampire." *London Times*, 18 February 1925, 12e.

21 "The cinema theatres are . . . beauties . . . history . . . romance. . . ." *London Times*, 5 November 1919, 8d.

21 "[Its] day was long ago. . . ." *Variety*, 14 July 1926, 18.

21–22 "symbolizes . . . sexual lust . . . so like the fires of hell," Higgins, 98, 106.

23 Re *white* professional. Cameron, *Into Africa*, 159–161.

24 "all big and little boys . . . what it is to-day." Quoted in review, *London Times*, 19 May 1919, 17b.

24   Early South African production. Tomaselli, "Capital."
24   See also Gutshe, *History*. Re *AQ* and *KSM*: Higgins, *Haggard*, 205, apparently confuses the African Film Productions films with Lucoque's purchase of rights; perhaps some deal between Lucoque and AFP was involved.
24   . . . no releases between 1925 and 1930. Tomaselli, *Cinema*, 261–62. See also Hennebelle, "Pretoria," 262, for early Afrikaans-English films.
25–26   "English film crowds . . . at close quarters." *London Times*, 19 May 1919, 17b.
26   African film extras. Tomaselli, "Capital," 36.
26   ". . . as good as, if not better than, *King Solomon's Mines.*" *London Times*, 3 November 1919, 10a.
26   "would require . . . romantic credulity." *London Times*, 21 October 1935, 12b.
27   "a request for the toning down of violence." Richards, "Palace," 149.
27   "European adventurers in search . . . give support." *London Times*, 26 July 1937, 10b.
28   "Mass stuff, unashamed hokum," *Variety*, 30 June 1937, 21.
28   "a vast panorama of Africa . . . native tribes" *New York Times*, 10 November 1950, 35:1.
30   "without her courage . . . the film would never have been finished." Granger, *Sparks*, 181.
31   "crudities of style. . . ." *London Times*, 26 July 1937, 10b.

Chapter 2 The Aristocrat of the Treetops

33   Burroughs's "twin sources." Etherington, *Haggard*, 115.
33   ". . . had done some reading . . . his writing career. . . ." Holzmark, *Burroughs*, 38.
34   "[His] comments about blacks . . . certainly very patronizing . . ." Holtzmark, *Burroughs*, 48.
34   "Burroughs implies . . . evolutionary trends. . . ." *Ibid.*
34   "I will obey the Chief. . . ." "Tribe of Tarzan" rules, in Fenton, *Swingers*, 70–71.
37   "The whites come . . . to the ground." Bazin, 83.
38   "the personification of Tarzan of the Apes as I visualize him . . ." Quoted in Fenton, *Swingers*, 130.
39   "enslaver." Ukadike, "Images," 34.
39   . . . a cruelty that is still an industry benchmark. Baxter, *Stunt*, 163. Cruelty to animals was not new. Elmo Lincoln supposedly stabbed to death a drugged, aged lion for a sequence in *The Romance of Tarzan.*
40   . . . a lawsuit started by Booth over her near-fatal illness. Legend has it that Booth died from her illness in the 1930s. In fact, she was still alive in Los Angeles in the late 1970s. Information supplied by George Bryan (author of *Stage Deaths*, et al.), personal letter to author.
40   Thalberg. See Schatz, *Genius*, 120.
40   Burroughs on Weissmuller. Holtsmark, *Burroughs*, 33.
41   "a faint but unmistakable unpleasantness." *London Times*, 16 May 1932.
43   ". . . with *Trader Horn* footage . . . the back projection screen." Baxter, *Stunt*, 165.

Chapter 3 Real Africa—But Not Really

45   Re "Buffalo" Jones and Kearton, see Cameron, *Into Africa*, 98–100.
46   "One gets a good idea . . . hundreds of natives. . . ." *London Times*, 10 February 1920.
46   "in the center . . . a white man's town. . . ." Johnson, *Lion*.
47   Re Lake Paradise and Marsabit, see Cameron, *Into Africa*, 90–92.
47   "received with constant outbursts. . . ." *New York Times*, 21 May 1923, 12:2.
47   "the plucky couple . . . into their film. . . ." *London Times*, 2 July 1924, 12d.
48   Re Kearton's "showmanship": *London Times*, 28 July 1924, 10d.
48   "was the first man to drive an automobile from Cape Town to Cairo." *New York Times*, 16 July 1952, 25:2.

48 "Nothing is arranged. . . ." *London Times*, 30 March 1925, 12d.
48 ". . . unique air views" and "The modern cities . . . the white man's initiative . . ."
      London Times, 14 June 1926, 16c.
49 . . . both apparently the work of the producer. . . . Personal letter, Kenhelm Stott,
      Jr., to author.
49 Re hiring Africans for the lion-spearing: Eastman, *Chronicle of a Second African
      Journey*, 54–55, 72.
49–50 "To show a film of Africa . . . tigers, or cheetahs. . . ." *New York Times*, 27 May
      1929, 22:1.
50 "fully-fledged feature film with native cast." Low, *1930s*, 66.
50 ". . . a native . . . another and became its chief." *London Times*, 15 July 1929, 12c.
50 "an original story by Mrs. Court Treatt. . . ." *London Times*, 8 January 1930, 10d.
50 "vitality of its conception. . . . Low, *1918–1929*, 290.
50 "lacking spontaneity and truth. . . ." *New York Times*, 28 April 1930, 24:5.
51 "so much time . . . wasted in outlining personal relationships . . ." *London Times*,
      25 February 1930, 12d.
52 "swell showmanship . . . a marathon of laughs." *Variety*, 26 July 1932, 17.
52 "will have achieved its end . . . films in the jungle." *London Times*, 27 January
      1936, 8b.
52 "Many of the scenes . . . iron bars." letter, E.E. Asten, in *London Times*, 10 April
      1934, 10c.
53 Re *Baboona* and Fox technicians: Personal letter, Kenhelm Stott, Jr., to author,
      January 1993.
53 "Sadly, we must report . . ." "dated, tiresome. . . . amateurish." *New York Times*, 24
      September 1940, 26:5; *Variety*, 25 September 1940, 15.
54 "Certainly the most beautiful . . . in this country. . . ." *New York Times*, 10
      October 1938.

Chapter 4 Pillars of Empire

59 "a flourishing cinema of Empire . . . beneficent and necessary. . . ." Richards,
      "Profit," 249.
59 ". . . the almost total absence of the reality of contemporary British life. . . ."
      Richards, *Palace*, 245.
59 ". . . inflaming" of native populations, and miscegenation. Richards, *Palace*, 137.
59 ". . . the social and political assumptions of the extreme right wing. . . ." Low, *Film
      Making*, 71–72.
59 ". . . to influence the use of films for the dissemination of true national culture and
      ideals." *London Times*, 2 October 1928, 14d.
60 . . . because they showed policemen and clergymen in "undignified" ways. Smyth,
      "Mandarins," 134–35.
60 ". . . to promote the better distribution...the native races." *London Times*, 19 April
      1930, 14b.
60 . . . all used film as propaganda. Smyth, "Mandarins," 132–41.
60 . . . the enshrining of conservative "good taste," Low, *1906–1914*, 85.
60 ". . . the social hierarchy must not be questioned." Low, *Film Making*, 68.
60 ". . . full-hearted cooperation of the army and the colonial authorities. . . ."
      Richards, *Palace*, 136.
60 "The novels of A. E. W. Mason . . . stage and screen. . . ." *London Times*, 23
      December 1954, 8e.
60 Lucoque seems to have made a version in 1915. Low, *1914–1918*, 286.
60–61 Stoll released its version in 1921, with some Egyptian location work. *London
      Times*, 16 May 1921, 6a.
62 . . . the Venice Bienniale's cup in December. *London Times*, 11 September 1939,
      6b; and 30 December 1939, 8a.
62 "[Alexander] allowed [Zoltan] . . . over the next thirty years. . . ." Korda, *Lives*,
      120.

62   "magnificent" Low, *Film Making*, 226.
62   ". . . disagreements . . . pro-Empire motion pictures. . . ." Korda, *Lives*, 108–109.
63   "the hero's study . . . withering repartee." *London Times*, 18 April 1939, 12b.
63   "the Kipling of Kinema." *New York Times*, 4 August 1939, 11:1.
63   "glib imperialism . . . another age." *London Times*, 31 August 1943, 8c.
64   "has been programmed . . . comic-strip patriotism." Kael, *State*, 374 and 375.
64   "a tribute to the 'keepers of the king's peace'." Richards, *Palace*, 286.
64   "comic role . . ." wanted Charles Laughton. Gilliam, *Robeson*, 73.
64   "with Zoli fighting . . . tribal institutions." Korda, *Lives*, 306.
65   "scenes of native warfare . . . big game." *London Times*, 1 September 1933, 10f.
65   completed his filming the following January. *London Times*, 30 January 1934, 19d.
65   "almost anyone . . . Kenyatta." Gilliam, *Robeson*, 73.
65   "If it is shown abroad. . . ." *London Times*, 3 April 1935.
65   ". . . protested that it brought disgrace. . . ." Low, *Film Making*, 170.
66   "more the triumph . . . dignity." *Variety*, 3 July 1935, 14.
66   governmental involvement in its inception, via the Ministry of Information. Richards, *Dickinson*, 110–111.
68   "twelve million native . . . pioneers and explorers." *London Times*, 29 January 1925. 10b.
68   "creaked with age . . . sadly unimaginative." *New York Times*, 25 March 1929, 32:2.
69   ". . . arranged with . . . Chief Scout." *London Times*, 19 July 1936, 11f.
69   "selected by the National Film Library to be handed down to posterity." *London Times*, 19 July, 1936, 11f; 28 August, 13e; 23 June, 14c.
69–70   "I think there is . . . call of the jungle." *New York Times*, 24 October 1939, 29:1.
70   "last expedition was tragic and villainous, tempered only by force." Waugh, *Tourist*, 75.

Chapter 5 Black Eve, White Grave

79   Bogle, *Toms*, has a detailed treatment of female black archetypes in American films.
79   "concubinage." Cameron, *Into Africa*, 75–77.
80   "The true-blue British hero repulses . . . 'I'm white!'" Low, *Film Making*, 89.
80   "More torpid than torrid . . ." *Variety*, 26 February 1930.
82   "a shining sign . . . Great Love." Izod, *Box Office*, 44.

Chapter 6 That's Africa For You!: Comedy Before 1950

89   *Old Bones of the River* . . . based on stories by the same author. Low, *Film Making*, 246.
93   Frank Buck and the drowned tiger. Denis, *Safari*, 68.

Chapter 7 The African Returner

97   Pierre Sorlin's analysis of the film. Sorlin, *History*, 83–102.
98   "The story of Lupelta . . . life of the jungle." Pressbook, reproduced in Null, *Hollywood*, 44–45.
99   "acceptance of servility . . . characteristic of the black race." Campbell, *Celluloid*, 35.
99   Re "savage dancing": Second-unit directors and documentary filmmakers were understandably seduced by the cinematic richness of exotic dances and the costumes that went with them. It is understandable, too, that when they encountered native people they arranged (i.e., paid) for such dances to be staged. The result, however, in the commercial world of replication, was that the footage was used over and over and was often imitated, on the basis that what has sold before will sell again. In this way, a stereotype was created and perpetuated.
99   "scenery props . . . menials." Vaughan, "Cinema," in Hughes, *Treasury*, 86.

99   "not invited to join . . . their concerts." Gilliam, *Robeson*, 15.
99   "For me, London . . ." Robeson, *Here*, 33.
99   "came to consider that I was an African." *Ibid.*
100 "I hate the picture . . . years later." Quoted in Ramdin, *Robeson*, 86.
100 "put [Robeson] to the task of convincing the world that Africa needed the British . . ." Vaughan, "Cinema," 87.
100 "artificial but well-handled musical drama." Quinlan, *British*, 149.
100 "misguided . . . far from flattering." Low, *Film Making*. 257.
100 "the first film . . . a real man." Quoted in Gilliam, *Robeson*, 85.
102 "strange film." Low, *1930s*, 63.
102 "the ambitions . . . the African Negro . . ." *London Times*, 8 April 1937, 14c.
102 "how Johannesburg has . . . has been gain." *Ibid.*
103 "heroic sentimental story." *Variety*, 9 August 1937, 18.
104 "playing their interminable . . . laughing." *London Times*, 1 November 1937, 12b.
104 "the genuine stuff. Their . . . for all classes." *Variety*, 9 August 1937, 18.
104 "Some of the most . . . 'The Sheik.'" *New York Times*, 17 August 1938, 23:4.
105 "has been trained by whites . . . savage natives." Bogle, *Toms*, 97.

Chapter 8 The Dangerous Africans

111   "European police . . . fighting in groups." *London Times*, 14 September 1950, 6f.
113 (fn)   "The Jim-goes-to-Jo'burg theme . . . fiction." Gerard, *Literatures*, 198.
118   Molly Haskell on sex objects. Haskell, *Reverence*, 230–35.
121   "pseudo-obectivité" Hennebelle, "Guerillas," 260. "L'analyse politique est remplacée par un pseudo-objectivité . . . qui élude les véritables questions de la colonisation au nom d'un 'humanisme' désincarné et d'un 'fraternalisme' suspect."
121   "it appears so confident . . . mute." *New York Times*, 3 June 1964.
123   Re white farmers: Even the white hunters were also farmers, many of them really farmers who did some guiding on the side. Cameron, *Into Africa*, 165.

Chapter 9 The Helper, The Simp, and The Oaf

128   . . . the British love of animals . . . British concern for mistreatment of wild animals in African and other films—those of Frank Buck were particularly noted—led to formation of a conference, then to two bills, in 1933–34 and to the Cinematograph Films (Animal) Bill of 1937. See *London Times*, 5 December 1933, 19f; 10 August 1934, 8c; 24 July 1937, 7c; etc.
128   *Where No Vultures Fly* was reportedly the idea of its director. . . . *London Times*, 16 October 1951, 8c.
130   . . . an action upheld by the Governor. *London Times*, 21 August 1954, 5f.
130   "There is nothing . . . equal partners in his land of hope." Vaughan, "Cinema," 89.
131   . . . by 1969, one had been found in critical condition and was returned to captivity. . . . *London Times*, 28 April, 1965, 11b; 3 June, 13d; 12 June, 11f; 28 August, 10f; 5 November 1969, 6f; 18 November 1969, 5h.
134   "The film has the same leaden pedantry as its source." Hammon, *Huston*, 92.

Chapter 10 Good Losers, Bad Winners

139   "glorious defeat in the best British tradition." Pakenham, *Scramble*, 495. This comment was made about the incident upon which *Shangani Patrol* was based.
139   Re South African military and mercenary films, see Tomaselli, *Cinema*, 21, and the "jeep opera," 135; and Spence and Stam, "Racism," 8. Gerard, *Literatures*, 209, mentions the "nefarious activities" of SA censorship. However, Tomaselli's *Cinema* should be read in its entirety for an overview of the SA industry, albeit from a largely unsympathetic viewpoint; Hennebelle's "Pretoria" should also be read, although it, too, is political. Gutshe's *History* is the standard work on SA film to 1940.

145 . . . censorship "at the script stage." Tomaselli, *Cinema*, 21.
150 "a swift and intelligent . . ." Kael, *Taking*, 167.
151 "A reasonably accurate test . . . triumphantly?" Kael, *State*, 116.

Chapter 11 Freedom *Now!*

158 "jeep opera." Tomaselli, *Cinema*, 135.

Chapter 12 Sighing For Yesterday

165 "British film renaissance." Sheila Johnston, "Charioteers and Ploughman," in Auty and Roddick, *Now*, 99.
165–166 ". . . doesn't seem to understand . . . scraggly mess." Kael, *State*, 148–49.
166 "Chimps of Fire." Ellison, *Watching*, 156.
169 South African input. Tomaselli, *Cinema*, 223.
172 "a total cipher . . . no role for [Redford] to act." *New York Times*, 18 December 1985.
173 Karen's supposed syphillis. See, for example, Aschen, *Man*.

Chapter 13 Conclusions

183 The real-life issue of white "professional hunters" remains unresolved; Tanzania, which tried to mandate the hiring of black professionals by white clients, encountered considerable resistance and withdrew the requirement.
184 "unintelligent menials . . . picturesque crowds with spears. . . ." Vaughan, "Cinema," 86.
184 South African influence on Mercenary fims. See Tomaselli, *Cinema*, 21, 135, and 262ff.
187 . . . praise at the Venice Film Festival. *London Times*, 4 September 1957.
188 The only positive black women in major roles. . . . Black female types known in other kinds of films were utterly absent. Recent scholarship has identified black female types in American film, but they are missing here: The Mammy is not found, nor is the Good Black Woman (except as the Black Wife of the Robeson films, a rather different type), nor is the Faithful Servant (the latter a fact that perhaps reflects the fact that in the real Africa of colonialism, most black servants were male). Esmerelda, the comic black maid of *Tarzan of the Apes*, stood alone, as did the young female lead of *Son of Ingagi* (who had nothing directly to do with Africa, anyway).
193 Molly Haskell, "the mammary fixation . . . history." *Reverence*, 105, 263.
193 "robbed of their identity . . . film." Mellen, *Wolves*, 16.
193 "alienated from the world." *Ibid.* 190.
194 For women and the Afrikaner myth, especially the *volksmoeder*, see Cloete, "Afrikaner Identity".
195 Françoise Pfaff's suggestion that the White Hunter was related to the Western hero because both were "strong, romantic and highly skilled at gun shooting" (Pfaff, "Hollywood," 115) is merely silly, but it is true that both types were classless. Otherwise, their differences were greater than their similarities: the double rifle as compared to the six-gun, competence and service as compared to extreme individualism, submission to law as compared to the bringing of law.
197 "Africa is seen by the West. . . ." *Ibid.*
197–198 South African censorship. Tomaselli, *Cinema*, 264.
197–198 See Hennebelle, "Pretoria," and Tomaselli's entries in the bibliography.

FILMOGRAPHY

Several criteria determined the selections: that the films were released in the United States or Great Britain; that they were feature films (an admittedly fluid idea in the early years of the century); that they were set in, or that they were about, Sub-Saharan Africa; that they were in English or, if silent, titled in English. Documentary or nonfiction films (including quasi- or pseudo-documentaries) are indicated by a †.

The contents of each column, and the abbreviations used, are as follows:

YEAR: year of copyright or release, where knowable.

COUNTRY: national origin, as follows:

US = United States;
GB = Great Britain;
CAN = Canada;
SA = South Africa;
FR = France;
AUS = Australia;
GER = Germany;
ITA = Italy.

ARCHETYPES: archetypes discussed in this book (initial caps); and stereotypes (lower case).

AVAILABILITY: the location of a viewing copy, or if on commercial videotape:

BFI = British Film Institute, London;
EH = International Museum of Photography at Eastman House, Rochester, NY;
JSM = Johnson Safari Museum, Chanute, KS;
LC = Library of Congress, Washington, D. C.;
MOMA = Museum of Modern Art, New York;
OCLC = on-line catalog (lists some local holdings);
UCLA = University of California at Los Angeles, film archives;
SANFVSA = South African National Film, Video and Sound Archive, Pretoria, RSA;
V = commercial video.

Title	Year	Country	Archetypes	Availability
Across the World with Mr. and Mrs. Martin Johnson †	1930	US	Explorers; savages, savage dancing, jungle, dangerous animals	JSM
Adventure in Diamonds	1939	US		
Adventures of Tarzan	1920	US	Jungle Lord; jungle, dangerous animals	V
Africa Addio (re-released as *African Blood and Guts,* 1970) †	1966	Italy	wild animals, savagery (revisionist)	V
Africa Erotica (*Happening in Africa, Karen the Lovemaker*)	1970	??		
Africa Screams	1949	US	White Hunter, Explorer (parodies); jungle, dangerous animals, savages	V
Africa Speaks †	1930	US	Explorer; savages, savage dancing, jungle	LC
Africa—Texas Style	1967	US	White Hunter (Americanized); dangerous animals	LC
Africa Today	1927			
African Adventure †	1937	GB	Explorer; jungle, savages	lost?
African Adventure †	1954	US		
African Bird and Animal Life †	1913	GB		lost?
African Diamond Conspiracy	1914	Italy	Savages, treasure	
African Dream, An	1988	GB	Helper (new South African version), Good African	V
African Elephant, The †	1971	GB	dangerous animals	V
African Holiday †	1937	US	jungle, savages, witchcraft	
African Lion, The †	1955	US	dangerous animals	LC
African Love, see: *The Renegade*				
African Manhunt	1957	US		
African Queen, The	1951	US	True-Blue White Woman, Imperial Man; jungle, insects, leeches	V
African Rage (aka *Target of an Assassin, Tigers Don't Cry, The Long Shot, Fatal Assassin*)	1978 (1976- Maltin)	SA	Helper-turned-killer	V
African Treasure	1952	US	Jungle Boy; jungle	
African World †	1913	SA	treasure	lost?
Afrikander Girl, An	1912	GB		lost?
Allan Quatermain	1919	SA	White Hunter, Good African; lost white civilization, savages	lost? Stills at SANFVSA
Allan Quatermain and the Lost City of Gold	1987	US	White Hunter; lost civilization; savages (some parody)	V

Title	Year	Country	Archetypes	Availability
Alone in the Jungle	1913	US	dangerous animals, jungle	EH (not viewable, 1991)
Always in the Way	1915	US	savages	
Amid Raging Beasts	1914	GB	dangerous animals	
Animals Are Beautiful People †	c. 1980	SA	animals, savages	V
April Folly		1920	US	LC
Ashanti, Land of No Mercy	1979	US/FR	Arab Slaver, Mercenary; slaves	V
Baboona †	1934	US	Explorer; savages, "strange ceremonies," dangerous animals	JSM
Back to the Primitive	1911 [1915?]	US		
Battle of Mafeking †	1900	US		LC
Bela Lugosi Meets a Brooklyn Gorilla	1952	US	jungle, dangerous animals	V
Below the Sahara †	1953	US	savages, savage dancing, dangerous animals, dark continent	UCLA
Beyond Mombasa	1956	US	American Oaf, Female Simp, White Hunter; savages, savage dancing, savage horde	LC
Big Game of Life †	1935	GB	dangerous animals, exotica	
Blue Lagoon	1923?	SA		
Boer War, The †	1905	US		LC
Boer War, The †	1914	US		
Boer War Commissary Train Trekking †	1900	US		LC
Boers Bringing in British Prisoners †	1900	US		LC
Boesman and Lena	1973			SANFVSA
Bomba and the Jungle Girl	1952	US	Jungle Boy; jungle	
Bomba and the Elephant Stampede	1951	US	Jungle Boy; dangerous animals, jungle	MOMA
Bomba and the Hidden City	1950	US	Jungle Boy; jungle, lost city	
Bomba and the Lion Hunters	1951	US	Jungle Boy; jungle, dangerous animals	
Bomba and the Lost Volcano	1950	US	Jungle Boy; jungle	
Bomba on Panther Island	1949	US	Jungle Boy	MOMA
Bomba the Jungle Boy	1949	US	Jungle Boy; jungle	
Born Free	1966	US	Helper; dangerous animals	V
Boy Ten Feet Tall, A (See: *Sammy Going South*)				
Breaker Morant	1979	AUS	revisionist (Boer War)	V
Building a Railroad in Africa †	1907	SA?		lost?
Bulldog Drummond in Africa	1938	US	wild animals (lion pit)	V
Buried City, The	1921	SA		lost
Burning, The	1968	GB		BFI

Title	Year	Country	Archetypes	Availability
Bushman, The †	1927	US	savages	lost
Bwana Devil	1953	US	Imperial Man; True-Blue White Woman; dangerous animals, savages, savage dancing (based vaguely on J. H. Patterson at Tsavo)	LC
Call of the Savage, The	1935	US	Jungle Boy	
Call Me Bwana	1962	US	White Hunter (parody); savages, savage dancing, fur and feathers	LC
Cannibal Attack	1954	US	White Hunter; savages, cannibalism, savage horde	
Cape to Cairo (see: *From Cape to Cairo*)	1906			
Cape to Cairo †	1926	GB	Explorer	
Cape to Cairo †	193?	SA?	march of civilization (railroad)	BFI
Captain Kate (same as latter part of *Capturing Circus Animals?*)	1911	US	Strong Woman; dangerous animals	BFI
Captive Girl	1950	US	White Hunter (Jungle Jim), White Goddess; savages	
Capturing Circus Animals in the African Wilds (see: *Captain Kate*)	1911	US	Strong Woman; dangerous animals	LC
Capture of Boer Battery [by British] †	1900	US		LC
Charge of Boer Cavalry †	1900	US		LC, BFI
Carry On Up the Jungle	1970	GB	White Hunter, Jungle Lord; savages, cannibals (all parodies)	LC (trailer)
City of Blood	1987	SA	urban revisionist	V
Clarence, the Cross-Eyed Lion	1965	US	Helper; dangerous animals, drums	V
Claw, The	1927	US		V
Coast of Skeletons	1965	GB	Imperial Male (Sanders spinoff)	
Cohens and the Kellys in Africa, The	1930	US	savages, savage dancing, evil Arabs, cannibals, dangerous animals	LC
Come Back, Africa	1959	SA	urban revisionist	V
Coming to America	1987	US	Reversed stereotypes: tamed animals, no jungle, palace, glitz	V
Common Beasts of Africa †	1914	US	jungle, dangerous animals	LC
Condemned to Live	1935	US	jungle, dangerous animals	
Congo Bill	1948	US	White Queen	
Congo Crossing	1956	US	jungle	
Congo Maisie	1940	US	Witty Woman; savages, magic	
Congolaise †	1950	GB?	dangerous animals, savages	BFI

Title	Year	Country	Archetypes	Availability
Congorilla †	1932	US	Explorer; dark continent, savages, dangerous animals, jungle	JSM
Country Lovers, City Lovers (US: *City Lovers*)	1982	SA	revisionist	V
Cradle of the World, The †	1923	GB	dangerous animals	
Creatures the World Forgot	196?	GB		
Cry Freedom	1987	US	Dangerous African, Helper	V
Cry, the Beloved County	1951	GB	Dispossessed	UCLA, BFI, V
Curse of Simba (US: *Curse of the Voodoo*)	1965	GB	dark continent, magic	BFI
Danger Island	1931	US		
Danger Quest	1936	US	diamonds	lost
Dangerous Adventure, A	1922	US	treasure quest, jungle, savages, dangerous animals	lost
Dark of the Sun (GB: *The Mercenaries*)	1968	US	Mercenary, Female Simp, Good Black; diamond quest, black horde	EH
Dark Rapture †	1938	US	dangerous and other animals, heart of darkness, savages	BFI
Darkest Africa (1949 re-release as *King of the Jungleland*?)	1936	US	Jungle Boy, White Goddess; dangerous animals, dark continent, jungle	V
Dassan, an Adventure in Search of Laughter †	1930	GB		
Daughter of the Congo, A	1930	US	jungle, savages; but unique in its black romantic leads	lost?
David Livingstone	1936	GB	Imperial Man	
Dawn	1917	SA/GB		
Death Drums Along the River (Same as *Sanders of the River*?)	1963	GB	Imperial Male (Sanders spinoff)	
Debt of Honour, A	1922	GB		
Debt of Honour	1936	GB		
Devil Goddess	1955	US	White Hunter (Jungle Jim); jungle	
Devil's Own, The	196?	GB		UCLA
Diamond City	1949	GB	diamonds	
The Diamond Hunters (*The Kingfisher Caper*)	1975	SA		
Diamond Safari	1958	US		
Dingaka	1965	SA	Dispossessed African; witch-doctor, savage dancing, fur and feathers	LC
Dogs of War, The	1980	US	Mercenary; black horde	V
Dry White Season, A	1989	US	Awakened White, White Torturer, Dangerous African; anti-apartheid	V

Title	Year	Country	Archetypes	Availability
Drums of Africa	1962	US	White Hunter, True-Blue White Woman; slavers, savages, dangerous animals—*KSM* spinoff (using 1950 footage)	LC
Drums of Destiny	1962	SA		stills at SANFVSA
Drums of Fate	1923	US		lost
Drums of the Congo	1941	US	jungle, savages, savage horde	
Duel in the Jungle	1954	US	American Oaf, Female Simp; drums, savage dancing, jungle, animals	LC
East of Kilimanjoro	1962	GB/ITA	Helper, White Hunter; savages, animals	V
An Elephant Called Slowly	1969	GB	Helper; dangerous animals	LC
Elephant Hunting in Victoria Nyanza †	1911		Hunter; dangerous animals	
Equatorial Africa: Roosevelt's Hunting Grounds †	1924	US	dangerous animals, jungle	lost
English Lancers Charging †	1900	US		LC
Explorer, The	1915	US		
A Far Off Place	1993	US	dangerous animals, savages	V
Fiercest Heart, The	1961	US	Good African; savages, black horde (Afrikaner myth-making)	LC
Five Weeks in a Balloon	1962	US	Slaver, Arabs	V
Flame and the Fire, The †	1965	FR	colonial gaze	
Forbidden Adventure	1915	US	may be India	
Four Feathers	1915	GB	Imperial Man; black horde	
Four Feathers	1915	US	Imperial Man; black horde	
Four Feathers	1921	GB	Imperial Man; black horde	
Four Feathers	1929	US	Imperial Man; black horde, animals	UCLA
Four Feathers	1939	GB	Imperial Man; black horde	V
From Cape to Cairo †	1906	GB		
From Red Sea to Blue Nile †	1925	GB		
From Senegal to Timbuctu †	1924	GB		
Game for Vultures, A	1980	SA	Mercenary (type), Dangerous African; black horde	LC
Gang Making Railway —South Africa †	1898	GB?		BFI
Gods Must Be Crazy, The	1980	SA	Good African; savages, skins, dangerous animals	V
Gods Must Be Crazy, The, II	1989	SA	Good African; savages, skins, animals	V
Gold and Diamond Mines of South Africa †	1917	US	diamonds	LC
Golden Dawn	1929	US	Black Eve, White Man's Grave; witch-doctor, savage dancing, jungle	LC

Title	Year	Country	Archetypes	Availability
Golden Idol, The	1954	US	Jungle Boy (Bomba)	MOMA
Golden Ivory (US: *White Huntress*)	1954	GB	elephants' burial ground, savage horde, dangerous animals	
Gorilla Hunt, The †	1926	US	Explorer; savage dancing, dangerous animals	lost?
Gorillas in the Mist	1988	US	Strong Woman, Helper; dangerous animals	V
Great Adventure, The	1950	GB	diamonds (SA)	LC
Great Kimberly Diamond Robbery, The (*Star of the South*)	1910	SA		
Greystoke: The Legend of Tarzan	1984	GB	Jungle Lord; jungle, animals (revisionist)	V
Guest, The	1984 (US)	SA		
Guns at Batasi	1964	GB	Imperial Man, Good African, Dangerous African; black horde	LC, V
Hatari!	1962	US	American Oaf; dangerous animals	LC, V
He Was Her Man (*We're Going To be Rich*)	US	1937	diamonds	
Hellions, The	1961	GB		
Hidden Valley	1916	US	lost land, savage sacrifice	
High Command, The	1937	GB	White Man's Grave; savage dancing	UCLA, V
Hippopotamus Hunt, The (*Hunting the Hippopotamus on the Upper Nile*) †	1910	GB?	Hunter; dangerous animals	BFI
Hold That Lion (*Ladies First, Hunting Trouble*)	1926	US	hunting, dangerous animals (only part Africa)	lost
Hunting Big Game in Africa †	1909	US	Hunter; dangerous animals	
Hunting Big Game Animals (*Big Game Hunting*) †	1929	US	Hunter; dangerous animals, savages	EH?
Hunting Big Game in Africa [With Gun and Camera] †	1922	US	Hunter, Explorer; dangerous animals	
I Married Adventure †	1940	US	Explorer; dangerous animals, savages, savage dancing, jungle	JSM
Illicit Liquor Seller, The (See: *The Liquor Seller*)				
In Tune With the Wild	1914	US	Strong Woman; animals, jungle	
Ingagi †	1930	US	savages, jungle, dangerous animals, ape-African mating	lost?
Interviewing Wild Animals †	1930	GB	animals	lost?
It Happened in Africa (See: *Women and Diamonds*)				
Jaguar †	1967 ("shot in 1953"			see OCLC

Title	Year	Country	Archetypes	Availability
Jericho (US: *Dark Sands*)	1937	GB	African Returner, Black Wife	V, BFI
Jim Comes to Jo'burg	1949	SA	Dispossessed	MOMA
Judgment of the Jungle	1914	FR	Strong Woman; dangerous animals	
Jungle Captive	1944	US	ape-woman	
Jungle Drums of Africa	1953	US	white witch-doctor	V
Jungle Gents	1954	US		
Jungle Girl	1941	US	Jungle Woman (female Tarzan)	V
Jungle Goddess	1922	US	White Goddess; jungle	
Jungle Goddess	1948	US	White Goddess; savages, treasure	UCLA, V
Jungle Jim	1937	US	White Goddess, White Hunter; jungle	
Jungle Jim	1948	US	White Hunter; jungle	EH (no viewing copy)
Jungle Jim in the Forbidden Land	1951	US	White Hunter; lost land; jungle	
Jungle Killer †	1932	GB		
Jungle Lover, The	1915	US	jungle	
Jungle Man	1941	US	Jungle Man; jungle, dangerous animals	
Jungle Man-Eaters	1954	US	White Hunter (Jungle Jim); jungle	
Jungle Manhunt	1951	US	White Hunter (Jungle Jim); jungle	
Jungle Master, The	1914	US		
Jungle Master	1956	GB	Jungle Lord, White Queen; jungle	V
Jungle Moon Men	1955	US	White Hunter (Jungle Jim); jungle	
Jungle Mystery, The	1932	US	ape-man, jungle	
Jungle Princess, The	1920	US	lost white civilization, jungle	
Jungle Princess	1936	US	White Queen; jungle	UCLA
Jungle Queen	1944	US	White Queen; jungle, savages	LC
Jungle Raiders	1945	US	lost city, jungle (may not be Africa)	
Jungle Siren	1942	US	jungle	
Jungle Skies	1932	GB		
Jungle Stampede †	1950	US	dangerous animals, savages (pygmies), savage ceremonies	
Jungle Trail, The	1919	US	white god, savages	lost?
Jungle Trail of the Son of Tarzan (condensed from serial)	1923	US	Jungle Lord; jungle, savages, dangerous animals, Arab slaver	

Title	Year	Country	Archetypes	Availability
Kaffir's Gratitude, The	1908	US?	Good African; diamonds (SA), dangerous animals	LC
Khartoum	1966	US	Imperial Man, Evil "Arab"; black horde	EH
Kill or Be Killed	1976	SA		SANFVSA
Killer Leopard	1954	US	Jungle Boy (Bomba)	
Killers of Kilimanjaro	1960	GB	White Hunter; black horde, witch-doctor, dangerous animals	LC
King of the Cannibal Island				
King of the Congo	1952	US	White Queen; jungle	V
King of the Jungle	1933	US	Jungle Lord; jungle (much of action in US)	
King of the Kongo	1929	US	jungle	V
King Solomon's Mines	1918	SA	White Hunter, Good African; savages, treasure	SANFVSA (almost complete)
King Solomon's Mines	1937	GB	White Hunter, Good African; savages, savage dancing, treasure	V
King Solomon's Mines	1950	US	White Hunter, Good African, True-Blue White Woman; savages, treasure	LC, V
King Solomon's Mines	1987	US	White Hunter, Good African; jungle, savages, dangerous animals	V
King Solomon's Treasure	1976	CAN	White Hunter, White Queen; treasure	V
Kingfisher Caper, The	1976	SA		V
Kings of the Forest	1912	US		BFI
Kitchen Toto, The	1987	GB	savage horde (Mau Mau), revisionist	V
Konga	1961	GB	jungle, dangerous animals (little African setting), monster from Africa	UCLA
Kongo	1932	US	White Man's Grave; savages, magic (same source as 1928 *West of Zanzibar*)	
Kongo Express	1940	US		
Kwaheri †	1964	US		
Lad and the Lion, The	1917	US	dangerous animals, Arabs	
Lady Mackenzie's Big Game Pictures (*Lady Mackenzie in Africa*) †	1915	GB	jungle, savage dancing	
Lady Who Lied, The	1925	US		lost
Land of Zinj, The	1933	GB		
Lassoing Wild Animals in Africa †	1911 (made in 1909)	GB	dangerous animals	lost?

Title	Year	Country	Archetypes	Availability
Last Lion, The	1972	SA		
Last Rhino, The	1961	GB	dangerous animals	
Last Safari, The	1967	US?	White Hunter (revisionist); dangerous animals, savage dancing, savages	UCLA, BFI
Law of the Jungle, The †	1936	GB	jungle (revisionist)	lost?
Leopard Men of Africa †	1940	US	witchcraft, jungle, savages, dark continent, fur and feathers	UCLA
Leopard Woman, The	1920	US	Imperial Man, Vamp, Arab; savages, fur and feathers	LC, V
Leopard's Foundling, The	1914	US	Jungle Woman (female Tarzan); dangerous animals	
Life's Crossroads	1928	US	jungle	lost?
Life in Senegal †	1910	GB?		
Lion, The	1962	US	White Hunter (revisionist); dangerous animals, savage dancing	LC
Lion Hunter, The †	1914	US	Hunter; dangerous animals	
Lion Hunters †	1913	GB	Hunter; dangerous animals	
Lion Hunting in East Africa †	1917	GB	Hunter; dangerous animals	
Liquor Seller, The (*The Illicit Liquor Seller*)	1916	SA		stills at SANFVSA
Living Free	1972	US	Helper; dangerous animals (revisionist)	V
Livingstone (US, 1929: *Livingstone in Africa*)	1925	GB	Imperial Man; Arab slavers, dangerous animals	
Lord of the Jungle	1955	US	Jungle Lord (Bomba)	
Lost at Sea	1926	US	(not much Africa)	
Lost City, The	1935	US	lost civilization, savages	V
Lost City of the Jungle	1946	US	Not Africa?	V
Lost Empire, The †	1929	US	savages, jungle—only part Africa (same expedition as *Four Feathers*?)	
Lost in the Desert	19??	SA		
Lost in the Jungle	1911	US	Strong Woman; jungle, dangerous animals	EH (unavailable for viewing)
Lost Jungle, The	1934	US		V
Lost Tribe, The †	1929		(only part Africa)	
Lost Tribe, The	1949	US	White Hunter (Jungle Jim); lost white civilization, jungle	
Macomber Affair, The	1947	US	White Hunter, Good African; dangerous animals	LC
Magic Garden, The (*Pennywhistle Blues*)	1952	SA	Dispossessed African	V
Mamba	1930	US	White Man's Grave, Black Eve	LC (fragment)
Man and Beast	1917	US	dangerous animals (SA setting)	

Title	Year	Country	Archetypes	Availability
Mapantsula	1988	SA	Dangerous African; urban anti-stereotypes	V
Marigolds in August	1984 (US)	SA		
Mark of the Gorilla	1950	US	White Hunter (Jungle Jim); dangerous animals	
Mark of the Hawk	1957	US		
Marriage	1927	US	dangerous animals	lost
Master of Beasts, The	1922	US		lost
Masters of the Congo Jungle †	1959	US		LC, V
Men of Two Worlds	1946	GB	Educated African, Imperial Man, Crowing Hen; witch-doctor, savages	LC, BFI, V
Mercenary Fighters	1988	US/SA	Mercenary; savage horde	V
Mighty Gorga, The	1969	GB	dangerous animals, treasure, lost world	
Mighty Jungle, The	1964	US	jungle—only part Africa	V
Midnight Madness	1928	US	diamonds, wild animals	
Military Drill of Kikuyu Tribes and Other Native Ceremonies †	1914	US	savage dancing, fur and feathers	LC
Miracles of the Jungle	1921	US	dangerous animals	
Missing Link, The	1927	US	Hunter; dangerous animals, man-ape, savages	LC
Missionaries in Darkest Africa	1912	US	miscegenation fear	lost?
Mister Johnson	1990	GB	Good African, Imperial Man	V
Mister Moses	1965	US	American Oaf, Helper, Good African, Dangerous African; savages, magic	UCLA
Modern Monte Cristo, A (*Diamond Frontier*)	US	1940		
Mogambo	1953	US	American Oaf/White Hunter, Witty Woman; dangerous animals, savages, savage dancing	LC, V
Monster from Green Hell	1958	US		V
Mountains of the Moon, The	1990	GB	Imperial Man (revisionist); savages (revisionist)	V
My African Adventure	1987	US	wild animals	
My African People †	1930s?	GB?	savage dancing, fur and feathers (revisionist)	LC
My Song Goes Forth †	1937	GB	revisionist: South Africa as it is	BFI
Nabonga (aka *Nabonga, Gorilla*)	1944	US	Jungle Girl; dangerous animals, treasure	LC, V
Nagana	1933	US	dangerous animals, savages, savage ceremonies, witch-doctor	
Naked Africa †	1954	US		
Naked Prey, The	1966	US	savages, dangerous animals, slavers; white reversion to savagery	V

Title	Year	Country	Archetypes	Availability
Naked Terror	1961		"ancient traditions and superstitions of the African Zulu tribes"	
Nature's Zoo †	1913	GB	dangerous animals— not all Africa	
New Explorers, The †	1955	GB		
Night in the Jungle, A	c. 1912	US		
Nionga †	1925	GB	savages, savage dancing; but interest in "local customs"	
No Room for Wild Animals †	1958		anti-hunting	See OCLC
Nun's Story, The	1958	US		V
Odongo	1956	US	American Oaf, Female Simp; dangerous animals	LC
Old Bones of the River	1939	GB	Imperial Man (parody), Good African, Educated African; savages, fur and feathers, savage horde	BFI
On Safari †	1932	GB		
On the Equator †	c.1923	GB		BFI
One Exciting Night	1922	US	(little Africa)	MOMA
One Step to Hell	1969	US/ITA		V
Ostrich Farming, South Africa †	1917	US		LC
Out of Africa	1985	US	Good Black, White Hunter, True-Blue White Woman; dangerous animals	V
Palaver	1926	GB	Imperial Man; savages, witch-doctor	
Panther Girl of the Congo	1955	US		
Paul Rainey African Hunt Pictures †	1912	US		LC
Perils of Pauline	1967	US	White Hunter (parody); dangerous animals, Arab slavers	LC
Perils of the Jungle	1953	US	dangerous animals, savages, witch-doctor, drums, confused geography	LC
Phantom, The	1943	US	lost white civilization	V
Place of Weeping	1986	SA	Strong Black Woman	V
Ponjola	1923	US		lost
Poppy	1917	US	savages	
Power of One, The	1992	GB	White Torturer, Awakened White, Good African; anti-apartheid	V
Prester John	1920	SA		
Primitive Man's Career to Civilization, A	1911	GB	savages, savage dancing, benefits of civilization	
Pygmy Island	1950	US	White Hunter (Jungle Jim)	
Queen for a Day	early silent			
Rainey's African Hunt †	1914	US	dangerous animals	

Title	Year	Country	Archetypes	Availability
Rastus in Zululand	1911	US		
Red Cross Ambulance on Battlefield †	1900	US		LC
Red Scorpion	1989	US/SA	Mercenary; savages	V
Renegade, The (Re-released as *African Love*, 1922)	1915	US	Arab slavers (mostly North Africa and England)	LC
Return of Tarzan (aka *Revenge of Tarzan*)	1920	US	Jungle Lord; jungle, dangerous animals	
Rhino!	1964	US	Helper/American Oaf, Female Simp; dangerous animals, fur and feathers	LC
Rhodes of Africa (US: *Rhodes*)	1936	GB	Imperial Man, Crowing Hen; diamonds, savages	BFI, V
Rivers of Fire and Ice (aka *African Safari?*)	1963?	US/ SA?	dangerous animals, savages, savage dancing	LC
Road to Zanzibar, The	1941	US	Witty Woman, Arab Slaver; savages, savage dancing, cannibals, animals	UCLA, V
Romance of Tarzan	1918	US	Jungle Lord; jungle, dangerous animals	
Roots of Heaven, The	1958	US	Helper; dangerous animals (revisionist)	EH
Rose of Rhodesia, The	1917	SA	Good African; savages	
Round Africa With Cobham †	1928	GB		LC (part, in their "Aviation")
Royal African Rifles (GB: *Storm Over Africa*)	1953	US		
Safari	1937	GB		
Safari	1940	US	White Hunter, Good Black; dangerous animals	UCLA
Safari	1956	GB/US	White Hunter, Dangerous African, Female Simp; savage horde (Mau Mau)	LC
Safari Drums	1953	US	Jungle Boy (Bomba)	MOMA
Samba	1928	SA?		
Sammy Going South (US: *A Boy Ten Feet Tall*)	1962	GB?	White Hunter (revisionist), Good African	UCLA
Sanders of the River	1935	GB	Imperial Male, Good African, Black Wife; savages, fur and feathers, savage hordes	V
Sanders of the River	1964	GB/SA		
Sands of the Kalahari	1965	SA/GB	Female Simp; dangerous animals, white reversion to savagery	UCLA
Savage Girl	1933	US	Jungle Woman	
Savage Mutiny	1953	US	White Hunter (Jungle Jim)	

Title	Year	Country	Archetypes	Availability
Savage Splendor †	1949	US	dark continent, dangerous animals, savages, savage dancing, ethnic misrepresentation	LC
Scenes of African Animals †	1911	US	hunting, dangerous animals	LC
Secret Service in Darkest Africa, The	1943	US		
Serengeti Shall Not Die †	1960	GER?	revisionist view of animals, population problems	LC, EH
Shaft in Africa	1973	US	Dangerous African	LC
Shangani Patrol	1971	SA	Imperial Man; savages	SA
She	1908	US	White Queen	lost?
She	1911	US	White Queen	V
She	1916	GB	White Queen	lost?
She	1916	GB	White Queen	lost?
She	1917	US	White Queen	lost?
She	1925	GB	White Queen	V, BFI
Sheena	1984	US	Jungle Queen	V
Shooting Big Game With Camera †	1928	US	dangerous animals	lost
Simba, the King of Beasts: A Saga of the African Veldt †	1928	US	dangerous animals, savages	JSM, V
Simba	1955	GB	Dangerous African (Mau Mau); savages, savage ceremonies	LC, V
Skabenga	1955	SA	dangerous animals	
Skeleton Coast	1987	SA	Mercenary, Dangerous African; savage horde	V
Slave Girls [US: *Prehistoric Women*]	1967	GB	Amazons, lost land	
Slaver, The	1927	US	Good Black; savages, savage dancing	LC
Slavers	1977	GER	Arab slaver	V
Snows of Kilimanjaro, The	1952	US	White Hunter (minor), True-Blue White Woman; dangerous animals (not all Africa)	V
So This Is Africa	1933	US	Jungle Lord, White Amazons, Explorer (parodies); savages, animals	LC
Something of Value	1957	US	Dangerous African; savage horde (Mau Mau), savage ceremonies	V
Son of Ingagi	1940	US	man-ape (no action in Africa—all U.S.)	V
Son of Tarzan	1920	US	Jungle Lords (2); jungle, dangerous animals, Arab slaver, savages	EH (incomplete)
Song of Africa	1946	SA	Dispossessed	LC

Title	Year	Country	Archetypes	Availability
Song of Freedom (US: *Big Fella*)	1936	GB	African Returner, Black Wife; savages (revisionist)	V
Source of the Nile, The †	1924	SA?		
South to Karanga	1940	US	savages, savage horde	
Southern Star, The	1969	US?	True-Blue White Woman, Good African; diamonds	LC
Sport and Travel in Central Africa †	1914	FR?	savages	
Stampede †	1930	GB	animals	EH, BFI (fragment)
Stanley and Livingstone	1939	US	Imperial Man; savages, dangerous animals	LC
Stark Nature †	1930	GB	animals, savages, savage dancing	BFI
Storm Over the Nile	1955	GB	Imperial Man; savage horde	LC
Struggle for Life †	1935	GB		
Sundown	1941	US	Imperial Man, Black Eve (fake), White Hunter; savage horde	V
Swallow	1922	SA		stills at SANFVSA
Symbol of Sacrifice	1918	SA	Strong Woman; savage horde	SANFVSA
Taffy and the Jungle Hunters	1965	US		
Tanganyika	1954	US	White Hunter; savages, jungle	
Tarzan and the Amazons	1945	US	Jungle Lord, Jungle Boy, True-Blue White Woman; jungle, Amazons	LC
Tarzan and the Huntress	1946	US	Jungle Lord, Jungle Boy, True-Blue White Woman; jungle, dangerous animals	
Tarzan and the Leopard Woman	1945	US	Jungle Lord, Jungle Boy, True-Blue White Woman; jungle, dangerous animals	
Tarzan and the Mermaids	1947	US	Jungle Lord, True-Blue White Woman; jungle, dangerous animals	
Tarzan the Ape Man	1932	US	Jungle Lord; jungle, savages, savage horde	UCLA , V
Tarzan and His Mate	1934	US	Jungle Lord, Wild Mate; jungle, savages, dangerous animals	BFI, EH (not available for viewing), V lost
Tarzan and the Golden Lion	1927	US		
Tarzan and the Jungle Boy	1968	US	Jungle Lord	
Tarzan and the Jungle Goddess	1950	US	Jungle Lord, Jungle Goddess; jungle	
Tarzan and the Lost Safari	1957	US	Jungle Lord	

Title	Year	Country	Archetypes	Availability
Tarzan and the She-Devil	1953	US	Jungle Lord; jungle	
Tarzan and the Slave Girl	1950	US	Jungle Lord; jungle	
Tarzan and the Trappers (same as *Tarzan's Fight for Life*?)	1958	US	Jungle Lord	V
Tarzan and the Valley of Gold	1967	US	Jungle Lord	
Tarzan Escapes	1936	US	Jungle Lord, Wild Mate; jungle, dangerous animals	EH, BFI, V
Tarzan Finds a Son	1939	US	Jungle Lord, Jungle Boy, True-Blue White Woman; dangerous animals	V
Tarzan of the Apes	1918	US	Jungle Lord; jungle, dangerous animals, savages, Arab slavers	LC, V
Tarzan the Ape Man	1959	US	Jungle Lord	
Tarzan, the Ape Man	1981	US	Jungle Lord, Wild Mate; savages, savage horde, jungle	LC, V
Tarzan, the Fearless	1933	US	Jungle Lord; jungle, dangerous animals, lost city, savages, savage dancing, savage horde, treasure	EH, UCLA, V
Tarzan the Magnificent	1960	GB?	Jungle Lord	
Tarzan the Mighty	1928	US	Jungle Lord	
Tarzan the Tiger	1929	US	Jungle Lord	V
Tarzan Triumphs	1942	US	Jungle Lord, Jungle Boy, True-Blue White Woman; dangerous animals, jungle	
Tarzan's New York Adventure	1942	US	Jungle Lord, Jungle Boy, True-Blue White Woman; dangerous animals, jungle	V
Tarzan's Desert Mystery	1943	US	Jungle Lord, Jungle Boy, True-Blue White Woman; jungle, dangerous animals	
Tarzan's Fight for Life	1958	US	Jungle Lord; savages, witch-doctor	
Tarzan's Greatest Adventure	1959	US?	Jungle Lord	
Tarzan's Hidden Jungle	1955	US	Jungle Lord; jungle	
Tarzan's Magic Fountain	1949	US	Jungle Lord; jungle, woman who never ages	
Tarzan's Peril	1951	US	Jungle Lord	
Tarzan's Revenge	1938	US	Jungle Lord	V
Tarzan's Savage Fury	1952	US	Jungle Lord	
Tarzan's Secret Treasure	1941	US	Jungle Lord, Jungle Boy, True-Blue White Woman; dangerous animals	V
Tembi †	1929	GB	animals	
Tembo †	1951	US	savages, savage horde, Leopard Men	
Theodore Roosevelt in Africa (aka Roosevelt in Africa) †	1910	GB	savages, hunting, dangerous animals	LC

Title	Year	Country	Archetypes	Availability
Terrors of the Jungle	1913			
Thoroughbreds All	1919	SA		lost?
Thou Shalt Not Covet	1916	US	jungle	MOMA
Through Central Africa †	1915	US/GB	dark continent, dangerous animals	
Through Darkest Africa . . . in Search of the White Rhinoceros †	1927	US	jungle, animals	lost?
Tim Tyler's Luck	1937	US	elephant's graveyard	V
To the Mountain of Mystery—Kilimanjaro †	1924	GB	animals, savages	
Torn Allegiance	1982	AUS	Strong Woman	V
Toto's Wife	1924	GB	animals	
Trader Horn	1931	US	White Hunter, White Goddess; dangerous animals, savage horde	BFI
Trader Horn	1973	US	White Hunter; savages, savage dancing, dangerous animals, jungle, treasure	LC
Trader Hornee	1970	US?		
Trailing African Wild Animals †	1923	US	Explorer; jungle, dangerous animals, savages	lost
Untamed	1955	US	Afrikaner myth-making	LC
Untamed Africa	1933	US		
Unto the Darkness	1915	US	dangerous animals	
Up the Congo †	1930	US	savages, savage dancing	
Valley of the Headhunters	1953	US	White Hunter (Jungle Jim); savages	
Vast Sudan, The †	1924	GB	dangerous animals, savages, savage dancing (but included building of a railroad and a dam)	
Vengeance of She, The	1967	GB	White Queen	LC
Voice of the Hurricane	1964	US	Dangerous African; savage horde (Mau Mau)	LC
Voodoo Tiger	1952	US	White Hunter (Jungle Jim)	
Voodoo Vengeance	1913	US	savage horde, savagery, "nascent Mau Mau conspiracy"	
Vulture's Prey, The	1922	SA	diamonds	Stills at SANFVSA
Wakamba	1955	US	jungle	
Watusi	1959	US	White Hunter; dangerous animals, savage horde, savage dancing, treasure	LC
Way of the Wild †	1934	GB		
West of Zanzibar	1928	US	White Man's Grave; savages, savage dancing, magic	EH, V
West of Zanzibar	1954	GB	Helper; Arab slaver, dangerous animals	LC

Title	Year	Country	Archetypes	Availability
Where No Vultures Fly (US: *Ivory Hunter*)	1951	GB	Helper; savage dancing, dangerous animals	EH
White Barbarian, A	1923	GB	"white royal family" of African tribe, savages	
Whispering Death	1971	SA	Dangerous African (as monster), Good African, Mercenary; savagery, savage horde	
White Cargo	1929	GB	Black Eve, White Man's Grave; jungle	BFI
White Cargo	1942	US	Black Eve, White Man's Grave; jungle	LC
White Hunter	1936	US	White Hunter	
White Hunter †	1964	SA	hunter (not White Hunter); dangerous animals	
White Hunter, Black Heart	1990	US	dangerous animals	V
White Man's Law	1918	US	White Man's Grave (but for the villain); animals, jungle	
White Mischief	1988	GB		V
White Witch Doctor	1953	US	Helper, American Oaf; jungle, dangerous animals, savages	LC
Wilby Conspiracy, The	1975	GB?	Dangerous African, White Torturer, Awakened White	V
Wild Geese, The	1978	US/GB	Mercenary; savage horde	V
Wild Heart of Africa †	1929	US	savage dancing, dangerous animals, hunting	lost
Wild Life (aka *Wild Animal Films?*) †	1913	GB	dangerous animals	
Wild Life Across the World †	1923	GB	only part Africa—animals	
Wild Men of Africa †	1921	US	savages, dangerous animals (includes pygmy footage)	
Wild Men of the Kalahari †	1930	US	dangerous animals	
Wild Ride, A	1913	US		BFI
Wild Women and Tame Lions	1918	US		
Wildest Africa †	1923	GB		
Wings Over Africa †	1933	GB		LC (fragment in their "Aviation")
Wings Over Africa	1939	GB	jungle	LC (not available for viewing)
Wings Over Ethiopia †	1935			
Winning a Continent (SA: *De Voortrekkers*)	1916	SA	Afrikaner myth-making, savages	SANFVSA

Title	Year	Country	Archetypes	Availability
With Cherry Kearton in the Jungle †	1926	GB	BFI	
With Cobham to the Cape †	1926	GB		
With Cobham to Kivu †	1932	GB		LC (in their "Aviation," fragments cut into 1933 *Wings Over Africa*)
With Edged Tools	1919	SA		stills at SANFVSA
With Eustace in Africa †	1922	US		lost
With Stanley in Africa	1923	US		
Women and Diamonds (*Conscripts of Misfortune, It Happened in Africa*)	1924	GB		
Won in the Clouds	1914	US	savages	
Won in the Clouds	1928	US	jungle	
Wonderland of Big Game †	1923	GB		
Wonderful Wife, A	1922	US		lost
World Apart, A	1988	GB	Strong Woman, White Torturer, Awakened White	V
Zanzabuku †	1956	US		
Zanzibar	1940	US		
Zulu	1963	US	Imperial Man; savages, savage horde	V
Zulu Dawn	1979	GB/SA	Imperial Man; savages, savage horde	V
Zulu King, The	1913	US		
Zulu's Devotion, A	1916	SA	Good African	stills at SANFVSA
Zulu's Heart, The	1908	US	savages	LC
Zululand	1911			

BIBLIOGRAPHY

Aros, Andrew A. *A Title Guide to the Talkies, 1975 Through 1985.* Metuchen, N.J.: Scarecrow, 1986.

Aschen, Ulf. *The Man Whom Women Loved.* New York: St. Martin's, 1987.

Auty, Martin and Nick Roddick, eds. *British Cinema Now.* London: BFI Publishing, 1985.

Baeta, A. R. "The Two Worlds." *Sight and Sound* 17, no. 65 (Spring 1948): 5–6. (Contains critique of *Men of Two Worlds.*)

Baxter, John. *Stunt.* Garden City, N.J.: Doubleday, 1974.

Bazin, Andre. *What is Cinema?* vol 11. Essays selected and translated by Hugh Gray. Berkeley: University of California Press, 1971.

Betts, Ernest. *The Film Business: A History of British Cinema, 1896–1972.* New York: Pitman, 1973.

Bogle, Donald. *Toms, Coons, Mulattoes, Mammies, and Bucks.* New York: Continuum, 1973; new edition, 1989.

Brown, Eric. *Deborah Kerr.* New York: St. Martin's, 1978.

Brownlow, Kevin. *The Parade's Gone By.* New York: Knopf, 1969.

Cameron, Kenneth M. *Into Africa: The Story of the East African Safari.* London: Constable, 1990.

Campbell, Edward D.C., Jr. *The Celluloid South: Hollywood and the Southern Myth.* Knoxville: Universiy of Tennessee Press, 1981.

Carroll, Noel. *Mystifying Movies.* New York: Columbia University Press, 1988.

———. *Philosophical Problems of Classical Film Theory.* Princeton: Princeton University Press, 1988.

Casty, Alan. *Development of the Film.* New York: Harcourt, Brace, 1973.

Cham, Mbye Baboucar. "Film Production in West Africa," in Downing, *Politics,* 13–30.

Cloete, Elsie. "Afrikaner Identity: Culture, Tradition and Gender," *Agenda* 13 (1992).

Connelly, Robert B. *The Motion Picture Guide, Silent Film, 1910–1936.* Chicago: Cinebooks, 1986.

Connolly, Brian M. "Southern Rhodesia—Is This Your Country?" *Sight and Sound* 17, no. 65 (Spring 1948): 7–9.

Corrigan, Philip. "Film Entertainment as Ideology and Pleasure: Towards a History of Audiences." In Curran and Porter, *History,* 24–38.

Cripps. Thomas. *Slow Fade to Black: The Negro in American Film, 1900–1942.* New York: Oxford University Press, 1977.

Curran, James, and Vincent Porter, eds. *British Cinema History.* Totowa, NJ: Barnes and Noble, 1983.

Davies, Philip, and Brian Neve. *Cinema, Politics and Society in America.* New York: St. Martin's, 1981.

Denis, Armand. *On Safari.* London: Collins, 1963.

Diawara, Mauthia. *African Cinema.* Bloomington: Indiana University Press, 1992.

Dimmitt, Richard Bertrand. *A Title Guide to the Talkies.* New York: Scarecrow, 1965.

Downing, J. H., ed. *Film and Politics in the Third World.* New York: Praeger, 1987.

Drew, Bernard A. *Motion Picture Series and Sequels.* New York: Garland, 1990.

Dunham, Harold. *Bertie: The Life and Times of G.B. Samuelson.* Privately printed (England), 1989.

Eames, John Douglas. *The MGM Story.* New York: Crown, 1975.

Eastman, George. *Chronicles of an African Trip*. Rochester, NY: privately printed, 1927.

Ellison, Harlan. *Watching*. Los Angeles: Underwood-Miller, 1989.

Essoe, Gabe. *Tarzan of the Movies*. New York: Cadillac, 1968.

Etherington, Norman. *Rider Haggard*. Boston: Twayne, 1984.

Fell, John, ed. *Film Before Griffith*. Berkeley: University of California Press, 1983.

Fenton, Robert W. *The Big Swingers*. Englewood Cliffs, N.J.: Prentice-Hall, 1967.

"Films for Africa." *Sight and Sound* 4, no. 13 (1935): 41.

"Films for Africans." *Sight and Sound* 12, no. 46 (1943): 39–40. "Reprinted by permission from Colonial Cinema."

French, Warren, ed. *The South and Film*. Jackson: University Press of Mississippi, 1981.

Furtaw, Julia C., ed. *The Video Source Book*. 15th ed., 2 vols. Detroit: Gale Research, 1994.

Gehring, D., ed. *Handbook of American Film Genres*. New York: Greenwood, 1988.

Gerard, Albert. *African Language Literatures*. Harlow, Essex: Longman, 1981.

Gifford, Dennis. *The British Film Catalogue, 1895–1970*. New York: McGraw-Hill, 1973.

Gilliam, Dorothy Butler. *Paul Robeson, All-American*. Washington: New Republic, 1976.

Gommery, Douglas. *The Hollywood Studio System*. New York: St. Martin's, 1986.

Graham, Shirley. *Paul Robeson, Citizen of the World*. 1946. Reprint ed. Westport, Conn.: Negro Universities Press, 1971.

Granger, Stewart. *Sparks Fly Upward*. New York: Putnam, 1981.

Grella, George. "The Colonial Movie and The Man Who Would Be King." *Texas Studies in Literature and Language* 22, no. 2 (Summer 1980): 246–262.

Grenville, J. A. S. *Film as History: The Nature of Film Evidence*. Birmingham: University of Birmingham Press, 1971.

Gutshe, Thelma. *The History and Social Significance of Motion Pictures in South Africa*. Cape Town: Timmins, 1972.

———. "South African Cinema." *Sight and Sound* 12, no. 46 (1943): 31–32.

Haggard, H. Rider. *Three Adventure Novels: She, King Solomon's Mines, Allan Quatermain*. Reprint. New York: Dover, 1951.

Hammon, Scott. *John Huston*. Boston: Twayne, 1985.

Hardwicke, Cedric. *A Victorian in Orbit*. "As told to James Brough." Garden City, NJ: Doubleday, 1961.

Haskell, Molly. *From Reverence to Rape: The Treatment of Women in Movies*. New York: Holt, Rinehart and Winston, 1973, 1974.

Hennebelle, Guy. "Pretoria veut construire un 'Hollywood' sud-africain. . . ." in Hennebelle, *Cinemas*, 261–66.

———. "Le Cinéma et les guérillas africaines." In Hennebelle, *Cinemas*, 267–78.

———. *Les Cinémas Africains en 1972*. In *L'Afrique littéraire et artistique*, no. 20. Dakar: Societé Africaine d'Édition, 1972.

Hepburn, Katharine. *The Making of the African Queen*. New York, Knopf, 1987.

Higgins, D.S. *Rider Haggard*. New York: Stein and Day, 1981.

Hirschhorn, Clive. *The Warner Brothers Story*. New York: Crown, 1979.

Holtsmark, Erling B. *Edgar Rice Burroughs*. Boston: Twayne, 1986.

Hughes, Langston, ed. *An African Treasury*. New York: Crown, 1960.

Izod, John. *Hollywood and the Boxoffice, 1895–1986*. New York: Columbia University Press, 1988.

Jewell, Richard and Vernon Harbin. *The RKO Story*. New York: Arlington House, 1982.

Johnson, Martin. *Lion*. New York: Blue Ribbon, 1929.

Jones, Eldred Durosimi, ed. *African Literature Today: 12*. London: Heinemann, 1982.

Kael, Pauline. *State of the Art*. New York: Dutton, 1983, 1984, 1985.

———. *Taking It All In*. New York: Holt, Rinehart and Winston, 1980–1984.

———. *When the Lights Go Down*. New York: Holt, Rinehart and Winston, 1975–1980.

Katz, Ephraim. *The Film Encyclopedia.* New York: Thomas Y. Crowell, 1979.

Kerr, David. "The Best of Both Worlds? Colonial Film Policy and Practice in Northern Rhodesia and Nyasaland." *Critical Arts, A Journal of Cultural Studies* 7, no. 2 (1993).

Klotman, Phyllis Rauch. *Frame By Frame: A Black Filmography.* Bloomington: Indiana University Press, 1979.

Korda, Michael. *Charmed Lives.* New York: Random House, 1979.

Kraemer, Siegfried. *Theory of Film: The Redemption of Physical Reality.* 1960. New edition, Oxford: Oxford University Press, 1971.

Krafsur, Richard P. exec. ed. *AFIC Feature Films, 1961–1970.* New York: Bowker, 1976.

Latham, G. C. "Films for Africans." *Sight and Sound* 5, no. 20 (1936–37): 123–25.

Lauritzen, Einr and Gunnar Lundquist. *American Film Index 1908–1915.* Stockholm: AKADEMIBOKHANDELN, 1976.

Leab, David. *From Sambo to Superspade: the Black Experience in Motion Pictures.* Boston: Houghton Mifflin, 1975.

Leach, Graham. *The Afrikaners.* London: Mandarin, 1990 [1989].

Lee, Walt. *Reference Guide to Fantastic Films.* Los Angeles: Chelsea-Lee, 1972.

Lerner, Gerda. *The Creation of Patriarchy.* New York: Oxford University Press, 1986.

Limbacher, James L., comp. and ed. *Feature Films.* 8th ed. New York: Bowker, 1985.

Low, Rachael. *Film Making in 1930s Britain.* London: Allen and Unwin, 1985.

———. *Films of Comment and Persuasion of the 1930s.* London: Allen and Unwin, 1979.

———. *The History of the British Film, 1906–1914.* London: Allen and Unwin, 1949.

———. *The History of the British Film, 1914–1918.* London, Allen and Unwin, 1950.

———. *The History of the British Film, 1918–1929.* London: Allen and Unwin, 1971.

——— and Roger Manvell. *The History of the British Film, 1896–1906.* 1948. New ed. New York: Bowker, 1973.

Maltin, Leonard, ed. *Leonard Maltin's Movie and Video Guide.* New York: Plume, 1992.

Martin, Angela, ed. *African Films: The Content of Production.* BFI Dossier no. 6. London: BFI, 1982.

Maynard, Richard. *Africa on Film: Myth and Reality.* Hayden, 1974.

Mellen, Joan. *Big Bad Wolves: Masculinity in the American Film.* New York: Pantheon, 1977.

Miles, Peter. *Cinema, Literature, and Society.* London and New York: Croom, Helm, 1987.

Monaco, Paul. *Ribbons in Time.* Bloomington: Indiana University Press, 1987.

Morley, Sheridan. *Tales From the Hollywood Raj.* New York: Viking, 1984.

Moses, Trevor. *Checklist of South African Films, 1910–Present.* Unpublished MS at SANFVSA, Pretoria. Kept current.

Munden, Kenneth W., exec. ed. *American Film Institute Catalog of Motion Pictures Produced in the United States: Feature Films, 1921–1930.* New York: Bowker, 1971.

Musser, Charles. "The American Vitograph, 1897–1901: Survival and Success in a Competitive Industry," in Fell, *Griffith*, 22–66.

Nash, Jay Robert and Stanley Ralph Ross. *The Motion Picture Guide.* Chicago: Cinebooks, 1985, etc.

Null, Gary. *Black Hollywood.* New York: Citadel Press, 1975.

Niver, Kemp R. *Early Motion Pictures.* The Paper Print Collection in the Library of Congress. Washington: The Library of Congress, 1985.

Ohrn, Steven G. and Rebecca Riley. *Africa From Reel to Reel: An African Filmography.* Waltham, MA: African Studies Association, 1976.

Pakenham, Thomas. *The Scramble for Africa.* New York: First Avon Books, 1992.

Pfaff, Françoise. "Hollywood's Image of Africa." *Commonwealth Essays and Studies* 5 (1981–1982): 97–116.

Pieterse, Jan Nedereen. *White on Black.* New Haven: Yale University Press, 1992.

Poitier, Sidney. *This Life.* London: Hodder and Stoughton, 1980.

Quart, Leonard and Albert Auster. *American Film and Society Since 1945.* New York: Praeger, 1984.

Quinlan, David. *British Sound Films.* Totowa, N.J.: Barnes and Noble, 1984.

Ramdin, Ron. *Paul Robeson, the Man and His Mission.* London: Peter Queen, 1987.

Relich, Mario. "Africans in Non-Standard English Playing Cards of the Restoration and Eighteenth Century." *Kunapipi,* 12, no. 1 (1990): 1–31.

Richards, Jeffrey. *The Age of the Dream Palace.* London: Routledge and Kegan Paul, 1984.

———. "Patriotism With Profit: British Imperial Cinema in the 1930s." In Curran and Porter, *History,* 245–56.

———. *Thorold Dickinson: The Man and His Films.* London: Croom Helm, 1986.

Robeson, Paul. *Here I Stand.* 1958. New ed. Boston: Beacon, 1971.

Roddick, Nick. *A New Deal in Entertainment: Warner Brothers in the 1930s.* London: BFI, 1983.

Schatz, Thomas. *The Genius of the System.* New York: Pantheon, 1988.

Smyth, Rosaleen. "Movies and Mandarins: The Official Film and British Colonial Africa." In Curran and Porter, *History,* 129–43.

Sorlin, Pierre. *The Film in History.* Totawa, N.J.: Barnes and Noble, 1980.

Spence, Louise, Robert Stam, et al. "Racism in the Cinema: Proposal for a Methodological Evaluation." *Critical Arts* 2, no. 3 (1983): 6–12. (Issue reprinted December 1986.)

Stam, Robert, and Louise Spence. "Colonialism, Racism and Representation." *Screen 24* 2 (March/April 1983).

Strebel, Elizabeth Grottle. "Imperialist Iconography of Anglo-Boer War Film Footage." In Fell, *Before,* 264–71.

Thompson, Kristin. *Exporting Entertainment: America in the World Film Market, 1907–1934.* London: BFI Publishing, 1985.

Tomaselli, Keyan G. *The Cinema of Apartheid: Race and Class in South African Film.* London: Routledge, 1989.

———. "Capital and Culture in South African Cinema." *Wide Angle* 18, no. 2 (1986): 33–43.

———. "The Cinema in South Africa Today." *Cineaste* 15, no. 2 (1986).

Ukadike, N. Frank. "Western Film Images of Africa: Genealogy of an Ideological Formulation." *Black Scholar* 21, no. 2: 30–48.

van Bever, L. *Le cinéma pour africains.* Brussells: van Compenhout, 1950. Cahiers Belges et Congolais No. 14.

Vaughan, J. Koyinde. "Africa and the Cinema." In Hughes, *Treasury,* 85–94.

Waugh, Evelyn. *Tourist in Africa.* 1960. New ed. Westport, Conn.: Greenwood, 1977.

Weiss, Ken and Ed Goodgold. *To Be Continued.* New York: Crown, 1972.

Wenden, D.J. *The Birth of the Movies.* New York: Dutton, 1975.

Wiley, David S. *Africa on Film and Videotape, 1960–1981.* East Lansing: African Studies Center, Michigan State University, 1982.

INDEX